DISOBEDIENCE, SLANDER, SEDUCTION, AND ASSAULT

D1104704

∞

DISOBEDIENCE, SLANDER, SEDUCTION, AND ASSAULT

Women and Men in Cajamarca, Peru, 1862–1900

∞

Tanja Christiansen

UNIVERSITY OF TEXAS PRESS
AUSTIN

The Louann Atkins Temple Women & Culture Series is supported by Allison, Doug, Taylor, and Andy Bacon; Margaret, Lawrence, Will, John, and Annie Temple; Larry Temple; the Temple-Inland Foundation; and the National Endowment for the Humanities.

LIBRARY OF CONGRESS CATALOGING-IN-PUBLICATION DATA
Christiansen, Tanja Katherine, 1972–
Disobedience, slander, seduction, and assault : women and men in Cajamarca, Peru, 1862–1900 / Tanja Christiansen.
p.   cm. — (Louann Atkins Temple women & culture series ; bk. 8)
Based on the author's thesis.
ISBN 0-292-70288-4 (hardcover : alk. paper) —
ISBN 0-292-70563-8 (pbk. : alk. paper)
1. Working class—Peru—Cajamarca (Dept.)—Sexual behavior—History—19th century.   2. Sexual ethics—Peru—Cajamarca (Dept.)—History—19th century.   3. Social control—Peru—Cajamarca (Dept.)—History—19th century.   4. Honor—Peru—Cajamarca (Dept.)—History—19th century.   5. Cajamarca (Peru : Dept.)—Moral conditions—History—19th century.   6. Women—Peru—Cajamarca (Dept.)—Sexual behavior—History—19th century.   7. Women—Peru—Cajamarca (Dept.)—Social conditions—19th century.   8. Sex role—Peru—Cajamarca (Dept.)—History—19th century.   9. Man-woman relationships—Peru—Cajamarca (Dept.)—History—19th century.
I. Title.   II. Series.
HQ18.P4C48   2004
306′.0985′15—dc22
2003026045

∞

To my parents,

Lyndi and Jo

Contents

Photo section follows page xii.

Abbreviations

ADC Archivo Departamental de Cajamarca

BN Biblioteca Nacional

CSJ Corte Superior de Justicia

CC Causas Criminales

CO Causas Ordinarias

Acknowledgments

This book is based on my PhD dissertation and would not have come about without the support of a number of individuals. My supervisor, Alan Knight, offered encouragement throughout, and his flexibility in adapting himself to my circumstances was crucial. My examiners, Malcolm Deas and Lewis Taylor, offered insightful comments on the dissertation, and I would like to thank Lewis particularly for his gentle encouragement since.

Cecilia and Socorro Barrantes' hospitality and friendship nurtured me through the early stages of research, and they deserve special thanks. I would also like to thank the staff at the Archivo Departamental de Cajamarca (ADC) for good-humored and patient help. Clift Barnard, Steinar Nordhaug, Veda Rajagopal Brubakk, and Fiona Wilson read various parts of the manuscript, providing valuable nonspecialist perspective and linguistic assistance, and Anette Oldenborg helped me with the maps and illustrations. Thanks are also due to David Rumsey for making his collection of maps available.

The greatest debt I owe is, of course, to my parents, who have supported me in every imaginable way throughout the last few years.

Finally, I would like to thank my son, Lucas, for accompanying me through my travails and forcing me to maintain a measure of sanity throughout.

General map of Peru

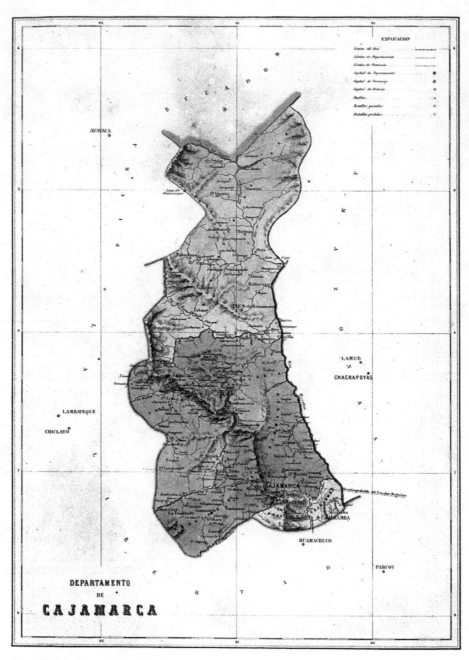

Department of Cajamarca

Topographic map of the city of Cajamarca, by Antonio Raimondi

Santa Catalina church and Aguas Termales de Cajamarca (today the Complejo Belén and the Baños del Inca)

Two Indian women, by A. Pincon

Indian man, by A. Pincon

A group of Indians, by A. Simeon

General image of altitudes in Peru

DISOBEDIENCE, SLANDER, SEDUCTION, AND ASSAULT

Introduction

PRESENTING THE CASE

This book considers how lower-class Peruvians reconciled everyday behavior with the strict norms established by church, state, and the public at large. While the state and church in late-nineteenth-century Peru established premarital virginity, patriarchal sovereignty, and the indissolubility of marriage as absolute norms, most Peruvians were unable to follow such rules. Public preoccupation with virtue and honor is evident in contemporary literature and contributions to national and regional newspapers, where the ideal woman was described as the guardian angel of the home.

Despite such concern for moral norms, the near-unattainable standards set by public discourse were defied in everyday life by the population in general. Among the lower classes, many women worked outside of the domestic arena, moving freely in the streets and markets. Young women sold their family's produce at the market or ran errands, unchaperoned, exposing themselves to contact with potential seducers. Couples cohabited without ecclesiastical blessing and separated from spouses despite formal wedding ceremonies in a church.

Regardless of these departures from publicly accepted norms, however, lower-class women and men displayed great concern for their reputation, as can be seen from criminal trial transcripts preserved to the present day. How did they reconcile their behavior with the norms that they purported to adopt as their own?

This book seeks to offer insights into the tensions that developed as a result of multiple, overlapping gender codes in a northern *departamento* (largest administrative unit in the Peruvian state, divided into provinces and districts) of nineteenth-century Peru. By studying criminal trial transcripts in the Archivo Departamental de Cajamarca, I have been able to analyze intimate gender relations and how Cajamarcans of different social standing dealt with codes of honor and respectability. One of my main concerns has been to understand official, state-sanctioned gender discourse, the ways in which lower-class practice differed from this, and how the encounter between official norms and popular practice was negotiated in the legal arena. To this purpose I analyze marital practice, the role of honor in provincial society, premarital sex, and relationships among women.

The predominant theme—the tension between official and popular gender norms—lies embedded in the very nature of the sources. While using judicial records for historical research can be an exercise mined with difficulties, I use these sources to explore the dialogue between the state's and the plebeians' often contradictory understanding of gender. Official gender norms—outlined in legislation and often reiterated by judges as they passed sentence—met popular gender practice in its many variations in litigants' and witnesses' depositions. In court, the many varieties of gender practice encountered and confronted each other. Although gender was constructed through interaction between men and women everywhere and continually, only a fraction of these encounters have been recorded; meetings within the judicial apparatus are among the few instances of gender negotiation which resulted in written documentation and, as such, are an invaluable source for the historian seeking to access subaltern understandings of gender.

Litigants came from a broad social spectrum and ranged from Cajamarca's more respectable citizens to (more typically) small-scale landowners, artisans, petty merchants, market women, agricultural laborers, and servants. As the events described in the proceedings clearly illustrate, lower-class everyday lives did not reflect state-defined gender norms. Young couples engaged in premarital sex; many, in fact, chose not to marry at all. Women lived on their own, many with illegitimate children, often fathered by different men, and those who cohabited with spouses countered their husbands' discipline with an array of responses, including violence.

The lens of the legal arena reveals, then, the gap between elite visions of society, as encoded in legislation, and actual gender practice. In addition to enabling us to study plebeian norms and lives, the trials reveal litigants' attempts at reconciling their behavior with the law.

HONOR: DEFINING PERSONAL WORTH

Assessment of right and wrong, and also of individual worth, was pivotal to legal proceedings. Judges passed sentence on defendants and, implicitly, on plaintiffs when they rejected suits or simply allowed them to grind to a halt.

They evaluated witnesses' statements, often allowing their assessment of the witnesses' moral worth to influence them in calculating the value of the testimony. Plaintiffs and defendants, in turn, sought to persuade judges—and the attentive public outside of the courtrooms—of the propriety of their own actions. Trials often turned into complex arguments about appropriate behavior, including questions such as how much abuse a wife should bear before she was justified in leaving her husband. Conversely, when did a husband have the right to chastise his wife? Among the most frequent issues debated were matters of honor: What were the criteria for possessing honor? Could women who worked in the fields, or who sold *chicha* (traditional Indian alcoholic beverage made from corn), claim to be honorable? Were there extenuating circumstances when women bore children out of wedlock, and could those women regain their honor? How did women's sexual behavior determine their husbands' and families' honor?

The complex debates contained in the trials, as well as recent research, indicate that perceptions of honor varied and were subject to the influences of time. In elite eyes, legitimacy, purity of blood, social status (ideally, a noble title), and wealth were prerequisites for honor; female chastity was a central corollary to this. Premarital virginity and matrimonial fidelity ensured legitimacy, endogamy, and the transfer of property within the peer group; the seclusion of women as a means of guarding female chastity in the private sphere served to mark the social distance from the masses. As Nazzari has pointed out, because upper-class women had servants to protect their honor, "the system of honor and shame upheld not only morality but also reinforced social stratification."[1] Virginity was more than a physical condition; it signified chastity and obedience to the church's moral canons. Its loss (at least, if publicly known) signified a fundamental lack of *vergüenza* (shame) in the woman in question.[2]

With independence, titles of nobility disappeared as a marker of social status, and illegitimacy and color ceased to be absolute barriers to certain posts and professional activities. Whereas illegitimates or individuals tainted by more than one-eighth of nonwhite blood could not be admitted as *abogados* (lawyers) or to official posts in the colonial bureaucracy, such limitations disappeared during the nineteenth century. Gradually, the code of honor changed to increasingly emphasize personal virtue—defined as self-discipline for men and sexual morality for women—rather than ostentatious display of wealth. Chambers argues that this more egalitarian definition of honor "was rooted in the claims of common folk who, by shifting the emphasis from status to virtue, both made sense of and influenced republican discourse."[3]

While Chambers considers this transformation to be a result of pressure from below, other authors have suggested that elite concerns for regulating society in a period of social and economic change—manifesting itself as a rise in racial mixing—prompted a shift in the interpretation of honor. The concomitant was a more stringent moral climate, with stricter public regulation of individuals' comportment and an assertion of patriarchal authority in the home.[4]

Regardless of whether the impetus for these changes sprang primarily from above or below, a more egalitarian definition of honor began to prevail throughout the nineteenth century—a transformation which also implied a stricter code of morality for women and increased subjection to patriarchal authority in the home.

Scholarly work since the 1990s has shown that people from all social classes were concerned about honor, although Latin American elites traditionally reserved honor for themselves.[5] Honor was variable and determined by situation, depending on social milieu, geography, and period. Despite colonial laws that equated honor with whiteness and legitimacy, colored individuals who were not free and who were illegitimate defended their honor. Notwithstanding elite disdain, members of the middle and plebeian classes asserted their claims to honor; these claims uncover differences in their perception of status based on race, family occupation, wealth, and gender. As Lipsett-Rivera and Johnson point out, subtle and by no means firm differences separated plebeians from the poorest, and a reputation—including a reputation for defending one's honor, violently if necessary—could be an important safeguard against association with the latter group.[6]

Lipsett-Rivera and Johnson's volume and Stern's *The Secret History of Gender* have amplified Peristiany's and Pitt-Rivers' original definition of the honor-shame complex described for the Mediterranean,[7] and all three authors convincingly conclude that no single code of gender behavior existed in Latin America. Rather, the various codes of different social groups and the numerous loopholes contained in each code allowed women and men considerable space for maneuver.

DEFENDING HONOR: SLANDER AND LIBEL TRIALS

Honor was central to many of the trials held in the provincial court of Cajamarca, and Chapters 5 and 6 deal extensively with two sets of such trials. Of the 234 trials I studied in detail,[8] 30 dealt with crimes of slander and calumny and asked for the restitution of reputation to the plaintiff and his or her family. A further 15 lawsuits were filed against alleged rapists, abductors, and seducers. In most of these, too, honor was the central issue. In addition, questions of honor proved pervasive themes in many other trials, demonstrating how perceptions of honor pervaded Cajamarcan society at all levels.

Incidents of rape and seduction dealt with actual and locally well known incidents of loss of honor and the victims' attempts to minimize this loss. The slander trials, on the other hand, addressed the unwarranted broadcasting of often fictitious misconduct. Plaintiffs, in other words, went to court in order to publicly deny the rumors which were being spread about them, or, if those rumors were rooted in reality, to set right the public's perception of events. Damage to one's name had extreme and real consequences: victims feared social ostracism; artisans complained of lost business; wives reported that their husbands had left or beaten them as a direct result of slander.

Talk did not emerge out of thin air. Most trials of *injurias verbales* (slanderous insults) resulted from heated arguments in the course of which one or both of the parties insulted the other, initiating new rumors or giving new life to half-forgotten ones. Insults could be directly related to the dispute at hand: where money was owed but not repaid, the creditor called the debtor a thief; women who were rivals for the same man called each other whores. Insults were chosen for their efficacy rather than their accuracy, or were picked at random. Offenders were the most powerful, however, when they alluded to past transgressions and rekindled almost forgotten tittle-tattle. The voicing of insults that implied dishonest or sexually promiscuous behavior triggered damaging rumors that threatened reputations unless they were publicly challenged.

Without doubt, most such insults and the resulting scandal were dealt with outside of the legal arena. Further arguments might follow, possibly settling the dispute; opponents might come to blows, thus establishing their readiness to defend their honor; public retractions might be obtained with or without the use of force and threats. Many, lacking the resources to combat gossip and public suspicion, presumably had to live under their shadow. In some cases, however, victims of insult and slander went to court in order to clear their names, leaving behind written records of their battles for reputation and allowing us a glimpse of their understanding of honor. The fact that women and men, many of whom were illiterate, opted for this path testifies to the importance they placed on honor—and to the opportunity the legal system afforded them.

The courts were not always sympathetic to charges of *injurias*, particularly as the litigants were mostly small fry. Several judges unceremoniously ordered plaintiffs to take their complaints elsewhere and warned them off further litigation with the threat of jail and hefty fines. More commonly, trials ended inconclusively, either with the defendant's acquittal or, equally unsatisfactory, with no conclusion at all. Nevertheless, going to court appears to have offered plaintiffs something of what they wished: even if they did not succeed in punishing their opponents, they obtained the public's ear and demonstrated that they valued their honor enough to press charges in a criminal court.

While what took place outside of the court is, of course, hidden from the eye of the historian, the fact that a number of estranged husbands accompanied their wives after they had initiated legal proceedings speaks for itself. They at least felt that their wives' fidelity had been vindicated sufficiently to appear at their side again, and therefore the husbands' manhood was reasserted. Even if the courts were ineffective as an instrument of legal redress, they represented an avenue for vindication for victims of slander.

Interestingly, it seems as if the legal system functioned as such an arena almost in spite of itself. Several of the litigants who sought to defend their honor would, at first sight, appear to have little to defend by way of reputation. Market women, women who had borne children out of wedlock, and impoverished widows were among those who left their imprint in court documents. Even according to the more egalitarian—but morally more exacting—code of honor of the nineteenth century, these women did not qualify as honorable. Nevertheless, they not only claimed to possess honor, but they also defended their claims with some success in court. Although several of these women had dubious pasts, which placed them under suspicion of continued immorality, they succeeded in using the legal arena to demonstrate to the public and the judge that their later lives entitled them to respect. By emphasizing those parts of their life histories that entitled them to honor, they were able to shift the balance in their favor, thereby revealing that honor could be an elastic and negotiable commodity.

DEFENDING HONOR:
TRIALS OF RAPE, SEDUCTION, AND ABDUCTION

The art of retelling life histories was also central in the other group of trials that dealt with honor, namely, rape and seduction suits, which I analyze in Chapter 6. Only a minority of the criminal cases dealing with rape, seduction, and abduction dealt with actual instances of sexual crime; most related the histories of consensual affairs, in the course of which the woman had given up her virginity willingly only to be abandoned later by her lover.

As in the slander trials, going to court in these instances was often less about punishing the offender than about shifting public attention. Plaintiffs went to court on behalf of their daughters and young female dependents in order to force absconding seducers to the altar or, failing that, to force public acknowledgment of the girl's remaining honor. In order to achieve this, they retold their version of events, asserting that the victim had been coerced through force, threats, drugs, or deceit. In this fashion plaintiffs aimed to shield the young women from public perceptions of complicity in their own downfall; by portraying them as innocent victims of abusive and immoral seducers, their personal virtue could be made to appear intact. Although virginity was indisputably lost, blame might be shifted to the fickle lover, and a measure of honor thus renegotiated.

Legal terminology reflected this concern with honor. The legal categories of *estupro, violación,* and *rapto* (rape and abduction) were defined specifically as crimes against honor. The victim's personal suffering received scant attention in the legal literature, except insofar as it went to prove that she was innocent of any complicity. The central criterion for establishing the defendant's guilt was therefore proving that the victim had upheld honor and been a virgin prior to sexual relations.

Needless to say, this posed a number of challenges for litigants. Defendants did their best to discredit their victim's reputation. Plaintiffs counterattacked by producing evidence to the contrary: adducing their ward's tender age and any other claims to respectability the family possessed, they insisted that the girl in question had lived a sheltered life and could therefore be presumed to be a virgin.

The courts discriminated against women from the lower classes by requiring a greater burden of proof of virginity. Only women belonging to the local elites had an automatic claim to the presumption of virginity and honor; plebeian women were assumed to be prone to an immoral lifestyle. Women who left the seclusion of their homes to work exposed themselves to suspicions of sexual misconduct, and complainants struggled to explain a ward's behavior in honorable terms. This bias is reflected in the near-absolute absence of trials dealing with the rape of peasant women. Very few charges were filed or otherwise recorded (e.g., in police records). Of the few that were filed, most were either not followed up on by the police or rejected by judges.

Although the antecedents of the histories recounted in court are often obscured by the litigants' disputes over honor, transcripts reveal that many of the young women in question were active parties to their own seduction, and that several consciously used a relationship in order to free themselves of irksome patriarchal control. As well as engaging in lengthy debates about honor, defendants and plaintiffs both struggled for moral superiority and accused one another of abusive behavior and neglect, on the one hand, and miserly and excessive patriarchal control, on the other.

While the details of sexual practice and the way in which young women and men saw it are therefore hidden from view, the trials show how their elders sought to resolve the evident gap between formal gender ideology and actual practice. In the course of the legal proceedings, plebeian litigants sought to justify their behavior in elite terms and attempted to reconcile divergent gender practices. The category of *rapto*—translated literally as abduction—was often used to mediate this tension. The tradition of eloping for strictly romantic reasons or in order to force parental agreement to a union, making it a fait accompli, had long historical roots in Peru, as, indeed, in the rest of Latin America,[9] and the penal code made special allowances for such cases. *Rapto* assumed that a woman had been forcibly abducted and held against her will prior to being robbed of her virginity. The description of elopement as *rapto* therefore exonerated the woman from personal responsibility for events and was a term frequently used as a euphemism for love affairs.

DEFINING THE PARAMETERS OF MARRIAGE:
WHAT CONSTITUTED MARRIAGE, AND HOW WAS IT LIVED?

Where premarital sex led to formal marriage or, at least, a long-term consensual union, no attempts at vindicating honor were made or, usually, required. Common-law marriages were so prevalent as to almost constitute a social norm among the popular classes. In Chapter 4 I look at plebeian marital practice and the frequency of common-law unions versus formal matrimony. The national census conducted in 1876 indicates that less than half of the adult population of Cajamarca was married; presumably, a large part of the remainder lived in consensual unions. While ecclesiastically blessed marriages gave greater status, common-law unions did not lead to any great social stigma among the lower segments of Cajamarcan society, instead offering the stability and support of formal marriage. Such unions resulted in close ties between families, and many were formalized on the deathbed of one of the spouses. In a sense, informal unions offered women certain benefits: common-law wives escaped damaging relationships with comparative ease, whereas formally married wives were legally obliged to reside with their husbands and were expected by the state to put up with abuse.

Not only did plebeians often choose not to marry, unlike the local elites, but their marital differences occasionally resulted in criminal prosecution. Trial transcripts dealing with marital conflict offer insight into some of the internal dynamics of marriage. They uncover some of the causes of conjugal conflict and its derivative, spousal abuse, as well as giving an insight into the strategies that women resorted to in combating violence. Rising elite concern for the maintenance of patriarchal authority and the sanctity of the private sphere clashed with popular practice. Although wives tolerated a measure of abuse at their husband's hands, they countered violence with different mechanisms. They fought back; fled for varying periods of time, sometimes leaving their husbands permanently; refused sex; and appealed to their families for support. Contrary to judges' repeated injunctions, relatives—usually parents or brothers—intervened in marital conflict in order to safeguard the wife. Their assistance ranged from physically protecting the victim to beating up the husband, thereby providing, it was hoped, a warning. Less often, outsiders took action in order to block battery by interfering in the domestic affairs of mere acquaintances or even complete strangers. Errant wives, on the run from abusers, sought refuge in neighbors' and acquaintances' homes. Without minimizing the pain, danger, or ever-present sense of threat induced by domestic violence, we can nevertheless conclude that victims had strategies of resistance and were not totally bereft of practical or moral support.

Although women resisted abuse and found support within the local community, judges were reluctant to meddle in matrimonial conflicts. Violent husbands were rarely reprimanded or punished; wives, on the other hand, were admonished to obey their husbands and to refrain from involving outsiders. In-laws and other family members who intervened in order to protect victims of abuse were warned not to repeat such actions and were threatened with jail and fines.

Recurring themes in marital squabbles were problems related to alcohol, husbands' failure to provide economically for their families, and infidelity. A husband who suspected his wife of adultery felt justified in chastising her and was backed by the courts. Wives tolerated male infidelity up to a point; where male philandering threatened the family's existence, however, they took action in a number of ways. These included the small weapons of daily interaction such as acrimonious language; the withholding of food, domestic services, or sex; gossip; public scenes; attacks on their rivals; or outright violence against husbands and their mistresses. Husbands did not take kindly to any of these and frequently opted for violence in response to any challenge to their authority, particularly if it took place in public.

QUESTIONING SISTERHOOD:
SOLIDARITY AND CONFLICT AMONG WOMEN

In resisting husbands' abuse, wives drew on networks of solidarity and co-operation, usually relying on primarily (but not exclusively) female kin and neighbors. Conversely, rivalry over men brought women into conflict with each other. Such relationships of solidarity and conflict are the topic of my penultimate chapter.

As trials dealing with oral and physical confrontations between women testify, despite the importance of female support networks, women were not always in agreement. Tension among women expressed itself in multiple ways: they wielded sticks, threw stones, pulled each other's hair, and stabbed one another. Such brawls resulted in miscarriages, the death of infants carried by warring women, or, sometimes, the death of one of the participants. Gossip, slander, and the resulting public scandal could inflict as much—or more—damage as physical blows. Although witchcraft and poison appear to have been used rather less than the fear of them might seem to warrant, they clearly figured in the popular imagination, and the threat of poison was perceived as serious. Finally, women (and men) resorted to the courts not only in order to obtain vindication, but also as a means of avenging themselves on enemies.

The frequent resort to violence reflects both its overall prevalence in Cajamarcan society and the depth of hatred borne by some women. Tensions could simmer for years, expressing themselves in occasional oral confrontation and threats, as well as the more common (and wiser) device of avoiding one another. Usually, however, such tactics culminated in periodic confrontations that, if serious enough, made their way into court records.

In general the conduct of women who were fighting reveals a separate, distinctly plebeian, code of behavior that bore no relation to elite norms. While many plebeians strove to emulate elite conduct—or at least to maintain the appearance of doing so—others did not bother, preferring to lead a life unfettered by the pursuit of honor as defined by the elite. As these men and women produced written records only in exceptional cases, their understanding of appropriate conduct, including gender codes, is extremely difficult to access and can be documented only in piecemeal fashion.

The most common reasons for quarrel identified in these cases—to the degree that the trial transcripts reveal motives at all—are rivalry over men, disagreement over property (in the form of debt, inheritance, border disputes), and women's struggle to protect their children from harm. Eruptions of anger often followed incidents in which a family's domestic animals, usually pigs, had overrun another family's fields, with women, whose duties included caring for domestic animals, serving as targets. While women competed for men in other periods and regions as well, it appears that female competition over men was exacerbated in late-nineteenth-century Cajamarca by growing seasonal migration to the coast. This led, quite simply, to a shortage of men as well as to a loosening of emotional bonds for those men who were (formally or informally) married and growing insecurity for their wives. Women fought each other rather than confront their men both in order to reduce conflict with their spouses and in order to ward off potential rivals.

Women did not fight alone, however. They commonly allied themselves with sisters and other (mostly female) relatives or friends and confronted their enemies in groups. They aided each other in other ways as well: older relatives in particular often defused such conflicts by persuading one of the women to desist from further argument and leading her away. Networks of solidarity and cooperation tied communities together and expressed themselves in small, everyday acts of assistance and in long-term solutions to the problem of orphans. Although women socialized and gossiped, solidarity tended to express itself through concrete acts, such as assistance in times of illness or childbirth in the form of small loans and the sharing of domestic tasks such as preparing food or washing clothes. Reflecting these activities and women's everyday tasks, certain sites were typical meeting places. Both social contact and confrontation often occurred where women met in their daily duties: at the *pileta* (water fountain), washing clothes; in the fields, tending to crops and animals; on the paths connecting the villages to surrounding fields.

Studying conflict and friendship among women offers an ample window into their lives, allowing us to understand some of the complexity of their everyday life as well as the strategies they developed to cope with the many pressures of their usual impoverishment. The ways in which these women fought is revealing of their view of their place in society: while some opted for legal action as more effective, others opted for head-on confrontation. Although judges and other members of the ruling class presumably shook their heads in disbelief at such behavior, these women acted in defense of their families, the material goods these required, and their position in society.

FILTERING THE JUDICIAL SOURCES: UNDERSTANDING THE
MECHANICS OF LEGAL ACTION AND MEETING THE LITIGANTS

Working with judicial sources is challenging. With plaintiff, defendant, and witnesses contradicting each other, who should the historian believe? How can he or she ascertain what actually happened? How valid are conclusions based on such a (of necessity) biased sample? Despite these limitations, trial transcripts are among the few sources that give men and women of all social classes a voice.

Pointing out that the social history of subaltern women cannot be inferred from the national elites' attempts to govern their normative ideas about sex and gender, Klubock observes that women's and men's day-to-day responses to and negotiation of patriarchy and gender ideology tend to remain hidden. Going further, he questions whether sources documenting the more intimate aspects of gender relations, including sexuality, can be accessed by historians and notes how histories of gender can encompass both subaltern practice and formalized discourses of patriarchy as enunciated by national elites.[10] With these questions, Klubock cuts to the very core of important issues facing social historians. How, indeed, are we to find sources which can shed light on plebeians' subjective experience of their life? And, if they exist, how are we to interpret these sources? This work seeks to offer some answers.

Even where subaltern challenges and responses to official normative discourses are documented, the records are not complete, unbiased, or, often, entirely truthful. Few possessed the means to initiate and pursue legal action, and the sample of litigants cannot be assumed to be wholly representative of a cross section of Cajamarca's society.

Even on the few occasions when plebeian women and men spoke with a degree of honesty about intimate matters, as—we must assume—they did in court, their statements were never entirely free from self-censorship. Statements were tailored to suit elite perspectives, and ulterior motives underlay most litigants' accounts. Plebeian gender norms were rarely revealed frankly and openly; usually, women and men were all too aware of the many discrepancies between elite gender discourse and lower-class practice.

In addition to self-censorship, a range of other factors impeded the free flow of information. Scribes often passed over details when taking witnesses' statements. Occasionally, ethnicity is evident from the fact that litigants or witnesses needed interpreters, but, unlike in the colonial period, ethnic identity was not usually recorded in late-nineteenth-century legal proceedings. Investigations were often superficial; judges rarely inquired into underlying causes. Many criminal trials and investigations were never concluded, and records remain incomplete. As a result, the events which underlay legal proceedings were often not uncovered, and stories were not fully told. Nor was any official reaction recorded in such cases. Instead, the reader is left with a nagging sense that much transpired outside of the courts. Why did the plaintiffs lose interest? What hidden agenda motivated the judge to discontinue the case? Were matters between the parties settled amicably out of court, or was one of the parties threatened into silence?

While many a story is not fully told and pertinent details may have been omitted and others embellished, we can nevertheless work critically and constructively with such sources. By carefully sifting through legal records, we can document moments of tremendous tension in an individual's life, as well as a wealth of apparently mundane details—which, when pieced together, offer a richer picture of everyday life. Not only do criminal trial transcripts offer stories of plebeian life experiences, they also place these within the context of the legal apparatus, the disciplinarian instrument of national elites par excellence. Judicial records therefore enable us to study the intersection of subaltern actions and experience, on the one hand, and the disciplinary discourses which form part of the process of state definition, on the other. This work therefore aims to make visible both discursive and legal constraints acting on plebeian life and plebeian efforts to reconcile everyday gender practice with official gender discourses.

My main sources are the criminal trials from the period 1862 to 1900 that are preserved in the Archivo Departamental de Cajamarca (see Appendix C). I have read all trials which explicitly deal with gender issues from the years 1862–1863, 1872–1873, 1882–1883, and 1892–1893, as well as any trials from the intervening years which were of obvious interest, such as those dealing with rape, slander involving women (and occasionally men), and domestic violence. Very few trials have been preserved from the early 1880s, reflecting the breakdown in political, legal, and social order during and following the War of the Pacific (1879–1884).[11] More trial records exist from the postwar period, probably because much of the existing documentation was destroyed during the Chilean invasion. Altogether I have analyzed 234 criminal trials. Most of these are from the province of Cajamarca; only in the cases in which the proceedings were of particular interest—such as the trial dealing with one husband's adultery and violent behavior—have I included trials from neighboring provinces (Cajabamba, Celendín, Contumazá, San Marcos, and San Pablo.)

I have also read civil proceedings, which—in most cases—shed less light on the daily functioning of gender relations, and 374 wills and a smaller number of notarial records. I have also looked at some of the local—predominantly urban—police reports that were filed daily and contain information on—mostly—relatively minor incidents of violence, excessive drinking, and theft. Even in those cases in which the reported crimes were serious—such as rape, assault, and murder—there is no overlap between police reports and criminal trials, indicating that only a fraction of the total cases filed and investigated have been preserved.

The trials I have studied deal with a variety of offenses, some of which I have already mentioned, such as rape and seduction, assault, slander, murder, theft, and spousal battery. Other recurrent categories are cattle rustling, burglary, the provocation of miscarriages through violence, and the abduction of servants. Naturally, some of these categories tell us more about gender relations than others, but some of the trials dealing with apparently gender-neutral crimes, such as burglary and cattle rustling, also contain relevant detail on gender relations. Plaintiffs who accused other peasants of stealing their only cow indicated—by virtue of going to court at all—how valuable a cow could be to a destitute Indian widow. Most of those accused of cattle rustling were, not surprisingly, men; but sometimes women, too, were blamed for the loss of cattle, usually if they were related to or were otherwise associated with—usually through common-law marriage—the alleged rustlers.

Smaller matters—including the infliction of minor injuries and the theft of property worth less than fifty pesos—were settled at the district level by a local *juez de paz* (justice of the peace, usually at the district or *caserío* [a smaller village within a district] level). Litigants could file complaints by speaking to the justice of the peace, and plaintiff and defendant met in court, with adjudication within few days. The justice of the peace recorded proceedings in the *libro de juicios verbales* (book of oral suits), or, in the case of reparations, in the *libro de conciliaciones* (book of conciliations). If either of the parties decided to appeal, the proceedings were copied by the justice of the peace and transferred to the *corte de primera instancia* (provincial court) in the provincial capital.

More serious matters, including assault, rape, slander, the theft of more valuable property, and murder, were dealt with in the provincial capitals by the provincial court. If the crime had taken place in a more remote location, the initial investigation and interrogation of witnesses was carried out by the resident justice of the peace and written reports were remitted to the judge of the provincial court as soon as possible.

The authorities, usually following an official report by police or political authorities, prosecuted *delitos exceptuados* (crimes against life or property, such as theft, robbery, assault, and murder). The court appointed a public defender, and victims or their relatives participated in the trial to varying degrees. Relatives might seek to speed up proceedings or obtain the release from jail of the defendant pending prosecution (tasks which were time- and money-consuming, and usually thankless) with repeated letters and petitions, or appear merely in the role of witness.

"Crimes against honesty," such as rape, seduction, slander, and adultery, could be prosecuted only at the instigation of the victim, and proceedings could be halted at any moment should plaintiff and defendant reach an agreement. However, as in crimes involving theft and violence, plaintiffs had to work continually to ensure that proceedings did not draw to a halt.

All criminal trials began with a formal accusation, denunciation, or complaint. Charges of assault usually began with a formal complaint by the victim; the prosecutor's office usually assumed responsibility after the case was reported. After investigating the crime in question, the court proceeded to ascertain the guilt or innocence of the accused before sentencing. In the course of the investigation, witnesses were interrogated and medical experts consulted, all of whom had to provide their name, age, origin, domicile, occupation, and marital status. Prior to signing their statements, witnesses had to read through them, or have their depositions read to them if they were illiterate. Witnesses were called to shed light on the events surrounding the crime, or, if it was a crime against honor, on the moral character of the complainant and, sometimes, the defendant. Spouses, siblings, parents, and offspring were not expected to testify against their relatives. Opponents often questioned the testimony of more-distant relatives, such as uncles, aunts, and godparents, of servants, other dependents, and debtors. Proceedings were therefore punctuated and sometimes interminably delayed by wrangling over whose testimony was to be admitted in court. In most cases relating to theft or violence, the defendant was jailed (providing that he or she could be found), although bail was possible.

Once matters were brought before the provincial court, plaintiff and defendant rarely met in court. Both parties and their various witnesses testified individually, with scribes noting the particulars. Statements, letters, and petitions were collated and added to the growing pile of trial documents. In most trials, litigants submitted numerous requests designed to speed up or slow down proceedings, as well as questions and lists of witnesses, most of whom were duly interrogated. Plaintiff and defendant frequently tried to disqualify the opponent's witnesses, and weeks if not months could pass while the various parties wrangled over which witnesses and evidence were admissible in court.

As letters had to be filed and copies of all letters sent to all the parties concerned—who often lived in different villages or towns and who had to confirm that they had received the document in question—proceedings could continue for years. Probably as a result of these delays and the cost they entailed, many trials were never concluded. When the time span set by the judge for the collection of evidence elapsed—although it was usually extended through a variety of devices employed by the litigants and their lawyers—the prosecutor and defense counsel summarized their main points before sentencing. In the cases where a verdict was reached, appeals were frequent, and, occasionally, all documents were remitted to the high court in Lima for reevaluation. However, even trials with such determined litigants were likely to peter out eventually, adding to the total number of trials with uncertain outcomes.

Such involvement in legal proceedings was not without its costs: *papel sellado* (stamped paper) cost twenty centavos per piece (the equivalent of a day's wage for an agricultural laborer), and illiterate and semiliterate litigants usually had to pay a *tinterillo*, or scribe, to author documents for them.[12] In addition, litigation was time-consuming, especially for those living outside of the town of Cajamarca. In those cases stretching over dozens (sometimes hundreds) of pages and months or years, costs ultimately proved prohibitive, explaining why lawsuits were sometimes discontinued. Initiating a trial or defending oneself, however, was within the means of most urban residents and peasants, excluding only servants, *colonos* (tenants on an hacienda who usually obtained access to land and pasture rights in return for labor), and the poorer laborers.

As truth can be for the historian, justice could be elusive for litigants. The legal machinery was extremely slow and cumbersome, and, as noted earlier, most cases remained undecided. When a verdict was arrived at, it was not always acted on: numerous felons succeeded in escaping to the coast and evading punishment through prolonged absence; wealthy *hacendados* (owners of an hacienda or large estate) who had come into conflict with the law were usually safe on their estates—as were their peons. The court's ability to implement justice was limited.[13]

It follows that, with many investigations uncompleted or only superficially carried out, the facts that underlay the legal proceedings sometimes remain obscure. Even when criminal proceedings reached a conclusion, much remains hazy: trial transcripts are full of claims and counterclaims; litigants rarely agreed on the facts and presented competing versions of events, summoning numerous witnesses to back up their versions; the accused presented occasionally ludicrous, but often entirely believable, explanations for actions; defendants in rape trials sometimes claimed that the charges were mere attempts at entrapment into marriage. Several women and men who charged their enemies with attacking them either orally or physically turned out to be as guilty as the defendants of the very crimes of which they claimed to be victims. In some cases, what actually transpired is anybody's guess. Such uncertainty poses serious challenges to the historian, and the study of the legal process itself becomes an integral part of the analysis.

I occasionally cite witness statements and assume that, even if they fail to reflect the whole truth, it is clear that they were contrived to be believed by a judge. Thus I have chosen to report both the rape victim's description of her ordeal and her alleged rapist and detractor's counterclaim that the legal proceedings were merely a ploy to force money out of him. The latter's attempts to sully his alleged victim's reputation are relevant; if nothing else, they can tell us how pressing charges of rape could further endanger an already threatened reputation. At the same time, many statements are clearly best taken with a grain of salt.

Many litigants—and their witnesses—tailored their statements to suit the authorities' set of beliefs. In order to appeal to the dominant class' value system—and increase the chance of obtaining a favorable finding—plaintiff and defendant frequently twisted the truth. Both sides tried to allocate as much blame as possible to their opponents and the minimum to themselves. In addition, they tried to represent their own behavior as corresponding closely to upper-class expectations in order to advance their case. The representatives of rape victims' emphasized the girls' decorum; battered wives focused on their patience and forbearance vis-à-vis their husbands, which they contrasted with the latter's unwarranted brutality.

While these statements may often have reflected the truth, sometimes they were a mere sop to upper-class expectations. Litigants' attempts to conform to the ruling class' gender norms means that there is an inherent bias in the material toward overemphasizing the elite's definition of gender roles. James Scott notes that even close readings of historical and archival sources will tend to favor the dominant group's account of social relations. He argues that subordinated groups have an inherent self-interest in conspiring to reinforce the official transcript, and that the "public transcript" used by subordinate groups in their exchange with dominant groups is therefore a poor guide to their actual views.[14] Bearing this caveat in mind, trial transcripts must be read with great care. If analyzed carefully, they do, however, reveal a distinct lower-class gender discourse, as evident in both the trial participants' actions and, more rarely, their justification for these actions.

A further complication inherent in using trial transcripts as source is the inevitable privileging of deviancy and conflict. Clearly, using trial records dealing with spousal abuse provides a lopsided view of marriage. Similarly, the presence of dozens of trials dealing with conflict among women must not blind the modern reader to the presence of their networks of solidarity and support.

Despite these limitations, criminal proceedings are a valuable source: as well as offering valuable insights into the causes and nature of these conflicts and a host of apparently trivial but very relevant details, they pinpoint moments of tension in gender relations. As Martínez-Alier has noted, "these deviations from ideal behaviour, while by no means everyday occurrences, nevertheless highlight the conflicts obtaining in the system and make its norms all the more apparent."[15] While the nature of the sources impedes us from drawing conclusions about the prevalence of problems such as premarital sex, wife battery, and adultery, we can analyze the circumstances under which these took place and how society reacted.

One of the problems for the reader of these trial transcripts is to understand the social class, ethnicity, and cultural identity of the various litigants. The transcripts give basic information on literacy, age, marital status, and employment—as well as, in rare cases, linguistic status—but pinpointing the ethnicity and social class of individuals is usually difficult. In some cases references to everyday activities indicate that the person belonged to the less-privileged classes: a mother's comment that she was carrying her child on her back, washing baby clothes, or laboring in a field all identify her as one of the lower orders, very likely at least part Indian.

In most cases, however, information about social class is more ambiguous. Due to the low levels of general (and especially female) literacy, illiteracy cannot necessarily be taken as an indicator of low social status. Even if a woman was illiterate herself, a close relative—husband or son, sister or daughter—usually knew how to write. Natividad Arana, although married to one of the town of Cajamarca's *escribanos* (scribes), Baltazar Arce, was illiterate. Her daughter, Catalina Puga, however, could both read and write and signed her mother's documents and petitions throughout the legal proceedings.[16] In another case, an illiterate woman had her sister sign documents for her. While some sisters had had the benefit of basic schooling, others had not been so lucky.[17] In the province of Cajamarca, which had—and has—one of the highest rates of *mestizaje* (ethnic and cultural mixing; the term is commonly used to describe the acculturation of Indians into Spanish culture) in the highlands, low social status does not always indicate Indian ethnicity, further complicating the precise identification of litigants' social, ethnic, and cultural identity.

Moreover, prosperity (relative to the local community) and political influence did not necessarily imply a sophisticated lifestyle. One traveler, when passing through the village of Magdalena, met the daughter of the local *teniente gobernador* (governor of a *caserío*). He commented that "different fathers had made her the mother of a fairly large family. I met her squatting before her hearth, cooking and spinning, surrounded by several half-naked children."[18] Clearly, individuals could wield local political clout without boasting any of the accoutrements of elite culture. The lower end of Cajamarcan society was thus fluid, with literate citizens mingling with the illiterate, market women and artisans with scribes and their wives, and almost everybody—regardless of profession—engaging in some agricultural pursuits.

One defining characteristic of society as seen in judicial documents, however, is the absence of the upper classes from criminal litigation. *Hacendados* usually possessed alternative ways of exerting pressure and making their subalterns bend to their will; they did not need legal recourse. Instead, landowners and merchants appear fairly frequently in civil cases, where matters of property were more frequently debated. Propertied widows and single women also figured in these suits; however, they rarely engaged in criminal proceedings. Both plaintiffs and defendants tended to come from the nether end of the social scale.

As most of the trials I have studied were filed in the district and provincial capitals, the sample of individuals and stories I have assembled tends to represent the urbanized and semiurbanized mestizo population rather than the peasantry, without clear indicators as to which litigants pertained to which group. Even for the urban and mestizo parts of the population, however, taking legal action was not an easy step, requiring time and money. For most of the illiterate and semiliterate population the cost of a scribe came in addition to the court's fees. In many cases, persuading a judge to accept a case in the first place was difficult. Ensuring that the trial did not come to a halt was a constant challenge, and one that necessitated payment to lawyers and scribes, court fees, and bribes. Ready cash, albeit not always in huge sums—obtained through wage labor, the sale of livestock or agricultural produce, or the marketing of artisanal products—was thus a prerequisite for legal action.

For the peasantry, the courts' inaccessibility—both geographic and cultural—was an additional disadvantage. Despite making up almost a third of Cajamarca's population in 1876, hacienda residents are almost entirely absent from the court records. Hacienda tenants registered complaints only in exceptional cases;[19] they appeared more frequently as defendants accused of cattle rustling. Most internal disputes on haciendas were never reported to the authorities; instead, the *hacendado* or his deputy, usually a manager, administered a semblance of justice on the estate itself, obviating the need for and often denying access to judicial authorities. Few records of gender relations on the haciendas have therefore been preserved. Although battery, rape, and seduction unquestionably took place there, too, the virtual absence of hacienda residents in the trial transcripts can be explained by the role of the *hacendado* in controlling affairs on the estate. I included the documentation's few glimpses of hacienda life in the analysis where possible, to offer some insights into gender issues on Cajamarcan haciendas in the nineteenth century.

Although *colonos* and *colonas* and, with them, the poorest in Cajamarcan society, are underrepresented in the criminal trial transcripts, the transcripts nevertheless contain a wealth of detail on the lives of women and men of the lower and lower-middle classes. Small-scale landowners, petty merchants, market women, artisans, and even servant women figured among the lists of litigants and witnesses. Many appeared in court unwillingly, as defendants. Plenty, however, entered the legal arena in the role of plaintiff, demonstrating both the willingness and the ability to use the legal system toward their own ends. Some trials, especially those pursued by the state prosecutor— *el ministerio fiscal*—were the result of criminal acts so grievous that they could not be ignored, such as near-lethal assault, murder, or the rape and subsequent death of minors. Others—comparatively minor, but nonetheless serious offenses—were brought to court by victims who sought to punish their offenders. While many sought justice, others used the legal system as a further weapon in disputes.

While the courts did not promise an easy avenue toward the resolution of conflict, many people, after years of conflict, viewed them as a last resort. Filing charges against an enemy—whether a battering husband, an absconding fiancé, or a rival—could be one way of forcing public attention on the problem at hand. Even if the lawsuit did not produce the desired result (as, indeed, it rarely did), plaintiffs hoped to gain the public's ear in order to be able to explain their version of events to the local community. This was particularly important in those cases that dealt with "crimes against honesty," such as rape, seduction, and slander. These trials were often less about punishing the culprit than about clearing the name of the person whose honor had been attacked. Moving into the legal arena was a powerful statement, demonstrating the clear conscience and conviction of possessing honor which dishonored individuals needed to project in order to persuade the public of their position in society. Despite being notoriously ineffective, and in spite of the many deterrents associated with the legal system, the courts therefore became an arena where reputations could be publicly discussed.

CHAPTER 2

Cajamarcan Society under the Magnifying Glass

REGIONAL SOCIETY, ECONOMY, AND POLITICS IN THE NINETEENTH CENTURY

The department of Cajamarca comprises the provinces of Cajamarca, Celendín, Cajabamba, San Marcos, Contumazá, San Pablo, and Santa Cruz, as well as the provinces of San Marcos, Cutervo, and Chota, more remote from the provincial capital. Located between the coastal departments of La Libertad, Lambayeque, and Piúra, on the one side, and the tropical department of Amazonas, on the other, the department of Cajamarca spans a range of ecological zones. These include arid highlands and fertile valleys, as well as districts such as Magdalena and the province of Contumazá with a lush, semitropical climate.[1]

While cattle—and, eventually, labor—were the department's main exports in the nineteenth century, the various provinces in the department of Cajamarca produced a range of other products: wheat, barley, vegetables, fruit, maize, pulses, sugar, aguardiente, and *chancaca* (molasses). Haciendas usually covered several ecological zones and were thus able to produce potatoes, barley, wheat, oca, beans, maize, and quinoa, as well as cattle. While pastoral activities dominated the highlands in the province of Contumazá, the hot coastal climate near the banks of the two main rivers, the Jequetepeque and the Chicama, allowed for the production of rice, sugarcane, cassava, bananas, and mangoes. In addition, the harvest from fruit trees was an important source of cash income in the valleys of Cascas and Contumazá.[2]

Similarly ecologically diverse was the province of Hualgayoc, which produced aguardiente, molasses, and maize in the valleys, tubers and cattle in the highlands, and silver from the provincial capital's silver mines. Historically, the silver mines in Hualgayoc, a mining town at an altitude of 3,508 meters, and the smaller mines in Celendín and Cajabamba, were important centers of economic activity. Although mining declined throughout the nineteenth century, Hualgayoc continued to constitute a local market for foodstuffs, artisanal products, and timber and charcoal. Even in 1873, a year in which silver production hit an all-time low, the town required thousands of sheep and hundreds of head of cattle, thousands of arrobas of salted beef, cheese, butter, rice, citrus fruit, barley, maize, tubers, pulses, and vegetables, not to mention timber, charcoal, coal, firewood, and beasts of burden.[3]

Although contemporary observers tended to view Cajamarca as an economic backwater isolated from the coastal agro-industrial complex, the department boasted a diversity of agricultural and pastoral products, as well as a tradition of healthy interprovincial trade. Traditionally, Cajamarca has been viewed as a region in which precapitalist, even feudal, relations dominated economic activity and social relations until the 1930s. As a result of the paucity of historical research on the region until recent years, a number of stereotypes that more properly reflect reality in the southern highlands—absentee landlordism, *gamonalismo* (local "bossism"), and servile relations between *hacendado* and peasants—have been wrongly imputed to Cajamarca.[4]

In the late nineteenth century haciendas covered two-thirds of the province of Cajamarca. However, the apparent dominance of the hacienda is deceptive: only 29 percent of the rural population resided on haciendas. Divided among six hundred rural communities dispersed among the haciendas, 71 percent of the peasantry lived outside hacienda boundaries in rural hamlets and on independently farmed peasant smallholdings.[5] Nor did haciendas necessarily monopolize the most fertile land; in Hualgayoc, for instance, most hacienda land was dedicated to the pasturing of livestock, with little land under direct cultivation due to the shortage of water.[6]

By the early twentieth century only 2–3 percent of the department of Cajamarca's population lived in traditional indigenous communities. Even where these existed, all cultivated land was privately held and worked as early as the 1880s. The traditional peasant community was, in other words, virtually nonexistent.[7] Hand in hand with the disappearance of the Indian community went a pronounced process of cultural and ethnic *mestizaje*, with the result that by 1876 the mestizos' share of the population almost equaled that of the indigenous population.[8] According to the nationwide census of 1876, only 41.5 percent of the population was Indian, 30.9 percent was mestizo, and 26.8 percent was categorized as white.[9] While ethnic categories must not be treated as absolute, the figures do give an indication of how the rural society was perceived by census takers and provide an approximation of Cajamarca's cultural and ethnic composition.[10] Both the 1795 and the 1876 censuses reveal that Cajamarca counted significantly fewer Indians than was typical of the rest of the country.[11] The expansion of hacienda boundaries in the southern highlands had no parallel in the northern sierra; to the degree that conflict over land did develop, this resulted in intra-elite tension rather than hacienda expansion onto peasant land.

RESPONDING TO COASTAL DEVELOPMENT: CAJAMARCAN ECONOMICS FROM MID-CENTURY

By the 1860s the growth of the sugar- and cotton-producing hacienda sector on the northern coast had created a market for Cajamarcan exports, most notably, cattle and labor. With the expansion of sugar production from the middle of the nineteenth century and the resultant rise in coastal demand for foodstuffs and other goods, as well as labor and transportation services, *hacendados* and small-scale peasant farmers responded in multiple ways.

First and foremost, landowners sought to expand their control of labor in order to be able to produce more cattle and other goods. As both Taylor and Deere have noted, the first step toward more efficient production on Cajamarca's estates was often an intensification of apparently "feudal" labor relations. The use of sharecropping is a case in point. Given tenants' resistance to landlords' labor demands and to wage labor, taking on sharecroppers proved the most economically rational option for many landowners. Both in the late nineteenth and the early years of the twentieth century, a number of Cajamarca's haciendas—namely, La Pauca, La Colpa, Huacraruco, Sunchubamba, Jancos, Tuñad, Combayo, and Polloc—entered into sharecropping agreements with peasants who were not associated with an hacienda. In addition, landlords let land to *minifundistas* (small-scale landowners) outside of the hacienda's realm in return for various labor services. These might include a fixed number of days per month, participation in *faenas* (collective work parties during the harvest), or a commitment to transport the *hacendado's* goods to the markets on the peasants' own pack animals.[12] Through a variety of mechanisms, including wage labor, tenancy, and sharecropping agreements, *hacendados* succeeded in attracting peasants to their estates. For example, from 1876 to 1940 the number of residents on the hacienda La Pauca rose from 898 to 3,137.[13]

Contrary to the conventional view of life on the Peruvian hacienda—as described, for instance, in Ciro Alegría's novel *El mundo es ancho y ajeno* (Broad and alien is the world)—life on the Cajamarcan hacienda was not overly harsh. Indeed, from a peasant's perspective, hacienda life often involved less hardship than life as an independent smallholder. Hacienda residents were frequently better off than independent peasant smallholders, whose landholdings became increasingly fragmented as the nineteenth century advanced and the population expanded. Variations within haciendas were also large. Hacienda residents and tenants were highly differentiated groups, consisting of *arrendatarios cabezarios* (head tenants), *arrendatarios agregados* ("marginal" tenants), *colonos,* and *aparceros* (sharecroppers on large or medium-scale estate), each group with different rights and duties vis-à-vis their landlord. Peasants thus came in all shapes and sizes: while some lived in abject poverty, others enjoyed plentiful access to land and water and supplemented their income with the sale of wage labor and agricultural and artisanal products.

Although landowners attempted to squeeze more labor or higher rents out of their dependents, peasants resisted such changes. They made full use of the high degree of mobility they enjoyed in order to seek alternative employment. The many options open to both hacienda and free peasants allowed most residents of Cajamarca (*cajamarquinos*) to enter genuine negotiations regarding terms of employment. Some peasants—*colonos* and *jornaleros* (day laborers)—worked for local landlords and commonly received between one-tenth and two-tenths of a sol per day as well as a midday meal, which was valued at one-tenth of a sol. Women's labor was valued rather less; they were paid one-twentieth of a sol per day's labor plus the midday meal. Frequently, *hacendados* had to complement the offer of wages with access to land (ranging from small plots to several hectares) and pasturing rights for cattle and sheep in order to persuade laborers to work for them.[14]

An alternative to selling labor locally was periodic migration to the coast. Seasonal migration rose beginning in the 1860s. Taylor points to a partial dependence on wage labor, with 3,888 *boletos de ocupación honrosa* being issued in 1887 to men departing to work on coastal rice and sugar plantations for stretches of two to three months at a time.[15] *Enganche*—the "hooking" of laborers by advancing a sum of money—was common, but did not necessarily imply coercion.[16] Once contracted, laborers worked off their debt on one of the coastal estates, such as Casa Grande or Cayaltí, over a period of several months.

Enganche, however, was only one of several ways in which peasants made their way to the coast. Many left Cajamarca independently, negotiating their own terms of employment with coastal estates and staying for two to three months.

Migration produced a gender imbalance, as growing numbers of men traveled to the coast for months on end. Many failed to return to the highlands, succumbing to illness, opium addiction, or accidents on the coastal sugar plantations. For many men their stay on the coast—even if temporary—contributed to loosening emotional bonds to their formal or common-law wives.[17] The 1876 census reveals that although the distribution among women and men was fairly stable for age groups zero to fifteen, imbalances between the sexes appear from age fifteen to twenty and up. In the district of Cajamarca, for instance, 51.8 percent of the population up to fifteen years of age was male; only 42.8 percent of fifteen- to twenty-year-olds was male; among twenty- to twenty-five-year-olds the share dropped to 40 percent. In other districts, such as Chetilla, the differences were even more marked: only 31.6 percent of twenty to twenty-five-year-olds were male.[18] While male undercounting (resulting from fear of taxation and conscription) may account for some of this, it seems likely that seasonal migration—and in some cases permanent migration—explain part of this imbalance.[19]

Provinces were affected differently. Those areas close to the coast or on a trade route were the most strongly affected by wage labor and market production. Contumazá strategically located on two important trade routes (through the Jequetepeque valley via Chilete and Magdalena to Cajamarca and through the hacienda Casa Grande and via Ascope, Sinupe, Cascas, and Contumazá to the sierra via Asunción or Cospán) was one such area. Most of the province's population resided on peasant-owned smallholdings and medium-scale *fundos* (estates), with 76 percent of the province's population working their own land in 1876; in the district of Guzmango the percentage was as high as 90 percent. In the fertile valleys surrounding the small towns of Cascas, Trinidad, Guzmango, and San Benito, peasants produced wheat, maize, and vegetables, while the sale of fruit constituted an important source of cash income for the populace of the Cascas and Contumazá valleys. Residents of the districts of San Benito and Trinidad farmed garlic, onions, cabbages, and other vegetables, which they sold in local markets; in those years when the rains failed them, peasants were forced to seek off-farm income through wage labor and artisanal work. The region's involvement with the coastal markets intensified further after the construction in 1870 of the Pacasmayo railway, which finally reached Chilete in 1874.

Another source of cash income was the sale of artisanal products. Traveling in the last quarter of the nineteenth century, Ernst Middendorf noted that local artisanal production included the weaving of ponchos, blankets, women's coats in both wool and cotton, saddlery, and straw hats, albeit— according to Middendorf—merely for local use, not long-distance sale.[20] In Contumazá, peasants wove various types of cloth and mats, made shoes, and did carpentry work. The quilts and sheets produced in Contumazá—of thread bought in Ascope, Pacasmayo, Chepen, and Guadalupe—were marketed in the town of Cajamarca, and as far afield as Trujillo and Lima. Ponchos and saddlebags made of wool and cotton were sold locally and on the coast, and cotton shawls and clothes with fine embroidery were marketed further inland, in Celendín, Chachapoyas, Moyobamba, and Loreto.[21] The fairs in the various provincial and district capitals also constituted important centers of commercial exchange, where the above-mentioned products as well as indigo dye, cotton thread, hats, reed mats, and agricultural produce were traded. Subprefect Manuel Romero said that ponchos sold on the coast and in Hualgayoc fetched 2 soles apiece, a pair of gaiters, 1.6 soles, and a shawl, 8 soles.[22]

With the coastal markets at a remove of five days' mule trek from the town of Cajamarca itself, transport costs obviously affected the marketing of different products. While cattle could be profitably sold on the coast, products such as wheat, maize, and beans were usually destined for the local market. Butter and cheese fetched high prices, locally as well as on the coast, and while transporting wheat to the coast was too costly, it was often marketed in Hualgayoc, where the silver mines created an important local commercial center.[23]

Peasants thus made do through a combination of subsistence agriculture and paid labor. They sold agricultural or artisanal products, worked for wages for local *hacendados* or medium-scale landowners, transported goods to and from the coast (as *arrieros* [muleteers]), or undertook seasonal labor on the coast. The coastal markets increased not only labor burdens, but also opportunities for supplementing income.

The emergence of alternatives to residence on haciendas, caused by both the development of seasonal migration and other employment opportunities, helped peasants avoid increased labor.[24] Deere and Taylor have pointed out that the participation in multiple modes of production, that is, combining subsistence agriculture with wage-earning and market activities, helped peasant families make ends meet and thus secured the survival of the peasant household. Connected with the demographic pressure on land, the consequent fragmentation of landholdings, and the burdens of taxation, this commercial stimulus contributed to the gradual proletarianization of the peasantry. Taylor notes that most independent peasant freeholders in Hualgayoc participated in both agricultural and other economic activities by the 1870s.[25]

The economic dislocation that resulted from the War of the Pacific and the ensuing period of instability and insecurity further increased peasant dependence on alternative sources of income. Following decades of gradual integration, modernization and proletarianization progressed more rapidly from the 1890s onward, when the regional economy began to recover from the devastation wrought by the Chilean invasion. Meanwhile, the commercial stimulus from the monocultural plantations on the coast made itself felt in the form of increased demand for livestock, agricultural goods, and labor. By 1900 the province of Cajamarca and its neighboring provinces exported lard, butter, livestock, and labor to the coast, as well as textiles and other artisanal goods to a number of the surrounding provinces.[26]

POLITICAL REFLECTIONS: PROVINCIAL SOCIETY, CLIENTAGE TIES, AND LOCAL POLITICS

The socioeconomic developments outlined above were shaped by, and profoundly affected, the relationship between *hacendados* and the peasantry, on the one hand, and between peasants and the state, on the other. While hacienda tenants, *arrendatarios,* and other tenants had historically close ties to the landlord class, the processes I have described led the independent peasantry to depend increasingly on landowners. As population grew, so did pressure on land, and formerly independent peasants were obliged to enter rental agreements with local landlords in order to ensure sufficient access to land for themselves and their families.

Peasants obtained the rights to rent parcels of land, to be paid wages, to take out loans, and—crucially—to enjoy the protection of their patrons. In return, they offered labor and, usually, their loyalty to their *patrón.* As Taylor has noted for Hualgayoc, the pauperization of peasants in the 1870s led to increased dependence on landlords for access to land, and thus paved the way for closer peasant involvement in patron-client relationships—and, ultimately, in elite politics.[27]

Key in these relationships was the role of medium-scale landowners and merchants, a relatively new social group that emerged in the second half of the nineteenth century. Combining land ownership with commerce and, in some cases, mining, this "self-made village bourgeoisie" commanded both social and political influence because of its intermediary position between large-scale landowners and the land-poor peasantry. Through their activities in commerce, the provision of credit, and *enganche,* the petty bourgeoisie had close contacts with both their social superiors and the peasantry. Many cemented their position in village society by obtaining political posts.[28] The combination of political office and entrepreneurial activity, particularly *enganche,* offered considerable potential for capital accumulation.

A three-tier structure of patron-client relations, consisting of landlord, medium-scale landholder or merchant, and independent peasant, thus emerged. While peasants, at the bottom of this hierarchy, might be offered payment, access to land, tax exemptions, or exemption from conscription,

27

landowners—whether large scale or medium scale—could hope for political office, with all the associated economic advantages. Among the favors that might be exchanged in both directions was assistance with lawsuits: patrons might expect their clients to serve as witnesses on their behalf; they might also extend a loan or use their influence in order to promote their clients in legal proceedings. In return, peasants offered their labor and near-absolute loyalty to their patrons—even risking their lives and following them into battle. Ultimately, the involvement of the free peasantry in such patron-client bonds meant that they tended to become more involved in intra-elite, factionalist conflict.[29]

Simultaneously, intra-elite tensions were on the rise. With growing competition over land, water sources, trade routes, and, ultimately, political office, *hacendados* increasingly came into conflict with one another, resulting in local factionalist conflict. The conflict between Francisco Plasencia León and José Mercedes Alva in Contumazá illustrates how such tensions involved individuals from all walks of life through complex clientage ties. With his purchase of the hacienda Catudén in 1877, Plasencia became the largest property owner in the province of Contumazá. The rise of this small-scale trader from the district of Asunción threatened the commercial activities of other merchants and landlords in Contumazá, and competition between him and Alva, a leading member of one of Contumazá's principal landowning families, came to dominate the last decades of the century. The two men competed for political posts throughout the 1870s, with Plasencia occupying the post of mayor of Contumazá from 1872 to 1874, and Alva acting as the first subprefect of the province of Contumazá following its formation in 1872. Both were members of the Partido Civil, but they belonged to different factions within the party.

Tensions further heightened in 1877, when Alva was removed from the post of subprefect and replaced by Plasencia, and both competed for the post of deputy to Congress. Although Plasencia became both wealthier and more influential once he occupied the politically important post of subprefect, Alva enlisted the support of his extensive clientele and organized protest marches against Plasencia. He encouraged freeholders, artisans, and traders to refuse to pay the *contribución personal* (head tax). He also armed peasant freeholders who had clashed with Plasencia over land, which ultimately led to Plasencia's murder by peasants from Guzmango.

Tension between the opposing factions continued beyond the grave, however, and throughout the 1870s and the 1880s election to political office continued hotly contested partly because it meant control of the local state apparatus. Members of the opposing factions repeatedly settled elections at gunpoint.

The tiny electorates (limited to a few hundred men in each district given the vote under strict literacy and property requirements), a system of indirect election, and the post-1861 system of decentralized electoral administration made manipulation of the political system easy. The electoral roll was drawn up by district officials (the mayor, the governor, and the judge), allowing these men inordinate influence over election outcomes, as citizens could be stricken off the registers at will.[30] In the 1886 elections in Cascas, the Alva family's control of the bureaucracy ensured that virtually all supporters of the Iglesias family (who supported the Plasencias) were struck off the register of *electores propietarios* (someone entitled to vote by virtue of having met literacy and landownership criteria).[31]

Hacendados usually dominated political posts at the departmental and provincial levels, namely, the posts of *prefecto* (the political head of a department) and *subprefecto* (the political head of a province); positions at the district level, such as that of governor were usually held by owners of medium-sized agricultural enterprises. Smaller villages (*caseríos*) were administered by *teniente gobernadores*, who might be small-scale landowners, well-off campesinos, or scribes.[32] These posts gave local bosses (who usually owned land and held political office) considerable leverage, allowing them control of tax collection, conscription, the recruitment of corvée labor, as well as control of the town jail. Such authority could be used in order to provide their clients with favors, further strengthening clientelistic ties. Local bosses also used their authority to punish enemies through the simple devices of jailing them or allowing crime against them to go unpunished.

Another benefit of holding political office was the virtual legal immunity this signified. In Contumazá, harassment of local Chinese inhabitants and related crime were not prosecuted, because it was well known that these actions were carried out by relatives of the local magistrate. The Vásquez gang, comprising no fewer than sixty-four *bandoleros* (bandits) who rustled cattle in Niepos and San Gregorio and took them to the coastal hacienda of Cayaltí, enjoyed the protection of several landlords. In Contumazá, Taylor observes, thanks to the participation of unscrupulous lawyers and judges in the complex webs of patron-client relations, "felons with money or influential backers rarely found themselves sentenced to prison."[33]

Without a genuine monopoly of coercive power, equipped with few policemen, and often at the mercy of local *gamonales*, the state apparatus was neither neutral nor effective. It was not uncommon for *hacendados* to protect their dependents from state persecution for desertion, failure to pay tax, or cattle rustling. Well aware of the limitations of state power, particularly vis-à-vis local landlords, officials were often unwilling to take action against local bosses.

Given the failures of the judicial system, it was common for people to rely on private punishment, adding to the widespread use of violence. Moreover, local representatives of the state usually did their best to subvert the state's authority and make it serve their own ends, thereby depriving the state of what legitimacy it had. Taylor notes *hacendado* refusal to pay taxes in Hualgayoc.[34]

As can be seen from the example of Contumazá, local issues dominated the agenda, although national political developments did impinge on local politics. While local bosses clearly held disproportionate power, this does not mean that the rural population at large was uninvolved in politics. On the contrary (as Taylor found for Contumazá), a surprisingly large number of men from town and countryside were involved with the various political or factionalist groupings, usually through complex clientage ties.

THE WAR OF THE PACIFIC: WEAKENING THE LOCAL STATE APPARATUS

Local factionalist strife moved to center stage during the War of the Pacific, when intra-elite tensions were exacerbated. Unable to unite in the face of the enemy, the various factions battled out their disagreements inside the army, in that way, preventing the organization of an army for the defense of Cajamarca.[35]

Although conscription began in 1879, and the Chilean forces reached the north coast in 1880, Cajamarca was not directly affected by the war until 1882, when the Chilean army reached the highlands. The enemy forces imposed *cupos* (cash payments or ransom) on town and hacienda alike, demanding ransoms worth thousands of soles and plundering and torching those estates and towns that refused to pay. San Luis, San Pablo, and Cajamarca, all of which refused, were sacked, while Hualgayoc, San Miguel, Ichocán, and Bambamarca, which paid, were spared.[36] A number of haciendas met the same fate, as their equipment was sent to Chile and their animals were slaughtered to feed the soldiers. Both enemy and Peruvian forces scoured the countryside for provisions, and the Peruvian army recruited men and boys. The many petitions filed by mothers and wives with the prefect on behalf of their wrongfully recruited male relatives show that conscription was often carried out indiscriminately and violently.[37] Officials stormed villages in the middle of the night, breaking into houses and arresting prospective conscripts. Rumor of such attacks could spread rapidly, with the result that entire villages occasionally took to the surrounding mountains.[38] Conscription, the armies' demand for supplies, and the sacking of towns and villages all added to the suffering of the Cajamarcan population, in particular, the peasantry.

Women played an important part in peasant responses to the war. As well as contributing to the war effort as camp followers, many women fought conscription. In July 1880 two hundred women and fifty men armed with sticks and rocks attacked the governor of the district of Ichocán as he tried to lead a group of conscripts from the area; in San Marcos, no fewer than five hundred women and men fired at the provincial governor from the surrounding hills to protest his attempt to collect the head tax.[39] Women also fought for the exemption of their menfolk from conscription by submitting literally hundreds of petitions to that effect—although the responses were rarely recorded.[40]

Patron-client relations also played a key role in peasants' attempts to evade conscription: among the *hacendados* hiding peasants on their estates was José Mercedes Puga, the owner of hacienda La Pauca and a central figure in intra-elite factionalism in the province of Contumazá. Offering his dependents protection was a way of cementing patron-client relations and strengthening his position in the growing conflict with his main political rival, Miguel Iglesias. Iglesias' Grito de Montán in August 1882, in which he called for Peruvian capitulation to the Chilean forces, resulted in open division within the Peruvian military. With *hacendados* taking different sides in the ensuing struggle for control, civil war broke out. Having opposed the demands of the Peruvian state, it was only a small step for Cajamarca's peasants to follow their patrons into battle against the official Peruvian state representatives when the latter collaborated with the Chileans. The result was Puga's *montonero* (guerrilla fighters usually united under a common leader by bonds of clientage) following, which fought the *iglesista*, pro-Chilean forces and the Chilean occupation forces from 1882 on.

Conflicts between the various *hacendado*-dominated factions continued after the end of the war in 1883, resulting in civil war from 1883 to 1885 and producing a legacy of enduring factionalist strife in the department of Cajamarca, especially in the provinces of Hualgayoc and Contumazá. Groups of guerrillas plundered the countryside with impunity, occasionally forcing subprefects and other officials to escape district and provincial capitals. Contumazá was overrun several times by followers of the anti-Chilean leader Andrés Cáceres in 1884 and 1885, forcing the *iglesista* subprefects to flee on several occasions.

By the 1880s disorder had become institutionalized in both national and local politics. Locally, elections were commonly settled by armed battle; nationally, three of the four main political parties were dominated by caudillos, with the fourth party, the Partido Civil, torn apart by dissension.

Peasant resistance also manifested itself in a variety of forms. In 1887 Guzmango's peasants protested the levying of the head tax and resistance to the payment of taxes soon spread across the entire province.[41] Ultimately, factional violence and grassroots protest escalated, resulting in the guerrilla (*montonero*) revolt in 1894 and ensuing political violence from 1894 to the end of the century in Hualgayoc.

By the last third of the nineteenth century, political instability, intervillage feuds, and endemic banditry increasingly shaped Cajamarcan society and left their mark on the legal record. Accusations of cattle rustling, illegal conscription, politically motivated attacks by armed groups, and complaints concerning *abusos* (misuse of authority) by local officials abound in the trial transcripts. In a period of near-total erosion of state authority, economic dislocation, and a newly armed and highly mobile peasantry, it is perhaps not surprising that cattle rustling and *bandolerismo* became common ways of supplementing income for many peasants.

The economic impact of rising demand on the coast for foodstuffs and labor in the 1890s, combined with the political stability which followed the advent of Nicolás de Piérola's government of national reconstruction in 1895, marked the beginning of greater security for most of Cajamarca. However, internecine strife and banditry continued endemic in Hualgayoc until the 1930s.[42]

URBAN, SEMIURBAN, AND RURAL SOCIETY: EVERYDAY LIFE IN CAJAMARCA

Although urban women and men dominate the legal records, most people resided in the rural areas. According to Taylor, a mere 28 percent of Cajamarca province's population resided in towns. As Taylor also notes, even his reworked figures of the 1876 census overestimate the degree of urbanization in the region's economic and social life. For the province of Cajamarca, only three of the twelve towns listed in the 1876 census contained more than one thousand inhabitants.[43]

Even though smaller "towns" such as San Marcos and Asunción (housing

637 and 803 inhabitants, respectively) hardly merited the label "urban," they nevertheless possessed some urban characteristics. As minor political, commercial, and administrative centers they provided some of the services and functions associated with an urban lifestyle. They were also district centers in terms of trade and administration and attracted rural visitors and regional travelers.[44] This is where ponchos, mats, hats, dyes, and foodstuffs were traded on market days; where churchgoers attended mass, or at least funerals; where transport to and trade with the coast were arranged with muleteers; and where people filed complaints with the local magistrate.

Even that part of the population that resided in "towns," however, gained its livelihood in part from agriculture. Taylor notes that 80 percent of the population of the district capitals of the province of Contumazá, which was part of the province of Cajamarca until 1872, stated that they relied on agriculture for their livelihood.[45] One nineteenth-century traveler noted that orchards surrounded most houses in Cascas.[46] This continued to be true of the town of Cajamarca as late as the 1930s.[47] Several of the disputes which ended in court were related to the keeping of domestic animals in town,[48] and numerous testators recorded that they owned and lived in houses in the town of Cajamarca, but owned and farmed fields in its vicinity.[49] Rural and urban society were thus interwoven, with agricultural work such as feeding the chickens, tending the pigs, and working the fields forming part of women's everyday tasks even within the town of Cajamarca proper. For residents in other supposedly urban centers the overlap between rural and urban existence was even more marked.[50]

This, then, was the society in which litigants lived: most resided in or near these semiurban centers; they were a mixed lot and included small-scale (and not-so-small-scale) landowners, merchants, carpenters, shoemakers, shopkeepers, day laborers, domestic servants, brewers, soldiers, priests, and notaries; some were literate, most were not; most owned their own home, some plots of land, and some domestic animals, engaging both in the commercial economy and subsistence activities; above all, they mixed. As Chambers has pointed out, drawing clear lines between social classes or high and low cultures is difficult. In provincial towns and villages these groups exchanged gossip and, with it, social and political views, creating their own popular culture and definitions of social norms.[51]

The 1876 census provides some (perhaps not totally reliable) information on employment. As Taylor states in his study of Hualgayoc, the occupational categories given by the lower-class population tend to hide the multiple ways in which individuals earned a living. In a society where peasant farmers began to rely on seasonal migration, on the sale of agricultural goods, and on the production and commercialization of artisan products, the simple label "agricultor" failed to capture the breadth of activities in which an individual engaged in the course of a year. In the same way, many urban inhabitants who derived most of their income from their work as shoemakers or hat-makers, or from other artisan occupations, also owned and worked plots of land outside the town (or at least an orchard or vegetable plot within it).

Even though the labels given by women and men rarely tell the whole story of how they earned their income, the census does tell us something about the occupational structure of the region. Textile production occupied 11,255 women, or 81 percent of the female population of the province. Most of these (68.2 percent) were hilanderas (spinners); a further 14.4 percent (1,986) called themselves costureras (seamstresses). The group also included 2 modistas (dressmakers), 80 tejedoras (knitters), 23 bordaderas (embroiderers), and 37 tintoreras (dyers). Although most of these women also engaged in numerous other activities, including housework, cooking, child care, and, in many cases, subsistence agriculture, their self-description as textile workers probably implies that this was where they derived most of their cash income. As Ernst Middendorf noted in 1895, most peasant women were almost continuously spinning and weaving while walking or talking.[52]

Although the textile sector was dominated by women, some men participated, too: 128 men described themselves as spinners, 170 as sastres (tailors), 115 as knitters, 25 as dyers, and 99 as trenzadores (rope makers).[53] While most spinners and dyers were women, dyeing was a trade where men and women were represented almost equally: 37 of 62 dyers—or 59.7 percent—were women.[54]

Apart from textile production, 948 women (7 percent) described themselves as agricultoras (agriculturalists), and 373 (2.8 percent) as jornaleras (day laborers). Almost 10 percent therefore considered working the land to be their main occupation. Whereas the agriculturalists farmed their own land, day laborers received a daily wage for their labors.[55]

If we include dependents, washerwomen, cooks, and wet nurses in the category of domestic servants, 430 women—3 percent—of Cajamarca's working female population worked as domestic servants. This is only slightly above the percentage of male servants, 2 percent.[56] A further 1.1 percent (149) of women said they worked full time in food processing, namely, as chicheras (makers of traditional beer), dulceras (sweets makers), and panaderas (bread makers).

Food processing, like textile production, was dominated by women, with only 12 male bakers and one male sweets maker in the province. Only 23 women called themselves comerciantes (merchants), as opposed to 108 men.

On the other hand, 46 women said they were *vivanderas* (market women), implying that they engaged in petty commerce rather than large-scale trade. Authors who have worked on other regions of Peru and Latin America have observed a gender division between large-scale trade as a predominantly male activity and petty commerce as a typically female activity.[57] While it is possible that this is an accurate reflection of the scale of men's and women's operations, it seems likely that women's business enterprises were routinely labeled by census takers as petty commerce or market activities by virtue of their sex rather than by size of their business. Certainly no corresponding label for male petty trade emerges from the census, although it is unlikely that all of the 108 men who described themselves as merchants operated on a large scale. However, engaging in commercial business was easier for men than for women, who, if they were married, needed written permission from their husbands to enable them to do business. In addition, female literacy rates were substantially below those of men (see below), preventing most women from engaging in business on a larger scale, as they were unable to read or sign contracts or accounts.

If women dominated the production of textiles, men dominated most other artisan activities. There was one female hatmaker, whereas 210 males engaged in this activity; and of the most important artisan occupations, all shoemakers (289), painters (12), carpenters (148), smiths (60), silversmiths (48), sculptors (1), wire makers (19), watchmakers (5), wax chandlers (3), gunsmiths (9,) and basket makers (6) were male.

One final point worthy of note with regard to female occupations is that, excepting the three formally educated midwives who resided in the town of Cajamarca and presumably attended the moneyed classes, no women registered their profession as midwives. Although it is clear that numerous women possessed the relevant experience and knowledge to assist in birth, they did not earn enough from this to consider it their main occupation. Instead, it was, like agricultural work, washing, spinning, weaving, mending, and cooking, one of the many skills and tasks of lower-class women to which no special recognition was attached.

Variations among districts within the province of Cajamarca were marked. While domestic service was clearly more common for women in the district of Cajamarca (including the town of Cajamarca itself, as well as surrounding villages and hamlets)—with 310 women, or 6 percent of the working female population listed as servants, cooks, child care workers, and washerwomen—only 0.5 percent of working men in the district of Cajamarca said they worked as domestic servants. In addition, the incidence of more professional services was higher in the town of Cajamarca, where three

Lima-educated midwives, one seamstress, one *peluquera* (hairdresser), and ten female teachers (as opposed to one in most of the other districts) were to be found. Otherwise, however, there were parallels between employment patterns in the more urbanized district of Cajamarca and other districts: 79.2 percent of women were engaged in textile production, 1.2 percent in trade, and 2 percent in food-processing activities, primarily bread baking.

The census also provides information on male and female literacy rates. Whereas 38.9 percent of men in the province of Cajamarca over the age of fifteen could read and write, only 13.5 percent of adult women could do the same. A further 5.1 percent of men and 3.4 percent of women could read but not write, and 53.3 percent of adult men were illiterate, as were 85.7 percent of the women.[58] Female literacy was thus substantially lower than male literacy.

These provincial averages hide large local variations in literacy as a whole, and the gap between male and female literacy. In the district of Cajamarca, of the half of the population which resided in the town itself, 21.4 percent of the women were literate, as were 37.6 percent of the men. In more remote districts, however, literacy rates were much lower. In Llacanora, for example, only 8 of 357, or 2.2 percent, of women, could read and write; 95.8 percent of Llacanora's female population was fully illiterate. The same applied to 75 percent of the men; only 20.5 percent of Llacanora's men could read and write.[59] Proximity to urban facilities such as schools thus contributed significantly to shaping both women's and men's access to education.

As the literacy figures from the 1876 census indicate, men continued to be privileged over women with regard to literacy, although rather less so in the urban than the rural areas. While the provincial averages for literacy were 38.9 and 13.5 percent for men and women, respectively, the gap was smaller in the more urbanized district of Cajamarca. Whereas 37.6 men were reported as literate there, only 21.4 percent of women could read and write.

WOMEN'S LIVES ON AND OFF THE HACIENDA

Although nearly a third of the population lived on large estates, this group is underrepresented among trial participants. Poverty, distance, and the *hacendados'* authority over life on their estates all made it unlikely that tenants would resort to the courts. Few of the criminal proceedings in the Archivo Departamental de Cajamarca deal with internal hacienda issues; those that do are complaints lodged by abused peons against their landlord, revealing the less-benevolent aspects of patron-client relations. Tenants, sharecroppers, and laborers complained of beatings, having their cattle and beasts of burden confiscated, being subjected to false arrest, forced labor, and the arrest and sometimes abduction of their children.[60] Although wives and mothers occasionally pressed charges on a husband's or son's behalf (or, more rarely, a daughter's), such trials were usually halted shortly after being filed, and the transcripts contain little information on hacienda life. Disputes among tenants were usually sorted out internally, under pressure from the *hacendado* and his manager, thus leaving few written records. The lives of women and men on haciendas therefore remain hidden from view, and it is difficult to draw any conclusions about the lives of female tenants. However, Deere has researched the lives of peasant women both on and off large estates and offers some ideas about their lives around the turn of the century. Focusing on the gendered nature of peasant labor, she concludes that the undervaluation of women's labor facilitated the increased exploitation of the peasant household as a whole, and women in particular. Whereas formal agreements between hacienda tenants and landlords delineated and negotiated men's labor contributions, the labor demands placed on women were not made part of formal contracts or agreements.[61]

In addition, female labor was valued much less than men's: on the hacienda Combayo men received between two-tenths and three-tenths of a sol in cash each day they labored on the hacienda; women who were paid for carrying out tasks such as cleaning out the stables, milking, or production of dairy products such as butter and cheese received one-twentieth of a sol per day in addition to the daily meal, valued at one-tenth of a sol, which also formed part of men's wages.[62] When wages were introduced beginning in the early twentieth century, these were usually paid only to men; where wages were paid to women, these were a third of what men received.[63]

In general, the gender division of labor implied that men carried out agricultural work, whereas women took care of daily reproductive chores such as wood gathering, washing, cooking, child care, sewing, and mending, as well as looking after the family's domestic animals. In addition, women helped out with agricultural tasks such as planting, threshing, and harvesting and took over subsistence agriculture when the men were working for the landlord or earning wages. Writing in 1939, Eulogio Eléspuru Bernizón observed, "the women take care of the domestic duties and assist the men in planting and harvesting; they are also in charge of selling the produce. . . . Normally it is the women who hold the family's money. The men do the heavy work in the fields and pasture the animals."[64]

Anthropological studies of peasant communities from other regions of Peru note that, although men tend to define fieldwork and other agricultural tasks as almost exclusively male activities, women do almost the same amount of agricultural work in addition to their reproductive tasks. Even where the tasks of men and women are very similar, women's contribution tends to be underestimated by the peasants themselves and by researchers.[65] Several authors, including Deere, have remarked the importance of women's contribution to both peasant household and hacienda profitability.[66] Cajamarcan tenant women's tasks included spinning and dyeing a certain amount of wool for the landlord, making butter and cheese, and participation in *mingas* (collective work parties). Female tenants also had to provide domestic service for the landlord and his family for weeks at a time, either in the house on the hacienda or in the *hacendado*'s house in town.[67]

Based on evaluation of a Cajamarcan census and her own research on rural women's work in agriculture, Deere points out that peasant women's participation in agricultural production is easily underestimated, particularly among the near-landless and smallholding population. She argues that it was among these groups that women's participation in agricultural fieldwork and decision making within the familial labor force was most significant. She also points out that women's involvement in income-generating activities and agricultural work varied according to social class. The lower their social status, the more they tended to be involved in agricultural work.[68]

According to Deere, in the early twentieth century patriarchal norms were stronger on haciendas than in free peasant villages, where she observed smaller families and a higher frequency of separation. Certainly, the burden of work on women living on independent peasant smallholdings may have been slightly less onerous, even if their household rented land from an hacienda, since they were not expected to provide the landlord with domestic service as part of the rental agreement. On the other hand, life on independent smallholdings was often more arduous than on the great estates for both sexes. As access to land was channeled through the male head of household (i.e., the father or husband), women were dependent on their links to men in order to obtain land on estates. Widows were occasionally booted off the estate after their husbands' death.[69] Because women were economically dependent on their husbands, women on the estates found it more difficult to leave unsatisfactory marriages than did women in the free villages, who usually owned some land of their own. Young couples' dependence on the landlord's approval of their union and allocation of land in order to establish themselves also made for greater landlord authority over tenants' matrimony.[70] Women's freedom to choose or leave a husband was further restricted by landlords' tendency to arbitrate internal conflicts on their estates. To the degree that landlords imposed their own class' definition of gender relations on their tenants, this adversely influenced women's position.

For women the economic changes of the late nineteenth century meant that the labor demands on hacienda tenants of both sexes (and probably on peasant women outside hacienda boundaries as well) rose during the last two decades of the century, as their fathers, husbands, and common-law partners migrated to the coast for varying periods of time. Even married women lived for months without men. Ernst Middendorf, passing through the village of Tambomayo in the late nineteenth century, described the following scene: "Sitting in the yard, in front of an open door, was a woman surrounded by four young women. The former was the owner, the younger ones her daughters and daughters-in-law, all of whom lived with their mother. There was no man in the house, as all were absent from the village, either traveling as muleteer or working as laborer on the estates of others."[71]

At the same time, the growing commercialization of the region offered opportunities for peasant women not associated with the hacienda, who increasingly engaged in petty trade and marketed their agricultural produce and artisanal production. Although it is impossible, on the basis of the available material, to produce statistical evidence that women engaged more in trade toward the end of the nineteenth century than at its beginning, examples from the wills and criminal trials indicate that they did participate in the gradual expansion of commercial relations in this period. As economic opportunities diversified, so did women's options. While many more may have experienced spinsterhood, abandonment, single motherhood, and serial monogamy, women also developed alternative ways of dealing with the economic challenges which their being single—often with children—posed.

CHAPTER 3

Legislating Gender

THE LAW, OFFICIAL GENDER NORMS, AND NOTIONS OF HONOR

Elite gender norms permeated Peruvian society, influencing all classes in a variety of ways, but most concretely via legislation. The legal framework, revised several times in the course of the nineteenth century, codified elite views on gender and offers us a window to elite perceptions of gender.

The role and importance of the institution of matrimony, the position of women and men within marriage, and the place of women in society were all dealt with in legislation, as were matters of honor and respectability and how male and female comportment impinged on reputation. Although far from all social groups abided by legal precepts of appropriate gender behavior, legislation nevertheless influenced the definition of sexual norms. Further, elite gender norms shaped the legal arena from which the sources I examine in the next chapters are drawn. I therefore look at the evolving legal structures during the nineteenth century, the shifting balance of church and state authority over marital and gender-related matters, and, most important, contemporary legal definitions of women's and men's legal rights in reference to marriage, property, children, and honor. I also consider the Creole elite's assumptions with regard to gender, which underlay much of the legislation, and changing perceptions of women's role in society.

Although independence eventually led to the introduction of new bodies of law, women's legal situation underwent no drastic transformation during the nineteenth century.[1] In the absence of new laws, colonial antecedent shaped post-independence legal practice.[2] Women's position was somewhat modified by the introduction of the 1852 civil code and the penal code of 1862, both of which form the basis for all legal proceedings detailed in this book.

Some of the new provisions of the 1862 code extended women's autonomy. Widows were allowed to remarry within the first year of their widow-hood; mothers of illegitimate children were granted *patria potestad* (parental authority) over their children; and the murder of adulterous wives caught in flagrante delicto was no longer condoned by the law. Women continued to be excluded from the professions, however, and married women remained subject to their husband's authority. Most important, the 1852 civil code defined marriage as a religious sacrament, leaving the church to regulate who could marry, to formalize marital union, and, where deemed appropriate, to dissolve it. Despite the gradual estrangement of the Peruvian state and the church in the course of the nineteenth century, the two continued to cooperate closely in the regulation of matrimony.

VYING FOR SUPREMACY: CHURCH AND STATE IN NINETEENTH-CENTURY PERU

The church enjoyed close ties to the colonial bureaucracy and played a central role in extending colonial authority over Peru's population. In addition to levying tithes, registering births, marriages, and deaths, and exercising partial responsibility for drawing up tax registers, parish priests sought to inculcate the populace with Catholic sexual mores.[3]

Through sermons, confessions, and the prosecution of persons engaged in illicit sexual relations, the church worked—with varying degrees of success—to discourage consensual unions. Mannarelli notes the frequency of common-law unions in seventeenth-century Lima. Most cases of concubinage brought before the ecclesiastical court in Lima dealt with relationships of several years' duration, which indicates the high degree of popular tolerance for informal unions. Moreover, the significant number of defendants who reappear in the transcripts reveals that even sentences imposed by the ecclesiastical court did not fundamentally change plebeian life choices.[4]

While the church continued to play a significant role in overseeing sexual morality during the nineteenth century, the institution was progressively weakened after independence. The wars themselves, and the ensuing end to the flow of priests from Spain, led to a shortage of priests, which was exacerbated following the abolition of tithes in 1859. As this source of income was only partially replaced by the stipend which the Peruvian state supplied until 1887, the number of applicants to the priesthood fell dramatically. By the end of the nineteenth century, many rural *doctrinas* (parish administrative units) had to make do without a resident priest, especially in the highland parishes, which clerics viewed as unattractive.[5] The church found itself increasingly challenged by the liberal nation-state, as the latter abolished the *fueros* (corporate legal rights and privileges, e.g., those of the church) in 1856, prohibited the collection of tithes, canceled the interest on loans made by the church, suppressed private ecclesiastical courts, and ended the church's monopoly on education.

The church's wealth having been decimated by the nationalization of a number of monasteries in 1833 and the abolition of tithes in 1859, the state also took over a growing number of administrative tasks. In 1869 cemeteries were brought under municipal control and civil funerals permitted. In 1890 liberal concern over priests' overcharging for *aranceles* (fees for baptisms, marriages, and burials) resulted in an official proposal for reduced burial fees. This led to the state's setting the levels of these fees in 1891. The Civil Code of 1852 ordered the establishment of civil registers (*registros civiles*)—though these orders had to be reiterated in 1873, 1892, and 1928 because of the failure to actually establish registers in most districts.[6]

The largely unsuccessful efforts to set up a national civil register are characteristic of the tension between church and state in this period. Not always successful in its first attempts, the Peruvian state nevertheless gradually expanded its bureaucratic apparatus, contesting and eventually assuming control over the registration of births, marriages, and deaths; over education; and, in the course of the first half of the twentieth century, over marriage itself. Despite the fierce criticisms of clerical abuse by liberal intellectuals (expressed most vociferously by Manuel González de Prada, who accused a trinity consisting of justice of the peace, district governor, and priest of exploiting the highland peasantry), the Peruvian state was never anti-religion and fully endorsed church authority over matrimony well into the twentieth century.[7]

WOMEN'S POSITION IN PERUVIAN LAW

Until the recognition of civil marriage in 1897 (a gesture toward the growing presence of foreigners rather than a fundamental reevaluation of the official stance on marriage), the Peruvian civil code recognized marriage only as defined by the Council of Trent in 1563. Marriage was thus viewed as a religious sacrament and not a civil contract.[8] The church held jurisdiction over who could marry through its ability to grant dispensation in cases of physical or spiritual kinship or parental objections, and its power to grant annulment of marriage and divorce. In addition, parish priests, by means of the confessional, guided much of the population with regard to questions of marital conflict. Until 1918, when marriage was secularized, only a few of its legal aspects were dealt with by civil courts.

Until 1918 marriage could be instituted only by the church and was indissoluble. However, spouses could file for annulment or *separación de cuer-
pos* (defined not as the dissolution of the marital bond, but as the separation of bed and board). While annulment opened the path for remarriage,
separation of bed and board did not. Grounds for annulment were invalidity,
such as in cases of kinship, or lack of consent on the part of the parents,
the bride, or the groom. A separation suit could be filed on the basis of adultery (committed by the woman) or public concubinage (committed by the
man); brutality, attempted murder, or uncontainable hatred on the part of
one of the spouses, manifested in frequent fights; incurable vices such as
gambling, drinking, dissipation, or prodigality; a husband refusing his wife
maintenance or a woman refusing to reside with her husband or meet conjugal obligations; absence of more than five years; madness; chronic conta-
gious illness; or the condemnation of one of the spouses to a sentence considered degrading.[9]

Although separation suits could be initiated on the above grounds, they
were seldom successful. Even when they eventually resulted in divorce, the
path usually proved costly, long, and painful. The first step for a wife seeking divorce was to petition the ecclesiastical court for permission for the
wife to leave the conjugal home and move to a *beaterio* (a religious house),
or an "honorable" household. Once such a petition was granted, the interim
monthly allowance the husband had to pay his wife settled, and the wife
established outside the marital home, proceedings could move on. Spouses
could file an ecclesiastical suit for divorce and apply to the civil court to have
their conjugal assets divided.

Many suits never moved beyond the first stage, however. It was in husbands' interest to delay proceedings for as long as possible in order to retain
control of conjugal property. Once established in an honorable household,
would-be divorcées were dependent on monthly alimony from their husbands; in those cases in which husbands refused (or were unable) to supply
this amount, couples were often forced to reconcile. In some cases, this was
the result of poverty and material necessity; in others, wives were forced to
return by their husbands' refusal to pay up.

Regardless of whether their husbands paid a sufficiently large monthly
allowance, many wives found that seclusion in a *beaterio* hampered their
divorce efforts. They needed outside assistance, and only a very few could
afford a lawyer. In addition, the cost of filing a suit often exceeded their alimony. In the meantime, many wives found, husbands squandered conjugal
property. Hünefeldt notes that, as wives became more and more aware of
these limitations, the percentage of women who pursued divorce proceed-

ings before the ecclesiastical curia fell during the nineteenth century, as did resort to the *beaterios*. Instead, they tended increasingly to reside on their own during the proceedings, earn their own living, and thus fund their divorce proceedings in order to more quickly regain control of their share of marital property. Also, couples resorted more and more frequently to informal divorce, reducing the role of honorable households and civil and ecclesiastical courts, but increasing their own chances of economic survival.[10]

Whereas the church oversaw marital relations, the Civil Code of 1852 defined women's civil position, including legal subordination to their husbands. Like men, women came of age at twenty-one, allowing them to initiate legal proceedings, testify in court, write their own wills, inherit property, and conduct business—but not to act as witnesses to other people's wills, enter the legal profession, vote, or occupy any official position. "Women, in general, cannot be guardians due to their weakness and scant experience in business," García Calderón explained.[11] Nor could they act as representatives of others excepting only their husbands, who could expressly authorize them to act on their behalf. Once married, women were placed under their husbands' tutelage and could no longer conduct business or take legal action without the latter's written authorization. Lacking such an authorization (either because the husband refused or he was absent), wives could apply to the civil court for a *licencia judicial* (an authorization enabling them to represent themselves in legal matters). This allowed them to carry out business on their own and engage in legal proceedings. Women could defend themselves without their husband's intervention in criminal trials, but not if civil action was taken against them.

Women's legal status was determined by their marital status: "When they are single they hold the same status as men . . .; but when they marry they are subject to the man's authority and become a dependent," noted García Calderón.[12] Wives' legal and financial subordination to their husbands was seen as beneficial because women were considered less able in business matters, and because male management was assumed to entail an element of economic protection. Through marriage, the couple established a marriage partnership (*sociedad conyugal*) in which the property of both partners became part of the same enterprise. Upon the dissolution of this partnership, usually because of the death of one of the spouses, the property which each partner brought to the partnership was returned to the initial owner or his or her estate, and the remaining property, the *gananciales* (acquest), was divided between the two parties and, in case of death, their respective heirs.

One way in which the law protected women's property from dissipation by the husband was a stipulation that the wife's contribution to the capital of the marriage partnership had to be returned before the husband or his heirs could claim their share.[13] Although the dowry which women brought into the marriage, or their subsequent inheritance, belonged to them throughout, it was administered by the husband. Additional property, called *bienes parafernales* (any property the wife might bring into the marriage or receive other than her dowry) and *arras* (donations made by the groom to the bride prior to the marriage) could be administered by the wife herself if she wished, although it was more common for women to entrust these to their husbands. Husbands held parental authority over the couple's children. Mothers obtained parental authority over a child only by default, that is, if the child was illegitimate and not recognized by the father, or if the child's father was deceased.[14]

Women's position and options varied in accordance with their life stage: widows often possessed greater economic and legal freedom than married or single women.[15] Although widowhood offered release from several of the restrictions placed on wives, widows were nevertheless more circumscribed in their actions than widowers. While widows could engage in business, take legal action, and exert parental authority over their children, remarriage was frowned on, especially among the educated classes. The Catholic Church refused to bless such unions. If a widow exposed herself to suspicion that her (sexual) conduct was less than irreproachable, she ran the risk of losing custody of her children.[16] Although it is unlikely that such considerations were decisive for widows considering remarriage, there was a legal argument to be made for remaining single. Widows who remarried automatically lost the right to administer their children's property. While it was assumed that formal marriage protected the rights of both women and children, it could also work in the opposite direction, as in the case of widowed mothers who relied on the income of their children's inheritance from deceased fathers. Social differences shaped the ways in which women coped with their marital status: whereas widowhood may have been liberating for women of means, working-class and peasant women usually faced hard times.[17]

NURTURING THE PERUVIAN NATION:
MATERNITY AND MATRIMONY

The period's legal texts recognized and acknowledged that wives occupied a position inferior to that of their husbands. The rationale was that women were less able than men and that, in any case, they were compensated by receiving control over the domestic realm. This division of spheres was designed to reflect the strengths and weaknesses of the sexes. "The male,"

García Calderón wrote, "is inclined to direct his thoughts and feelings primarily toward the outside world, while women's nature inclines them to concentrate their affections in the intimate sphere of life. Therefore the husband represents the family in its dealing with the world, while the wife is in charge of administering all domestic business."[18]

By the second half of the nineteenth century the domestic realm was acquiring a new ideological significance for the national elite. Women's role as mother and safekeeper of the domestic arena became central to the formulation of the Creole intellectual elite's modernizing, nation-building project in Peru—as, indeed, in other parts of Latin America. The home came to be viewed as a haven from the aggressive, masculine, and conflictual outer world. Wives and mothers were given the role of guarding this domestic refuge and imbuing it with the "feminine" qualities of loving obedience, gentleness, morality, and religiosity. Most important, mothers were expected to pass precepts of religion, morality, and nationalism on to their children, and thus mold the country's future citizens. "Mothers exercise an important role in society, for it is they who form the hearts of their children," noted García Calderón.[19] As Denegri has observed, "feminine, maternal, educated and chaste domesticity was taken by the urban elite to represent the very essence of modern Peru."[20]

Education of females was central to the modernizing elite's conception of women's role in national development. Concern with female education originated in Enlightenment Europe, where it was hoped that educated and enlightened mothers would instill reason in their descendants. In order to fulfil their role as responsible wife, ideal companion for men and, most important, model mother, women needed to be educated.

In Peru, these ideas produced a series of decrees encouraging education of females and culminated in the Reglamento General de Instrucción Pública (General Law of Public Instruction) of 1876, which (in theory) made primary instruction compulsory for both boys and girls. By the 1870s the expansion of education (for elite females), combined with the spread of reformist ideas concerning women's role in Peruvian society, contributed to the emergence of a group of intellectual *literatas* (literati). These talented female writers for a period moved to the very center of the public cultural arena. At their *veladas* (soirées) writers and intellectuals of both sexes met regularly, exchanged ideas, and read each other's work. Through their books, articles, short stories, poems, and other literary contributions, published either individually or in one of the many newspapers and magazines in Lima, they commented on society and advocated women's mission in it. One of these authors, Teresa González de Fanning, linked the need for education with national development: "Education should be republican: it should inculcate love of the fatherland, morality, and simplicity of comportment."[21]

While advocating education for women, Peruvian intellectuals nevertheless defined woman's role in society in traditional terms: she needed education primarily in order to fulfill her function as daughter, wife, and mother.[22] This was also reflected in the curriculum at most schools for girls: as well as studying the Spanish language, geography, and history, girls had classes in drawing, embroidery, dance, or housekeeping, depending on social class.[23] Late-nineteenth-century Peruvian literature abounds with heroines whose prime mission was the preservation of domestic order as a palliative to the travails of public life to which their menfolk were exposed. Women were seen as possessing an innate moral superiority, which served as a "moral reserve" in a world of political instability and conflict.[24] The idealization of woman's role as mother went hand in hand with this and was paralleled in other Latin American countries. As Ruggiero has noted, late-nineteenth-century Argentinean society placed growing emphasis on woman's role as mother, partly because "the qualities of motherhood were considered to have a purifying effect on society as a whole."[25]

This new idealization of women represented a sea change from colonial Peru's tradition of satirical literature, which had portrayed women as the seductive, elusive, and immoral *tapadas* (literally, covered). In a period in which female seclusion was still a near-absolute norm for the elite, Creole women had obtained a certain freedom of movement by hiding in a *manto* (shawl) when leaving their homes, which concealed their identity while still indicating, by virtue of the shawl's costly materials, their social class. Disguised by a shawl, the *tapadas* made the best of their anonymity, and are described both in Peruvian colonial literature and by travel writers as involved in illicit intrigues, including flirting and occasional affairs. The disappearance in the 1850s of the traditional *saya y manto*, the overskirt and shawl behind which Peruvian women, especially those from Lima, hid when moving about in the streets, was emblematic of the elite's changing definition of women's role in Peruvian society. Instead of using the overskirt, women of all ages in Lima imitated European fashion. Increasingly, the Peruvian elite imagined the country as part of a group of white, Christian, capitalist, and (above all) modern countries, with women playing a central role in national development.[26]

Despite upper-class intellectuals' new valorization of women's potential, the balance of power between the sexes was not to be upset. The wife's subservient position in a marriage was of particular importance. "The male is the chief in the marriage partnership," García Calderón explained. He went on to add, "This superiority of the male is born out of nature herself, and the laws do nothing but recognize and regulate it."[27] The law stated even more explicitly, "The husband should protect his wife, and the wife obey her husband."[28] Peruvian legislators argued that ensuring clear lines of command was important in order to minimize marital discord. "If women were to be given the same authority . . . as their husband without subjugating them to their husband's will, both heads of the family might find themselves in disagreement as a result of the opposition of their wills." The same rationale was used to justify the denial of parental authority to married mothers: "In order to ensure the order of society, the mother's authority over her children is recognized only in case of the father's default."[29]

Marital harmony and male authority were regarded as essential to the preservation of the social order. As Lavrin has observed for the colonial period, church and state regarded the family as "the locus of moral and political socialization" and therefore dedicated considerable effort to ensuring male dominance within this institution.[30] The same was true for state bureaucracies across Latin America in the nineteenth century. In Mexico, Arrom observes, "the state required the obedience of wives as a guarantee of social cohesion"; nineteenth-century changes in Mexico's legislation tended to reaffirm women's oppressed position rather than to liberate them.[31] Linking concerns about threats to the patriarchal family to the Latin American tradition of corporatism, Dore says that Latin American leaders justified their authority by appealing to family patriarchs. "In the process of nation-building, elite discourses conceptualized the nation as a family ruled by a supreme patriarch." Thus Fruto Chamorro, an early president of Nicaragua, labeled himself the nation's father and the Nicaraguan people his children. Other politicians and religious leaders emphasized the importance of children's obedience to their parents and the institution of marriage. Any threat to the "institutions of patriarchy represented a fundamental challenge to the established order."[32]

In Argentina, as in other Latin American nations, official concern for social order resulted in growing state interference in lower-class families' private lives in the early nineteenth century. In Córdoba and Tucumán, regional authorities vigorously applied vagrancy laws to women deemed to be unemployed and, hence, potential prostitutes. Citing concern for unemployed women's morality, the police in the interior of the country forced them into state-approved paid employment.[33] Similar concerns for public morality also shaped official policy in Guatemala.[34]

Hünefeldt, working on nineteenth-century urban Peru, notes that traditional conceptions of honor and gender roles became more entrenched as a result of political and socioeconomic developments.[35] The increasingly visible presence of the urban masses occasionally manifested itself in noisy and even violent protests, such as in the artisans' protest against the importation of goods in 1859.[36] Together with the ongoing process of racial blurring, such social developments led to heightened elite concern for social order. By adding rules of honor and morality to the requirements of social status, elites re-erected social barriers which were perceived to be threatened. The lower classes' failure to comply with these rules was seen as proof of their inferiority and justification for their exploitation.

Chambers, using her study of the town of Arequipa, notes that the definition of honor was gradually transformed in the first half of the nineteenth century, becoming more egalitarian. As a result of plebeian pressure and negotiation, notions of virtue and self-discipline acquired preeminence over the more traditional criteria of purity of lineage and ostentatious display of wealth. According to Chambers, these changes meant that recognition of honor was ceded by regional elites to local, plebeian *hombres de bien* (men of honor) in return for which male artisans, farmers, and shopkeepers offered regional caudillos political allegiance. The recognition of honor was linked to notions of citizenship and the strengthening of patriarchal authority over the domestic sphere. Increased emphasis on female sexual virtue and obedience in effect justified women's exclusion from politics and subjected them to further scrutiny.

Alongside these attitudinal shifts, state intervention in cases of marital conflict among the popular classes rose after independence; granting "honorable" men rights accompanied the repression of women without "virtue."[37] In response to different pressures and processes, the moral climate and understanding altered toward the end of the nineteenth century, affecting plebeians primarily when they came into contact with official gender norms (for instance, when they came into contact with the legal system).

SAFEGUARDING THE SOCIAL ORDER: LEGISLATIVE RESPONSES TO ILLEGITIMACY AND CRIMES AGAINST HONOR

Compliance with the norm of formalized, church-sanctioned marriage was central to elite concern with lower-class sexual mores. Both church and state differentiated sharply between marriage and so-called *relaciones ilícitas*, illicit sexual relations, an expression which was used to describe all types of sexual liaisons outside formal marriage, including long-term common-law unions. Regulating informal unions into nonexistence proved impossible, however. Instead, civil law continued the colonial tradition of discriminatory inheritance rights for the offspring of such unions. It was hoped that such discrimination would discourage common-law unions. If legitimate children existed, the inheritance of *hijos naturales* (children born to unmarried parents), regardless of their number, could not exceed one-fifth of the testator's property. The remaining four-fifths accrued to the legitimate children. "Not all children are of equal rank, depending on the morality of their parents' relationship," legal commentator Manuel Atanasio Fuentes observed.[38] If the father failed to recognize his illegitimate children, or failed to number them among his heirs in his will, they were not entitled to any inheritance, merely to the provision of *alimentos* (alimony) up to a fifth of the paternal estate.

Similar arrangements applied to women's succession. Providing a mother had no legitimate issue, her illegitimate children (excepting those born of an adulterous relationship) automatically inherited all her estate. If a woman's illegitimate children competed with legitimate siblings, the former's share was reduced to one-fifth of their mother's estate. However, most illegitimate children (excepting *hijos adulterinos*—those born of an adulterous relationship) could be legitimized by their parents' subsequent marriage, which accounts for the practice of deathbed marriages. It was common for de facto spouses to formalize their union in moments of grave illness, usually on the deathbed, in order to legitimize any offspring the couple might have produced.[39] Lino Rodríguez wrote that he married his wife four days before making his will: "Before marrying my wife, I have had four children with her, of whom three have died, and one lives . . ., so that this son is now legitimized through our marriage."[40]

The greatest dishonor was attached to adultery. Illegitimate children born to adulterous mothers (*hijos adulterinos*) were discriminated against even more than other illegitimate children and possessed no automatic right to inheritance from their mother. Children of adulterous fathers, however, were not discriminated against relative to other children conceived out of wedlock and could inherit up to a fifth of their father's estate after his death, providing that he had acknowledged them or remembered them in his will.[41]

As is evident from the above, a wife's adultery was considered a more serious offense than a husband's. Reflecting canon law and colonial tradition, civil law differentiated between male and female adultery: while female adultery qualified as a crime and provided grounds for divorce, male adultery did not. Wives could file for divorce only if their husbands had engaged in adultery in the conjugal home or conducted the affair in such a way as to cause public scandal. Late-nineteenth-century Peruvian legislation thus perpetuated the double standard that demanded absolute sexual virtue from women while granting men the right to philander.

Similarly, divorced women could apply for custody of their children only if they could prove they led a virtuous life. A woman's moral character was thus a prerequisite for carrying out her role as mother.[42] There was no corresponding restriction on men's ability to acquire custody of their children. Legal commentators justified the double standard with a concern for the line of succession. M. A. Fuentes wrote that "the husband's adultery is considered less serious than the wife's because the former does not produce the grave consequences of the latter, which could introduce children who are strangers to the family into its fold."[43]

Concern for legitimacy was central to elite preoccupation with marriage and was doubly important: it guaranteed paternity—and thus served to regulate the transmission of property—and it was a precondition for possessing honor. As Martínez-Alier has noted for Cuba, "the device through which the purity of the group was achieved was virginity. By controlling the access to female sexuality, control was exercised over the acquisition of undesirable members by the group."[44] Since the Council of Trent (1545–1563) firmly established the link between dishonor and illegitimacy, the stain of illegitimate descent was linked with the lack of *limpieza de sangre* (purity of blood). In Spain and colonial Latin America such dishonor signified social stigma and implied exclusion from respectable professions. Illegitimate persons were not allowed to practice law and were barred from posts in the upper echelons of the colonial bureaucracy.[45]

Sexual purity (i.e., premarital virginity and marital fidelity) was the prime ingredient of female honor. As the honor of the family depended on the honorable behavior of its members, its female members in particular, women's behavior was closely regulated and supervised wherever possible. In practice, only wealthy families could afford the luxury of secluding and supervising their female members. As a result, social distinctions were reinforced between families that could protect their women from the suspicion of sexual contamination and those that could not.

Despite the strict criteria governing honor, it remained a pliable concept—especially for those with means. Twinam's analysis of the colonial elites' negotiation of honor through devices such as hiding pregnancies, the acknowledgment (or otherwise) of natural and illegitimate children, and the purchase of *gracias al sacar* (a royal decree legitimating those born outside of marriage) reveals how the definition of honor could be stretched. Although sexual deviance in the form of extramarital relations was common enough, it did not always diminish honor, providing that knowledge of the event was not made public and remained within the private realm. An event such as the birth of an illegitimate child might be known privately among colonial elites, but nevertheless not be publicly acknowledged; honor was thus retained for the child's mother, the child, and their family. As Twinam has pointed out, many of the illegitimate children who subsequently applied for *gracias al sacar* were the result of unions which should have resulted in formal marriage (and, hence, legitimization of the couple's offspring), but marriage was derailed for a variety for reasons. In some cases, the groom- or bride-to-be died (occasionally in childbirth); in others, the couple was estranged, usually with the lover abandoning his mistress and marrying another woman. The point here is that premarital sex was relatively widespread among the colonial upper classes, and illegitimacy necessarily remained a fluid notion, as its stain could usually be removed by the parents' marriage.

Although, after independence, the concern with purity of blood ceased to be upheld by the state as a formal criterion for judging the quality of the individual, concern with honor—and, by implication, sexuality—was deeply rooted in Peruvian society. This is evident from the way the courts dealt with incidents of sexual crime. *Estupro, rapto,* and *violación* were defined as crimes against honor rather than against an individual and could be prosecuted only at the insistence of the victim or her guardian.[46] There was no provision for a state-initiated prosecution.

At the same time, the law recognized a variety of offenses. The 1862 penal code contains several contradictory definitions of sexual crime. Articles 269 and 270 mention different forms of rape: that carried out with violence, with the woman's consent, through seduction, or through the abuse of power. While all of these were listed as crimes, consensual intercourse with a woman was considered a minor offense and not punishable. This multiplicity of definitions did little to enhance clarity. In his analysis, García Calderón resolved this problem by differentiating between the rape of virgins (*estupro*) and "the defloration of a woman who is not a virgin" (*violación*). Rape (both *violación* and *estupro*) was punishable by prison if carried out with the help of violence or drugs (including alcohol and sleep-inducing medications). Seduction or rape of girls below the age of twelve was considered tantamount to the violent rape of a virgin.

Although phrased with far from perfect clarity, the legal texts confirm that rape was regarded primarily as a matter of honor. In cases of rape, seduction, or elopement, the defendant could evade sentence by agreeing to marry his victim, providing that she gave her consent to the union. García Calderón explains: "The reason is that the punishment is imposed because the raped woman loses the option of marriage; and if the rapist marries her, there are no grounds for the penalty."[47] At stake were the woman's—and her family's—honor and reputation, rather than the personal trauma she might have undergone. Only if the woman in question refused the offer of marriage, if the felon were already married and thus unable to marry his victim, or if he refused was he expected to provide the woman with a dowry in accordance with his means and to serve his sentence.

Few cases of rape were brought to court, and even fewer resulted in sentences. Instead, the cases brought to court dealt almost exclusively with seduction and elopement (in effect, breach of promise). Plaintiffs' main objective was to force errant lovers to marry their mistresses, or, failing that, to establish the woman's honor.

For dramatic effect, these cases were labeled *estupro, violación,* or *rapto. Rapto* was the abduction of a woman from her home in order to "corrupt her or marry her."[48] Elopement was common not only in Peru, but all over Spanish America as a mechanism used by young couples who wished to force parental agreement to their unions.[49] Incidences of *rapto* were expected to end in marriage; if they failed to do so, the woman was dishonored, as she had given up her virginity and risked pregnancy without obtaining a husband. Chances of persuading a seducer or rapist to marry his victim were small in cases where he was of higher social status; at best, a girl might hope for a small monetary compensation.[50] García Calderón summarizes these women's dilemma in his description of marriage contracts (*esponsales*): "What recourse is left to a woman ridiculed by a man who gave his word that he would marry her? . . . If her credulity made her accept a promise, she pays for her ignorance . . . , and the guilty person remains unpunished."[51]

The defining feature of *rapto* (as opposed to *estupro*) was that it involved the abduction of a young woman and frequently her imprisonment for a limited period. In instances of *rapto* in which the accused refused to fulfill his promise of marriage, the option of marriage as a means of repairing the damage made sense. As the woman had, it must be assumed, eloped willingly, often hoping that a formalized union would follow, we can assume that marriage to the partner of her choice was acceptable to her.

Honor was threatened not only by sexual misconduct; the mere imputation of such behavior could be as serious a threat to family honor as any actual blemish on a family's sexual history. Twinam has observed that dishonor among colonial elites was usually brought about not by incidents of dishonorable conduct, but by the public (as opposed to private) knowledge of these.[52] Public accusations of illicit sexual activity (even if unfounded) could have implications for public reputation that could be as serious as genuine transgressions. The penal code therefore listed the crimes of *calumnia* (slander, libel) and *injurias verbales* (slanderous insults) as crimes against honor. According to García Calderón, "reputation and honor are more highly valued and desired than riches, because they win society's esteem," and crimes which diminished them were therefore punishable for the same reason as crimes against property.[53] However, as in the case of rape, charges of slander had to be filed by the victim, who could desist from further proceedings at any moment, usually after being satisfied by the offender's public apology. Failing such an agreement, slanderers could be fined and sentenced to prison sentences of several years' duration. If the defendant succeeded in proving what he or she had said was true, however, acquittal followed.

While insults were known as *injurias verbales, injurias graves* corresponded to assault and were usually pursued by the prosecutor's office, albeit often only after the victim had filed a complaint. Likewise, murder, theft, and robbery were all matters for the public prosecutor's office.

Even in the strictly criminal domain, women's status was different from men's. Although married women could not represent themselves in civil suits or press criminal charges without specific authorization from their husbands, they had the right to defend themselves against criminal charges. A wife who wished to file charges was either represented by her husband or obtained a *licencia judicial* authorizing her to conduct her own legal business.

Depending on the gravity of the crime, proceedings were carried out locally and face to face, with almost immediate decisions from the justice of the peace. Victims and defendants in more serious matters had to travel to the provincial courts in order to pursue charges and defend themselves. In honor trials the victims or their representatives had to press charges themselves; further, it was the plaintiff's reputation prior to becoming the victim of slander or rape that determined the outcome.

The legal definition of crime thus had a very real impact on people's lives and the legal records they produced. Despite the social distance between urban elites in Lima and Cajamarcan peasants, the former's views on gender and social class influenced the latter's lives—and most certainly the way in which we read the documentation left behind by these groups.

As important as formal structures and legal codes was legal practice. As I shall show, not all charges of assault or rape were admitted; it depended on the nature of the crime and the plaintiff's reputation. Even if admitted, far from all suits were settled; the outcome depended on the influence of the plaintiff or the defendant and on the judge's inclination. When crimes were proven and sentences pronounced, the latter often reflected the litigants' social status as much as the seriousness of the crime. While legislation and elite views on gender are therefore important, the interplay between legal codes and the actual encounter between lawyers, judges, and litigants is as significant. Trial outcomes could be influenced by different factors, not all of which can be identified using preserved documents. Nevertheless, the trials themselves are a mine of information on legal practice and the interplay between different social groups. They also tell us a lot about plebeian gender practice and how lower-class men and women portrayed their lives in their encounters with their social superiors. In the next chapter, we turn to an examination of these documents.

CHAPTER 4

Survival Strategies

NEGOTIATING MATRIMONY

This chapter analyzes marital relations and how popular and official views of consensual unions and formal marriage differed and were negotiated in practice. One of my recurring concerns is how socially differentiated marriage practices shaped women's and men's lives in practical terms. While state and church doctrine defined marriage as the only appropriate framework for sexual relations, procreation, and family life, consensual union was the norm for large sections of the population. Popular attitudes reveal little prejudice against what official ideology labeled "illicit sexual relations"; on the contrary, many common-law unions functioned as permanent unions. Formally married husbands and wives, on the other hand, occasionally defied the church's and the state's definition of marriage as an indissoluble sacrament and opted to leave unsuccessful relationships. Equally, the state's assumption that women should be subject to male authority and protection was not necessarily borne out in practice.

In the second section of this chapter, I look at the issue of marital conflict and domestic violence. The criminal trials which I use as sources tend to overrepresent incidents of extreme violence. Rather than focusing on the nature and frequency of such behavior, I analyze official and lower-class attitudes toward spousal abuse and the victims' strategies. I argue that the state's attitude toward wife beating differed from, and occasionally came into conflict with, popular views and practices. Although contemporary legislation defined spousal abuse as unacceptable, domestic violence against wives and children was—in practice—condoned by the state. Arguing that the sanctity of the home and the husband's patriarchal authority must be upheld, the courts rarely intervened in domestic affairs, even when violence assumed grotesque proportions. Intervening in-laws, for example, were severely reprimanded by judges. In reality, however, such intervention was—and continues to be—widespread and was expected and feared by abusive husbands. Legal fiction and lived reality existed side by side, mirroring socially differentiated gender practices.

The documentation reveals some of the causes of matrimonial disharmony and its eruption into physical confrontation. Alcohol frequently played a part in precipitating fights and removing inhibitions against violent abuse. Aggressors often cited infidelity as the cause of their anger, although it is not always clear whether this was fact or an attempt to justify violent behavior. While the sources shed some light on the mechanics of marital conflict, its deeper causes tend to be obscured by both parties' attempts to excuse their behavior before unsympathetic judges.

HOLY MATRIMONY VERSUS CONSENSUAL UNIONS: STATISTICS

Regardless of institutional attempts to encourage formal marriage, it is generally accepted that common-law marriage was the norm for many in colonial and nineteenth-century Latin America.[1] According to Mannarelli, cohabitation and the provision of mutual services were seen as proof of sexual intercourse by the ecclesiastical authorities in seventeenth-century Lima; nonmarital relations were endemic in the Peruvian capital.[2] In eighteenth-century Cuzco, a local priest asserted that as many illegitimate children were born as legitimate ones;[3] the same was true of early-twentieth-century Lima.[4] Among the rural population in Cajamarca, formal marriage continues to be the exception: Eléspuru Bernizón, writing in 1939, noted that among the Indians "usually the parents unite their children in concubinage";[5] and as late as the 1970s Cajamarcan anthropologist Ana de la Torre noted that marriage was only rarely formalized before the civil authorities.[6]

There is no statistical evidence of common-law unions, and only limited evidence of the frequency of marriage for the province of Cajamarca. I did not find parish records. The only available statistical source relating to the frequency of marriage is the 1876 census.[7] I use this census to suggest that formal marriage was chosen by a substantial part, but not the overwhelming majority, of the adult population. Although official Peruvian statistics are notoriously unreliable, they are often the only source of information for certain demographic and socioeconomic factors.[8] Taylor concludes that the census takers were unreliable and imprecise in their definition of rural and urban properties, thus affecting the statistical balance between urban and rural populations. Similarly, I am not convinced that all individuals who were reported as formally married had actually married in church. It strikes me as quite probable that some priests or *hacendados* may have reported that their parishioners or tenants were married in an attempt to place themselves in a better light as moral supervisors. It is therefore possible that the incidence of marriage was actually overreported in the census.[9]

The figures I have been able to gather from the census confirm that by no means all adult Cajamarcans formally married. According to the 1876 survey, 53.5 percent of the adult male population of the province of Cajamarca was married, and 6.8 percent was widowed.[10] Forty percent of the male population over twenty-five was hence unmarried and had never been married, and 48 percent of women over the age of twenty-one were single.[11] The figures varied a little from district to district, with no single adult men recorded in the village and surrounding area of Llacanora. If this is correct, 88.5 percent of the male adult population in that district was married, and 11.5 percent was widowed. There seem to have been more never-married women than bachelors in Llacanora, with 20.6 percent of women above the age of twenty-one in the village single.[12]

In other rural areas, such as Asunción, 51.8 percent of adult men and 57.6 percent of women were single.[13] In the town of Cajamarca, from which most of the trial documentation used in this study comes, 62 percent of adult men and 58.6 percent of adult women were single.[14] Surprisingly, given the greater availability of churches, priests, and cash with which to pay them, more people remained unmarried in the urban capital of the region than in its surrounding rural villages and hamlets. This may be due to the fact that a number of servants, who had few opportunities to formalize unions, lived in Cajamarca.[15]

The census data corroborate the court record data I am using. The statistical frequency of marriage in the sample of people I have drawn from the 234 criminal trials roughly parallels that found in the 1876 census. Of the people on whom I have collected data from trial records, data on marital status were available for 733. Of the adult men, nearly 50 percent were single, 45 percent were married, and 5 percent were widowed. The corresponding figures for women were 52 percent never married, 31.8 percent were married, and 15.4 percent were widows.[16]

Although there are therefore no hard data on informal unions, the figures suggest that these were common. As we cannot ascertain the frequency of such relationships, we must rely on a study of the attitudes toward them. While premarital sex and sex outside of marriage were not explicitly approved, they were accepted as part of life by the lower and middle social groups. The textual documentation from civil and criminal proceedings and wills supports my conclusion that informal unions were not stigmatized among the lower classes. As Lavrin remarks about illegitimacy and, by extension, informal unions in colonial Latin America, "Given its frequency, illegitimacy could not have constituted a very powerful social stigma."[17]

HOLY MATRIMONY VERSUS CONSENSUAL UNION: POPULAR PERCEPTIONS

The population at large did not endorse the state's strict differentiation between formal and common-law marriage. On the contrary, most lower-class people treated informal unions much the same as marriage. Although the Peruvian state regarded only marriages that had been ecclesiastically blessed as formal marriage, the Indian population had its own rituals, which were not recorded or accepted as valid by the state.[18] In the more remote areas, in particular, people attached little value to the formalities of marriage, regardless of social class.

Although the official term *"relación ilícita"* implied both the illegitimate and, by implication, the short-term nature of free unions, many were in fact of long duration. Sixteen of 374 wills I studied record that free unions were formalized during grave illness. Called *matrimonios en artículo de muerte*, such last-minute marriages were frequently concluded in order to legitimize offspring.[19] Manuela Abanto stated in her will that her eighteen children had been legitimated by her marriage *en artículo de muerte* to their father, Toribio Bringas, shortly before his death.[20] Similarly, Juan Tomás Gutiérrez married Petrona Sifuentes, with whom he had three living children, immediately prior to making his will;[21] Nicolás Silva Santisteban, who was connected to Cajamarca's upper class, married the mother of his five children during his last illness.[22]

Legitimizing children was not the only reason for such last-minute marriages, however. José Barrena Soto declared that he was "married . . . to señora Doña Petronila Arroyo after twenty years of illicit relations in which we have not had a single child."[23]

Although many common-law unions were long-term relationships, they could be, and often were, dissolved. Laura Escuza related that she had shared her life with Pedro Novoa Jiménez for nine years, after which she broke off the relationship.[24] Testators also recorded briefer unions in their wills, providing that these had produced children. José Sumarán noted that he had three children, by three women.[25] José Santos Zamora had had children by two women before he married, after which he had three children by his wife.[26]

It was not just men who had children from different relationships: Isabel Cotrina had four children by three fathers.[27] Thus *"relación ilícita"* described both short-term affairs and long-term unions that resembled church-blessed marriage in all but name.

A measure of how illicit sexual relations were perceived is the spouses' relationship with in-laws. Young men commonly referred to their partner's parents as *suegros* (in-laws), whether they were formally married or not. Manuel Inocente Gaona, for instance, described the mother of his common-law wife as "my mother-in-law Mercedes Castrejón."[28] Hilario Castañeda recorded that he and his sister's partner "treated each other as brothers-in-law as he has been living with my sister."[29]

The link between two families was also manifested in strong bonds of loyalty and support. Catalina Carbajal did not merely describe her daughter's partner as her son-in-law, but proceeded to lie in court in order to protect him from the legal consequences of his actions. Although several witnesses confirmed having seen Elías Arribasplata beat his common-law wife and mother-in-law, the two victims insisted that the argument had merely been "a quarrel of words."[30] No doubt the fact that Arribasplata was the father of her grandchild weighed heavily on Catalina Carbajal's mind.

Occasionally, common-law unions resulted in more formal family ties. When Manuela Chávez' mother died in childbirth, the girl's aunt's common-law husband, Simón Valera, became the child's godfather and assumed a share of the responsibility for the orphan.[31] Although the tie between Simón Valera and his common-law wife was not recognized by the authorities, his religious tie to the child was.

Although consensual unions were widespread, plebeians revealed an awareness of official condemnation of the practice. When they came into contact with the authorities, they demonstrated that they were well aware that the latter did not sanction informal unions. When accused of having severely wounded his common-law wife, Antonio Vargas admitted that he "had had illicit relations with her,"[32] adding that they had planned to marry —clearly in an attempt to make himself and the relationship appear in a more respectable light. In the same vein, Antolino Álvarez attributed an argument with his partner to the informal nature of their relationship: "induced by the temptations of Belial, I . . . illicitly seduced Tomasa and cohabited with her. As quarrels abound in such criminal unions, I had an argument with my companion [*acómplice*]."[33]

At the same time as public knowledge of illicit sexual relations implied reduced status for single women, public knowledge of the exact nature of their affairs brought them security: the more people in the local community who knew who the father of their children was, the less likely was he to abandon them.[34] The balance between security and honor was not simple.

While common-law unions were socially acceptable (albeit under a cloud), adultery constituted a social stigma so severe that almost no parents admitted that their children had been conceived in adulterous relationships. The only parent in the records I examined to openly admit to producing "adulterous" offspring was Manuel Miranda, who confessed, "I have had one son, José Circuncisión Miranda, who is now dead, apart of my wife."[35] His son, being dead, would not suffer from the dishonor associated with the label of *hijo adulterino*. Julián Rubio was less overt about admitting the origin of his children. Having been deserted by his wife, he cohabited with Martina Aguilar for several years. He left the "wooden bedstead in which I lie ill as well as the bedclothes to Doña Martina Aguilar who has served and assisted me. Everything else Don Lorenso, Don Manuel, and Don Gavino Rubio are to divide equally among themselves."[36]

Parents lied in order to hide the blemish of adultery, falsely claiming that their children were *hijos naturales* when they were in fact *hijos adulterinos*. This may have been the case for María Carmen Apaestegui, who carried her mother's name. Her father had never officially recognized her, possibly because he was married. Revealing the connection between father and daughter could only serve to damage her name.[37]

A number of the "adopted" children, or children who, according to testators, had been fostered (*criado*) by them, had similar origins.[38] The option of adopting their illegitimate children enabled parents to circumvent the associated slur on their children's reputation. Manuel Atanasio Fuentes, an intellectual and contemporary legal commentator in Lima, asserted, "Today adoption serves, in the majority of cases, simply to legitimate . . . natural offspring, and, even more frequently, adulterous offspring."[39]

Even where adoption was not formalized, de facto parenting implied its equivalent. Miguel Sánchez Castillo, a man of modest property, had six living children with his wife of twenty-nine years, among whom he divided his six horses, a house, two vegetable gardens, several plots of land, and some debts. In addition, "a little girl whom I have fostered called Matilde Pita" was to receive a horse, as did his other children, and a legacy of one hundred pesos.[40]

PARENTHOOD: CHILDBIRTH,
CHILD MORTALITY, AND ADOPTION

The birth, death, or absence of children fundamentally shaped married life. An idea of fertility and child mortality rates can be obtained from analyzing data provided in the wills. Parents listed their offspring, including, usually, how many had died in childhood or as adults. José María Gálvez Tirado, for instance, noted that he was "married to . . . Doña Sebastiana Golina, and during our marriage of sixteen years we had five children."[41]

Of the 374 wills I have read, 259 contain data on the testator's fertility. Testators had an average of 4.5 children each; these had a 45.5 percent chance of still being alive at the time their parents wrote their wills. While many children died during childhood, others reached adulthood. These figures do not, therefore, reflect child mortality rates. In most cases the information concerning the timing of testators' children's deaths is too imprecise to allow more precise calculation of child mortality rates.

Curiously, married and widowed fathers reported that 49 percent of their children had died, whereas married and widowed mothers recorded that 60.6 percent of their children had died.[42] It seems likely that mothers, due to the closer biological ties, were more likely to recall the exact number of pregnancies, stillbirths, and children lost in early infancy than were fathers. It should be noted that Deere, on the basis of her 1976 survey of peasants, concludes that the average peasant woman on a Cajamarcan hacienda gave birth to nine children, of whom five would have reached adulthood.[43] Although fertility therefore varied greatly, depending on social class, child mortality rates did not differ much by class.

The death of children caused parents tremendous pain and must have placed strain on their conjugal relationship. Rosa Rocha de Rangel, age fifty-four, stated that she had had fifteen children during her marriage, of whom only two were alive at the time her will was written.[44] Mariano Basauri noted that he had had eleven children in the course of his marriage to María Linares, only three of whom were alive when he wrote his will.[45] Manuel Quiroz and Jacoba Bermúdez lost all nine of their children; it is fair to assume that this figure includes miscarriages and stillbirths.[46] Not all couples were this unlucky, however: only one of Diego Rangel and his wife's nine children had died by the time he wrote his will.[47]

Some couples were barren. Gregorio Cubas y Rubio stated that he and his wife had had no children during their forty years of marriage.[48] Estanislao Álvarez noted in his will that he and his wife had had no children: "We have had no offspring except a miscarriage at the beginning [of our marriage]."[49] The couple seem to have been unusually fond of each other, as Álvarez left his wife all his property, also making her the executor of the will: "My wife . . . always lent me her care and services with the greatest solicitude throughout our marriage. [This] gives her an indisputable right to my property."

If the marriage itself had not produced offspring, couples occasionally searched for substitutes in the form of poor relatives, foster children, or, if one of the partners had children from earlier unions, stepchildren. Thus Rafael Tejada and Josefa Cachi had no children of their own during their twenty-year marriage; nevertheless he left all his property to his wife and her son, whom he also appointed as executors of his will.[50] Camilo Barboza and Josefa Rojas fostered and adopted a child who, Barboza wrote in his will, "was left at the door of my house when newborn."[51]

In line with the governing legislation, all or most of the property was left to the surviving offspring.[52] In most cases, after the deduction of the surviving spouse's share of the conjugally owned property, the rest of the property was simply to be divided equally; in others, certain types of property were left to certain children. Daughters and female relatives were likely to receive jewelry and equipment from the kitchen or furniture;[53] José Esteban, the only son of a shoemaker, was to inherit his father's workshop and tools.[54] Descendants who assisted in the care of their parents or grandparents were usually rewarded with an increased share of the inheritance. Francisco López Hoyos thus left a farm to his granddaughter Matilde Magna Vallejo "in appreciation of her personal services";[55] Josefa Horna wanted to give her granddaughter María Francisca Mestanza the *quinto* (one-fifth) of her property she was allowed to dispose of freely, "in recognition of the services she has provided and continues to provide, lavishing her filial love on me."[56] Melchora Corpa willed all her property to her son-in-law, following the death of her daughter, in recompense for all the help he had given her in her old age. Thus, relations between mother- and son-in-law did not have to be characterized by animosity.[57]

Deere also states that it was common practice among the peasantry for the youngest son to reside with the parents until they died and to be left their house in recognition of his services during their old age.[58] Antonio García opted to increase the inheritance due his three youngest children, who were not yet of age, at the expense of their elder sister, who was married and who was, in his eyes, provided for.[59] Parents therefore demonstrated concern for their children's material welfare after the parents' death, as well as the wish to reward the children for their help.

In addition to dividing up their property, male testators and widows appointed guardians for their children under age twenty-one in the eventuality of the parents' death. José María Gálvez Tirado therefore appointed his wife as their children's guardian, explaining that he had "complete faith [in her] . . . as I have no doubt that she will educate our children religiously and in a Christian way until they become of age, and administer the goods they may inherit."[60] His faith in his wife was not unique. When Mariano Eduardo Vargas dictated his will in 1864, he appointed his wife the guardian of their fourteen-month-old daughter and of the child which was due to be born in two months' time.[61]

Women who appointed their husbands as the guardians of their children did little more than confirm the legal predisposition for such an eventuality. Nevertheless, women who had children who were not of age usually stated that the children's father was to assume full guardianship[62]—which, in fact, he had had even during his wife's lifetime, as parental authority was vested in the father during his lifetime.

Several testators explicitly stated that they and their partner had been single at the time their illegitimate child (hijo natural) was conceived. Manuela Barrantes y Villanueva declared that "during the time I was single I had one daughter. . . . I procreated her with Don Francisco Jabier Odiaga . . . [who] at the time when he procreated my daughter was [also] single."[63]

Some of the children who were formally or informally adopted by their parents were the children of priests and should therefore be correctly described as hijos sacrilegos.[64] The priest José Pantaleón Palacios recorded that he had one natural daughter "whom I procreated when I was a layman; I also declare that I have six orphans . . . whom I . . . name as my heirs with the same rights as my natural daughter."[65] His colleague José Tadeo Pita was even more blatant. His protégés carried his surname, had been brought up by him "as if they were my own children," and were to inherit all his property.[66] Of the 374 wills I have read, 9 were authored by priests. Of these, 5 refer to women who seem to have been life partners or to children who carried the priest's surname.[67]

While consensual unions were condemned officially, they were common enough to be confessed openly in litigation and wills, and I have not found any litigant openly condemning common-law unions. Adultery, however, was frowned on and was disguised wherever possible, either by describing children as hijos naturales or by claiming them as foster children. And, although legally as serious an offense as adultery, the semimarital relations engaged in by priests were hidden under a mere veil of pretense, clearly following the reasoning that to leave their children property was more important than to safeguard their honor.

DOMESTIC VIOLENCE: METHODOLOGICAL NOTES

Few cases of marital conflict ever reached the legal arena. For good reason, wives were wary of reporting violent husbands: complaints were only rarely admitted and led to sentences only in extreme situations. Nor was punishment likely to improve the conjugal climate. Several suits ended with a reprimand for the wife for disobeying her spouse, thus provoking his anger.[68] However, those trials that do deal with spousal battery shed light on some of the causes of conflict and the responses of spouses and outsiders. It is possible to gauge victims' perception of abuse, aggressors' attempts at justifying their use of physical violence, and how outsiders, ranging from close relatives of the participants to the local community at large, viewed such incidents.

As these histories were recorded as part of criminal proceedings, the state's stance toward marital conflict and abuse, infidelity, separation, and abandonment can also be inferred from the documentation. That said, the material has its limitations with regard to quantity, range, and perspective. Clearly, the twenty-three references to marital abuse that I have found in the trial documentation cannot provide a representative or exhaustive picture of marital conflict in Cajamarca. Only the most extreme, and hence, by definition, atypical, cases of abuse reached the attention of the authorities. The bias in the sources can easily create an illusion of prevalent and extreme violence. I will try to counteract this by focusing less on the nature of abuse than on the response of the parties involved. Cross-referencing *guardia civil* (police) records, records of criminal and civil trials, and records from the trials adjudicated by the local justices of the peace reveals no overlap. This indicates that many, possibly most, trial documents from the relevant period have disappeared; what can be concluded is therefore only suggestive of trends.

In terms of social class, it seems that trial participants included both urban and rural residents, usually from the lower end of the social scale.[69] It is worth noting that I have found no case in which charges were filed following violence against children, excepting one incident in which a teacher was charged with having beaten a student excessively.[70] No parents or other relatives were prosecuted following incidents of violence against children.[71] Rather than assume that violence against children did not exist,[72] I take this absence of examples to mean that whereas spousal abuse was not universally tolerated, violence against children was probably seen as acceptable.

Only eleven trials between 1862 and 1900 were initiated directly as the result of spousal abuse.[73] Several of these incidents ended in the victim's death, such as in the case of María Huaccha.[74] Huaccha lived several hours after being stabbed, so was able to tell the tale, but Simona Cabanillas' death was almost instantaneous: her husband drove his knife into her "to the extent that her liver came out."[75]

I also found references to marital conflict—but not necessarily battery—in twelve other trials.[76] During a trial ostensibly dealing with the attack by Tomasa Arce and her husband on his former lover, Narcisa Mendoza, the latter made a chance remark revealing that Arce's marriage was far from tranquil. According to Mendoza, Arce had insulted her with the words, "Clear out you shameless whore. . . . It is your fault that my man has almost killed me twice." Despite the seriousness of her husband's aggression, Arce had not thought it worthwhile to take the matter to court.[77] Similarly, the violence experienced by Baltazara Minchán was recorded only because she tried to blame two Indian peons who had walked through her family's fields one evening for her miscarriage. The two men defended themselves, arguing that the miscarriage had been the result of a scene between Minchán and her common-law husband.[78] The revelation that Simona Paredes' partner beat her in a fit of jealousy emerged only during the investigation of a fight between two neighbors.[79] Perhaps most tellingly, there were six incidents in which women were victimized following the breakup of consensual unions.[80]

Further references to wife beating can be found in the records of the *guardia civil*, which functioned as the police for the town of Cajamarca. Typical entries concern the arrest of seven individuals for "passing through the roads at ungodly hours";[81] the arrest of three women for "carousing uproariously," or, in the case of María Espíritu Iras, "for brawling."[82]

As well as jailing drunken revelers, the local police occasionally detained abusive husbands. Bartolo Sánchez "beat his wife Leocadia Huycha with a stick, for which he was arrested and placed in detention."[83] Antonio Julcapoma was arrested in January 1878 "for having battered his wife."[84] Another husband taken into custody was Casimiro Vejarano, in this case, for "having broken his wife's head, as well as entering the house of Don Cavallero, where his wife had sought refuge, and offending the gentleman's family."[85] However, police records contain little information on the circumstances surrounding the incident of abuse; also, the records appear far from complete.[86] The only thing that I can conclude with certainty is that there were occasions when the local police took action, however limited, against wife batterers.

DOMESTIC VIOLENCE:
THE RATIONALE BEFORE AND AFTER BLOWS

It is impossible to draw any conclusions about the frequency of spouse battering on the basis of the available material. It may be useful, however, to
consider how people perceived physical abuse in the context of marriage and
common-law unions. In what contexts did such violence occur, and how did
batterer and battered make sense of these events? How did outside agents
such as the state and the local community respond to incidents of domestic
violence? And what strategies did the victims of abuse develop in order to
deal with it?

Defendants chose different ways of justifying their actions. In the process they revealed some of their attitudes toward the use of violence in a
relationship, as well as what they thought would be acceptable excuses in
the eyes of local judges. Some denied that violence had taken place. Several
claimed that the argument had been oral, not physical. One of these was
Antonio Minchán, suspected of murdering his wife, Josefa Chingal. Josefa
died shortly after Minchán was first jailed for battery. He insisted that the
conflict had been merely "a quarrel of words."[87] As the doctor decided that
Chingal's death was the result of illness, Minchán was absolved of responsibility and released from custody. Antolino Álvarez, too, claimed that the
argument with his partner, Tomasa Vásquez, "did not move from word to
action."[88] As there were several witnesses to the contrary, as well as to earlier
beatings, he failed to convince the judge. Another, even less convincing, defendant was Casimiro Chilcote, whose common-law wife, María Huaccha,
bled to death after being repeatedly stabbed by him. "On this day I was ill in
bed when I saw my wife . . . María Huaccha enter crying because she had cut
herself while chopping wood,"[89] he told the court. His brothers-in-law, who
had arrived in time to hear Huaccha accuse him before she expired, further
belied his already unconvincing version of events.

In several cases defendants tried to persuade the judge that the aggressive
behavior had been mutual. Accused of stabbing Vicente Briones, his girlfriend's uncle, Manuel Inocente Gaona implied that he was acting in self-
defense. Gaona asserted that a "family dispute" had occurred as he was eating
and holding his knife in his right hand. He claimed that he was set upon by
his girlfriend's relatives, and that Briones was hurt when the latter tried to
snatch Gaona's knife.[90] According to Lizandro Olivares, his wife had been
wounded in the course of a "marital squabble during which my wife also
raised her hand against me."[91] By defining the violence as mutual, aggressors

reinterpreted it as a fight, which implied equality of strength and culpability. As Hydén points out in her analysis of dialogues arising from incidents of extreme marital violence, the concept of "assault" is difficult to integrate into married life, whereas "fights" can be compatible with it.[92] By claiming that the act of violence was mutual, and not a one-sided assault, husbands both minimized and normalized the event.

Others justified their violence by accusing their wives of adultery. José Chávez Velásquez stated that he beat his wife because he "had suspicions of adulterous relations . . . between my wife and Manuel Chacón."[93] Similarly, Manuel de la Cruz blamed his attack on his former girlfriend, Antonia Lamar, on a fit of jealousy. Suspecting her of being involved with somebody else, he, "enraged . . . drew the knife he carried and threatened her with it, without the intention of hurting her," he explained.[94] When the young woman tried to escape, "I got even angrier, followed her, and no longer able to contain myself, wounded her." José Adriano Silva, who also claimed to be motivated by jealousy, asserted he was "blinded by anger" when he found his fiancée in an isolated spot, conversing intimately with another man, and allegedly making fun of him. Infuriated, he gave his fiancée "four little pricks," as he described the five wounds he inflicted on his victim.[95] Women, too, responded violently to infidelity. Manuela Agip crept up to her brother-in-law's house, where she knew her husband was staying with his mistress, and tried to stab them both, almost blinding him.[96]

Of the eleven aggressors who were brought to court for their abusive behavior, four justified their actions with suspicions of infidelity;[97] four denied having used physical violence;[98] and two argued that the violence had been provoked by their partners.[99] One of the defendants, Asunción Eustacio, fled and was therefore not interviewed by the court; another, Antonio Vargas, explained that he had acted in a fit of—to him—inexplicable fury when ill.[100]

It is unclear to what degree suspicions of adultery were justified, as the victims of violence invariably denied any sexual impropriety. Although wives undoubtedly were unfaithful on occasion, aggressors' accusations of infidelity need not always be taken at face value. Modern research as well as anthropological and historical studies concur that the "Othello syndrome" is common in abusive relationships, and although caution is advisable in transferring insights from research on modern western societies to the study of Peruvian history, this particular conclusion echoes the evidence.[101] Certainly the behavior of Manuel de la Cruz in refusing to accept his former girlfriend's desire to end the relationship and continuing to stake claim on her body seems to fit the description of possessive and jealous abusers. Cajamarcan anthropologist Ana de la Torre notes that couples described suspicions of infidelity as a recurring problem in relationships. According to her, such suspicions were frequently fostered by rumors spread by envious villagers.[102] Unfounded rumor was one of the more disruptive features of these small communities where everyone knew everyone else.

While some men hit because they (correctly or erroneously) believed their wives to be committing adultery, others consciously—and cynically—used such accusations to justify their behavior. One abusive husband, himself unfaithful, tortured his wife into confessing adultery—a confession which might then legitimate his use of violence.[103]

Judges did little to punish abusive husbands, particularly if the latter argued that they had been punishing adultery.[104] José Adriano Silva, who stabbed his fiancée four times, had his sentence reduced because he was acting "in defense of his personal honor, which had been attacked by a woman who, without respecting the contract of engagement, was shamelessly unfaithful with Mariano Muñoz."[105]

Physical abuse within marriage was even less likely to produce legal consequences. When José Chávez Velásquez justified the beating he gave his wife, Marcela Montoya, because he suspected her of infidelity, the judge ordered reconciliation. He demanded that the couple "mutually forgive each other's past offenses,... and start a new life together as a true married couple." Even though the couple argued throughout the session, the judge decided the husband had done sufficient penance with his arrest and exhorted the couple to resume their lives "in the marital home, providing a good example for the neighborhood."[106] He made it clear that any further offense would result in jail for both parties. In the same way, the charges pressed by Fernanda Rodríguez against her husband for *maltratos* (abuse or maltreatment) did not produce any legal consequences beyond the initial investigation. Although a doctor observed the "imprint of several kicks" in her ribs and signs of strangulation, and found that the "victim's pregnancy is [endangered] as it seems as if the foetus is on the verge of death within the mother, and may cause the mother's death," the judge concluded the proceedings with the statement: "It turns out that the bruises inflicted on Fernanda Rodríguez are light," and ordered all proceedings halted.[107]

Although aggressors were occasionally given a light punishment, judges made it clear that the legal authorities would not deal with open marital conflict. The principle of the indissolubility of marriage was to be upheld at all costs; separation was not tolerated. Instead, the state tacitly condoned the use of violence against wives.[108]

The same did not apply to consensual unions. When Manuel de la Cruz argued that he had acted in a fit of jealousy when stabbing his former girlfriend, Antonia Lamar, the judge found that "the jealousy by which he says he was carried away is no extenuating circumstance because of the unlawful nature of the relations with the victim."[109] Unlike violent husbands who had committed similar crimes, de la Cruz was condemned to a year of forced labor; unlike with wives accused of infidelity, a priest did not investigate Lamar's behavior. The court's approach shows that the state differentiated sharply between formal and informal marriage.[110] If couples were married, the courts consistently encouraged reconciliation,[111] even in cases in which it was clear that a genuine resumption of marital life was likely to lead to further conflict and violence. Violent spouses were prosecuted and punished only after their abuse had led to the death of the victim, as happened in the murder of María Huaccha.[112]

Formally married husbands therefore knew that they could beat their wives with impunity, and many took full advantage of this freedom. Lizandro Olivares was so confident of his right to discipline his wife that he assumed responsibility for the injuries that his mistress and her sister inflicted on his wife. His mistress and her sister were acquitted, and no charges were pressed against him.[113]

Given the state's insistence on reuniting warring couples, it was extremely difficult for either spouse to leave the relationship. Beyond the personal dilemma and dishonor involved, divorce proceedings were costly and lengthy, only rarely producing the desired results. I have not been able to establish how common such proceedings were in Cajamarca. The archive of the archbishopric, where applications for ecclesiastical divorce would have been filed, was not accessible, and there is only one (incomplete) reference to divorce proceedings in the civil court records,[114] indicating that divorce applications were much rarer in highland Cajamarca than in urban Lima.[115]

Although there is no evidence of formal divorce proceedings, this does not mean that couples did not split, or at least try to. However, leaving a violent relationship was not easy. A husband whose wife had left the home could demand her arrest.[116] Victorino Miranda reported his wife, Juana Mercado, to the local priest when she left him to return to her brother's home. The priest placed her in *depósito* (under arrest) in his own home for several days and subsequently ordered her to return to her husband.[117]

As well as revealing the degree of power which husbands could exercise over their wives, this incident also hints at local power conflicts between church and state. Although Miranda, the priest, and several witnesses believed that the priest was within his rights to punish a woman suspected of adultery, the local justice of the peace disagreed. Exploiting this dissension, Juana Mercado's brother filed a complaint and charged the priest with unlawfully arresting his sister, thus obtaining her release. In this case, Mercado's husband and brother applied to different authorities in order to obtain, in the husband's case, her arrest, and, in the brother's, her release, exploiting the confusion over who held jurisdiction in matters of sexuality and marital relations, the church or the state. The fact that the local priest and the justice of the peace were, according to the priest, *enemigos capitales* (deadly enemies) further complicated the issue.[118] The tension between an expanding state administration and a church which traditionally held jurisdiction over issues related to morality, sexuality, and matrimony (combined with local power relations wherein public officials and priests competed over land and trade routes) could impinge directly on couples' marital negotiations and be exploited by either party—or, as in Juana Mercado's case, both.

I have found three references in the testamentary evidence to spouses separating. These indicate that successful separation was possible only by fleeing the province or even the department and by severing all ties to the region.[119] Wives who left their husbands had limited options, and many faced poverty. When Asunción Ramírez tried to escape from her abusive husband she went into hiding and sought employment as a domestic servant. When she was discovered after some months, a local judge compelled her to return to the conjugal home.[120] When María Albarrón separated from her husband, she was left homeless. She was said to have "wandered about for some time" before she was lucky enough to strike up a relationship with a new man, who took her in.[121]

Running away from an unsuccessful marriage could be difficult, but being left behind was no easy matter, either. Matea Gallardo explained that she had been abandoned by her husband many years earlier and had had to hand over her daughter to wealthier acquaintances, who reared the girl and employed her as a servant. Both the child and her mother suffered abuse at the hands of the girl's employers. Thus the personal costs of separation were borne both by the partner who left and the one who was abandoned.[122]

Nor did separation always imply freedom. Even in cases in which couples had been separated for years, formally married wives still felt subject to their husband's authority in respect of their sexuality. When María Jesús Salazar became pregnant by another man three years after separating from her husband, she tried desperately to induce an abortion, fearing her husband's punishment for what constituted, legally, an act of adultery.[123]

Given the official constraints on marriage it is not unreasonable to assume that common-law unions were seen as preferable by many. Several individuals commented on both women's and men's freedom to choose their partners, providing they did not marry. Mariano Montoya described his break with his *amacía* (lover), Antonia Méndez, in the following fashion: "The separation took place . . . with no disagreement. She, as a free woman, did not want to continue [our] relationship, so [I] left her."[124] Although the rejected partner did not always share this view, as can be seen from the numerous cases of both male-against-female and female-against-female violence following broken relationships, its wide currency did ensure greater freedom of choice for common-law spouses than for formally married partners.

A seventeenth-century resident of Lima quoted by Mannarelli probably anticipated the concerns of nineteenth-century women when she stated she did not "know if she should get married, as she did not know if her husband would give her a *mala vida* [bad life]."[125] Stern, working on colonial Mexico, also underlines the difference between formal and informal unions. Whereas wives did not break out of marriages, lovers "strove to carve out a more consensual, female space, a lesser pact," in their relationships with men, ranging from uncompromising relationships to common-law unions.[126] Although informal unions may have offered women more freedom, he also notes that such relationships "constituted an ambiguous cultural terrain," and the chance of abandonment—including being left with the sole responsibility for children—was greater in consensual unions.[127]

For women informal unions could also mean more rights over their children. Providing that the child was not formally recognized by the father, single mothers retained parental authority, whereas this authority automatically pertained to the children's father when the parents were married.[128] A wife who wished to separate from her legal husband was seen as loose, and the children therefore had to stay with the father, who held parental authority. Single mothers, on the other hand, succeeded in retaining formal parental authority over their children even where paternity was established. Thus Santosa Quispe reclaimed custody of her daughter after leaving her common-law husband, Carlos Alcántara, by asserting that he was not the biological father. Notwithstanding years of coparenting, Santosa Quispe's legal representative claimed on her behalf that "the girl is not the daughter of Alcántara, but hers; as a single woman she knows how she got this child, and that her father is not Carlos Alcántara."[129]

While the state thus differentiated sharply between formalized marriage and illicit sexual relations when it came to male expectations of a partner's fidelity, men in consensual unions staked out the same claims to their partner's sexuality as if they had been formally married. For women there was, ultimately, little difference: whether in formal or informal unions, they risked violence, particularly if they had aroused suspicion of infidelity. Matters of honor and reputation excepted, common-law unions offered one advantage: either party could leave such unions without the huge personal cost entailed by breaking out of formal marriage.

DOMESTIC VIOLENCE: CAUSES OF MARITAL CONFLICT

The batterer's defense opens a window on marital conflict and physical aggression in the home, allowing a glimpse of some of the immediate causes of violence. The underlying causes are more difficult to guess at, partly because defendants were more preoccupied with justifying themselves than with proffering facts, but largely because courts were perfunctory at best in their investigation of matrimonial conflict.

Alcohol played a role in precipitating many of the cases I found in *guardia civil* records and in criminal charges dealing with spousal abuse. Couples who caroused together frequently ended up at loggerheads. One witness described a fight between a common-law couple: "Sebastián N., Minchán's young man, battered her on the Sunday during carnival . . . as both of them were drunk, cutting up her face" and causing her, a few days later, to lose the child she was carrying.[130] Angelina Chávez confessed that her husband had threatened her with a knife during a quarrel that developed when they were both drunk; she claimed that she stabbed him in self-defense.[131] The tendency of alcohol to remove inhibitions against violence was widely acknowledged: following his sister's death, José María Huaccha told the court that her common-law husband "pretends to be crazy, but he is not and never has been ill . . . Every time he got drunk he lost control, and he has frequently beaten my sister."[132] José María Fernandes lived with Andrea Díaz, the mother of his children, and regularly beat her whenever he was drunk, as she told the court after she ended the relationship.[133]

Not only wives and mistresses were at risk; children too were beaten. When Nicolás Malca came home drunk one afternoon, he grabbed his stepdaughter and flung her across the room, leaving her crying in a corner.[134]

Alcohol thus posed a treble risk: quarrels were more likely to occur if one or both partners were drunk; some men regularly became violent when drunk; and the consumption of alcohol could in itself become a point of contention, resulting in a potentially violent argument. The incident in which Elías Arribasplata punched his common-law wife is an example. Realizing that Manuela Valderrama, his partner, was "somewhat drunk, he took her outside . . . and a little while later we heard a fight from their house," a witness commented.[135]

A number of studies confirm the role of alcohol in precipitating marital violence.[136] Interviews conducted by anthropologist Ana de la Torre in rural

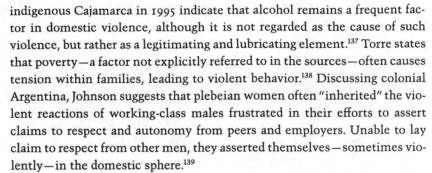

indigenous Cajamarca in 1995 indicate that alcohol remains a frequent factor in domestic violence, although it is not regarded as the cause of such violence, but rather as a legitimating and lubricating element.[137] Torre states that poverty—a factor not explicitly referred to in the sources—often causes tension within families, leading to violent behavior.[138] Discussing colonial Argentina, Johnson suggests that plebeian women often "inherited" the violent reactions of working-class males frustrated in their efforts to assert claims to respect and autonomy from peers and employers. Unable to lay claim to respect from other men, they asserted themselves—sometimes violently—in the domestic sphere.[139]

Johnson reminds us that poverty created at least two types of pressures, which may in turn have increased the level of tension and violence to which women (and children) were exposed. In addition to the hard work, insecurity, and constant economic hardship associated with poverty, it implied being at the bottom of the social scale and thus vulnerable to a series of indignities and insults at the hands of local power holders—for our purposes, landlords, political officials, and their minions. Both of these pressures may well have increased women's and children's risk of abuse at the hands of their male relatives.

Apart from whatever steam husbands may have wished to let off, an understanding that men were entitled to wield power in the home (if nowhere else, as was the case for plebeian men) was fundamental to subaltern masculinity.[140] Men could command female deference, and wives' failure to display due respect gave rise to conflict. Sexual availability was a central corollary to this: a husband's sexual rights over his wife extended beyond commanding her absolute fidelity; the wife was also seen to owe her husband sex. As Tinsman has noted, "Sex lay at the heart of a campesino husband's assumed right to command authority over other aspects of a woman's labor and person."[141] Women's sexual subservience was pivotal to men's authority over them, and female challenges to male sexual rights were perceived as a challenge that went beyond the immediate disappointment of wishes denied, as is evident from the case of Raymunda Goicochea and her husband, Melchor Figueroa. The trial is unusual in being one of the few that details marital tensions prior to violence. Goicochea accused her husband of abandonment, prolonged public adultery, and assault.[142] Throughout the proceedings she complained about his daily visits to confiscate what she regarded as her property: "My husband comes to my house every day in order to take some object or animal that I have worked for"; "my situation is all the more pitiful, because of my poverty and abandonment, with no help to provide for the children which I have borne the adulterer." Reflecting her concern for day-to-day survival, much of the proceeding focused on who owned two oxen that she had sold in order to feed and clothe her children. Figueroa's mistress also claimed ownership: allegedly she had received the *junta de bueyes* (yoke of oxen) from him as a gift. The debate concerning the oxen illustrates why women feared and fought infidelity as much as they did: above anything else, male adultery threatened the daily survival of the family.

Wives fought male adultery tooth and nail, especially when it led to economic neglect or even total loss of support for them and their children. Stern notes that the high incidence of female *celos* (jealousy) cases in colonial Mexico—accounting for 51.5 percent of all cases in which spouses ended up in court over conflicts related to infidelity—forces us to question traditional notions of a double sexual standard in Latin America. Even if wives accepted men's right to philander, they drew the line when male amorousness threatened the family economy. Whereas female infidelity was charged with symbolic meaning, male adultery signified largely at the point when it threatened family survival. Where husbands, whether formal or common-law, failed to contribute to the family's expenses and provide for their children, wives and mothers put their foot down. As Stern observes, women were willing to accept male infidelity up to a point; however, "if a man's extramarital sexual liaisons implied economic negligence, domestic violence or abuse, or open cultural humiliation, then a woman had to assert boundaries of permissible male sexual behavior even when male sexuality as such was not the main point of concern."[143] Boyer notes that colonial Mexican women defined "*mala vida*" as the cessation of economic support from their husbands, tracing it to the presence of another woman.[144]

Some wives, including Raymunda Goicochea, argued with and berated their husbands, restricted sexual access, and insulted them until the situation escalated into one of extreme violence.[145] Others attacked their rivals.[146] Fernanda Rodríguez told the court her husband had beaten her and taken a knife to her, asking her "why she bothered Hernanda Potosí, his mistress. Potosí had told him to hit his wife so that she would not provoke Potosí again."[147]

Unfounded suspicions of infidelity and ensuing quarrels between lovers produced violent repercussions, too. When María del Carmen Ducos started an argument with Isidora Paico, accusing the latter of flirting with her common-law partner, Julián Marín, "he got up threatening to hit her in the presence of the entire neighborhood, and took her home where he dealt her several blows."[148] Whether Marín had been flirting with Isidora Paicos or not, he certainly did not relish his wife's behavior, which, we must presume, embarrassed him in public.[149]

Husbands often had a very different view of the origin of marital conflict. Melchor Figueroa's description of events differed significantly from his wife's, for example. He denied committing adultery or threatening his wife and justified his prolonged absence from home by the need to tend his *sembraditas y animales* (sown fields and animals) in Sorochuco. He also insinuated that illness had prevented him from returning home promptly after he finished his work in the fields. After the judge peremptorily ordered the couple to resume marital life, Figueroa stated that "my wife annoys and wearies me daily for no reason at all."[150] He told the court that she had refused to go to bed with him and "called me a rapist and pulled my hair." Clearly, one of the points of contention was his expectation that his wife should be sexually available, whereas she thought it within her rights to refuse. Figueroa was frank in his description of events: "I managed to bring my wife to our bed, reminding her again and again that we had made our peace, and that the judge had said she should obey me . . . as she was my wife and had no reason to call me a rapist."[151] Figueroa thus felt entitled to demand sexual favors, arguing that the judge had ordered his wife to obey her husband.

Although he had initially stood accused, it was Melchora Goicochea's husband, Figueroa, whose position was strengthened by the judge's ruling. Raymunda's view of the matter is revealed through her refusal to bed with her spouse.

Such willfully conflicting interpretations of official gender discourse were not unusual. Tinsman notes that Chilean husbands and wives also defined the gender mutualism promoted during the agrarian reform in contrasting, gender-specific ways: "Whereas wives interpreted the ethos of gender mutualism to mean that husbands should give them more respect and autonomy, men often interpreted it to mean that women should support and obey their husbands."[152]

Despite her husband's insistence, Raymunda Goicochea continued to resist his sexual advances and finally won the day (or, in this case, the night). As Melchor laconically told the court, "I rolled up my poncho and lay down in a corner."[153] Figueroa was clear about his sexual claims on his wife; he also argued that he had fulfilled his part of the deal, namely, providing for his family. "After the advice we had been given by the judge," he declared, "I went alone to Sorochuco to look after my fields, and returned with two reales' worth of bread for my wife and children." Whether he spoke the truth when he claimed he was traveling in order to work and support his family is irrelevant for the purposes of my argument; clearly, he thought he was advancing his case by describing himself as a hard-working and conscientious father and husband. His wife, on the other hand, did not, in his eyes, fulfill her part of the bargain when she greeted him with continued hostility on his return from Sorochuco. Figueroa told the court that his wife met him coldly (*"con desprecio"*) and only reluctantly prepared his breakfast. "I asked her for breakfast, and she prepared it, and then made soup with half the bread I had brought, and served it with the other half." Raymunda therefore took all of the bread he had brought for her and the children and served it to him, implying that she wanted nothing from him.[154] Figueroa went on to describe how he finally managed to persuade his wife to join him for the meal, which she reluctantly did, only to escape from the house at the first opportunity. He declared that her behavior—*"malos manejos conmigo"* [poor behavior toward me]—demonstrated her "resentment against me, and the loathing she bears her husband."[155]

By describing his wife's hostility, which she expressed in verbal and nonverbal insults[156] (such as returning all the food he had purchased for the family), Figueroa gives us an insight into what Stern calls the weapons of "daily social interaction."[157] Figueroa sought to convince the judge that he was not to blame for the failure of his marriage. "I have borne her bad behavior, and enduring my unfortunate fate, have continued fulfilling my duties."[158]

This exchange of views reveals some of the potential points of contention in male-female unions: wives expected husbands to contribute economically and refrain from excessive violence; husbands shared this view, at least in theory (or thought it was expedient to give the impression that they did). This is clear from Figueroa's assertion that he had conscientiously provided for his family, tolerated his wife's coldness, and refrained from violence. Wives, for their part, were expected to be sexually available, to provide domestic services such as cooking and laundering, to assume primary responsibility for children, and to display obedience. Figueroa insisted on exercising his right to his wife's services regardless of his behavior, whereas Goicochea made it clear that the provision of these services, domestic and sexual, was conditional on his fulfilling his part of the marriage pact. Women regarded sexual and economic rights as interlinked in what Stern calls a "contested patriarchal pact." In the eyes of Goicochea and her counterparts, the husband's sexual rights were contingent on fulfillment of certain economic obligations. Stern observes that failure to provide for their families economically resulted in the withdrawal of sexual access; in extreme cases, women felt justified in entering relationships with other men if their husbands failed to provide for them.[159]

While abandoned wives in Cajamarca also entered new relationships, occasionally with a clear economic rationale underlying the decision, they did not try to justify their action. Rather, they seem to have been driven into economic dependence on other men by sheer destitution and desperation, as in the case of María Albarrón, who wandered about homeless until she was taken in by Manuel Torres.[160] Whatever their private thoughts on the rights and wrongs of ending their husband's sexual monopoly, wives who had left did not share those thoughts with the authorities, probably knowing full well that they would receive little sympathy. Husbands, aware that they could count on official support for their stance, displayed no such reticence in asserting their absolute sexual rights over their wives.

As Goicochea's and Figueroa's statements show, there is no doubt that men and women did have different, and conflicting, views of male and female rights and duties in marriage. Although many husbands clearly thought that their rights were absolute (and not conditional, as most women defined them), Figueroa's efforts to make his behavior palatable to the authorities illustrate that he recognized that he had overstepped a boundary. Although this did not change his behavior, it shaped his portrayal of events in court.

Raymunda Goicochea did not mince words when telling her husband what she thought of him, but at least she did so in private. Wives' public expression of contempt and disobedience was certain to provoke male displeasure. Gregoria Astopilco claimed that Lizandro Olivares beat his wife "because she seeks to quarrel with him and anybody else."[161] Similarly, Julián Marín Plasencia beat his partner, Carmen Ducos, after she challenged him in public by beginning an argument with a suspected rival.[162] For purposes of comparison it is worth recalling Johnson's comment about late-colonial Buenos Aires: "An overly assertive or combative wife was a threat to the reputation of any man."[163] Challenging a husband's demand for deference could be the result of negotiating Stern's "contested patriarchal pact" and part of an ongoing negotiation over rights and duties within the framework of marriage.[164] However, individual differences in temperament also played a role. Even within societies governed by patriarchal norms and expectations of female deference, some wives were likely to be less subservient than others.

Regardless of the reason for wifely fury, it constituted a threat to husbands' authority and hence their honor. As Chambers has observed, "masculine honor depended, in part, on the image of a patriarch in control of his household";[165] hence, a wife who brought marital disputes out into the open or in other ways challenged her husband's authority threatened all husbands' social standing within the local community. Men therefore sought to control their wives by stopping them from gossiping excessively and squashing any open challenge to their authority, as, for instance, public intervention in a husband's sexual affairs.[166]

Violence was one way of asserting control. In this, men were backed by the state. Beyond countenancing male violence, the courts repeatedly ordered couples to settle marital disputes in private, and without involving third parties—a topic I discuss in the next section.

Marital conflict was not necessarily as extreme as the examples I deal with in this chapter. In order to avoid open provocation, and the threat of violent repercussions, women often relied on the marital counterpart of what James Scott has labeled the "everyday weapons of resistance": coolness toward their husbands, slowness (or even failure) to fulfill domestic duties; or denial of sex. Although Scott notes the difference between gender-based domination and other relations of subordination—gendered domination tends to be more personal and intimate—I believe that some of his terminology and ideas are useful for understanding both the weapons employed by women in their marital struggles and the ways in which they portrayed their behavior to the authorities. Since, as Scott argues for peasants, subordinate groups, in order to avoid punishment, prefer everyday resistance to open challenges to the system, these small daily battles between men and women have gone largely unrecorded. Women's experience of marital relations and their way of rationalizing them are particularly elusive. Although they may have shared their thoughts with intimate friends and female relatives, any hidden transcript is "specific to a given social situation and to a particular set of actors," and hence not easily visible and identifiable—especially for the historian who must rely on written sources. Moreover, as Scott also notes, everyday resistance is often masked by symbolic conformity, further obscuring both women's acts of everyday resistance and their hidden transcripts.[167] As a result, most examples of women's everyday resistance, although evident to their husbands, have not been preserved for the historian.

DOMESTIC VIOLENCE: PLOTTING SURVIVAL STRATEGIES

If women took legal action against their spouses only in cases of long-term or serious violence, and men sought to justify their violence in terms of their wife's capricious behavior, what other strategies did these women use to deal with abuse, and how did outsiders respond to them?

While women were frequent victims of domestic violence, they were not always passive victims, and—in some cases—not victims at all. Manuela Agip, for instance, drove a knife into her husband's body after finding him in bed with another woman.[168] When common-law spouses María de los Santos Chávez and Felipe Leyva fell to arguing over an item of gossip, he (although blind) raised his stick in order to beat her, and a violent struggle ensued during which he broke his ankle.[169] If they had the advantage of a weapon or a physical advantage, women did, therefore, occasionally succeed in turning the tables and victimizing their partners. In his study of battered wives in the 1980s, Gayford says that women usually succeed only by negating the male's physical advantage through the use of a weapon or when he is physically disadvantaged by illness or alcohol.[170]

Even if women in Cajamarca did not always gain the upper hand, they did not shy away from retaliating with physical violence. Several trials record full-blown fights in which both sides used violence. The incident that led to Baltazara Minchán's miscarriage took place when both partners were drunk during Carnival and involved mutual violence.[171] When her common-law husband attacked María Castañeda with a sword, the couple rolled "some distance below the house, as she had fought her way there."[172] Martina Terán was even arrested following the death of her common-law husband, as it was suspected that the wound she had inflicted on him during a domestic quarrel—"una reyerta doméstica"—might have caused his death.[173] One modern student of domestic violence states that "in contrast to the common idea that female interaction is characterised by politeness and an aversion to fighting, I found my female informants equally competent in this kind of activity as were the men."[174] Closer to home, in Ocongate, near Cuzco, Harvey confirms that women often give as good as they get.[175] Torre also confirms that Cajamarcan women occasionally, although rarely, respond with violence, often using their rueca (distaff) as a weapon. However, female resistance to abuse also produces the most extreme escalations of conflict, often endangering battered women even further.[176] Nevertheless, the modern anthropological evidence and the examples taken from the trials show that women in the nineteenth century were not necessarily passive victims of violence.

As we have seen, some women chose to take legal action. Being a difficult and rarely fruitful process, this course was chosen only in extreme cases. Only two of eleven trials dealing with marital violence were initiated by female victims.[177] Male victims started two.[178] The two women who did press charges had suffered severe battery over a protracted period. Marcela Montoya stated, "I am no longer able to bear the suffering to which my husband has reduced me . . . and therefore bring legal action against him." She went on to describe how he had attacked, beaten, and tried to stab her after an argument concerning his mistress in the town of Cajamarca.[179] Raymunda Goicochea, who charged her husband with attempted murder, was driven by a multiplicity of causes: the wish to protect herself from further abuse; protection of her property; and the desire to persuade her husband to provide for their children.[180] Relatives of the victim started four trials,[181] and the authorities, due to the serious nature of the crimes, instituted another five.[182]

The threshold for battered wives formally to accuse their husbands of abuse was therefore extremely high.[183] As Boyer has noted for colonial Mexico, although women did try to resist marital violence by seeking redress from the authorities, there was no effective way of protecting themselves from battery.[184] Instead, they sought alternative strategies. Some tried to leave the relationship they were in. Research in other regions and periods indicates that applicants for divorce were primarily female, and that domestic violence was a frequent reason given for such petitions. Hünefeldt has studied no fewer than 1,070 conjugal suits brought in the archbishopric of Lima in the nineteenth century. Some dealt with violence, some with economic neglect and adultery.[185] As I have been unable to study any ecclesiastical records for Cajamarca, I have not found any divorce petitions; nor have I found any applications for *separación de bienes* (separation of goods) in the records of *causas civiles* (civil suits). Divorce suits usually included an ecclesiastic petition for the dissolution of the marriage and a civil suit for the division of property; the absence of such trials in Cajamarca seems to indicate that divorce was more rarely resorted to in highland northern Peru than in the capital, Lima. We can only speculate as to the reasons, but presumably the weaker presence of the state in the provinces played a role, as well as possibly more limited access to cash to pay for such proceedings.

With reduced state and church surveillance of the region's inhabitants' marital and sexual activities, it is possible that it was easier for spouses to escape unsuccessful relationships without having to initiate divorce proceedings. Men simply left, often migrating to the coast; women, too, left. Asunción Ramírez endured her marriage to the violent Aurelito González for some time before she decided to escape and left the district in order to seek work as a servant.[186] Sometimes couples separated, but continued to live near each other. Andrea Díaz told the court that José María Fernandes "has lived as my companion many years, beating me every time he got drunk. . . . When I could bear no more I dismissed him from my house."[187] She finally brought him to court some years after the relationship ended, since he continued to harass and threaten her and her children.

As Fernández' continued persecution shows, ending a relationship was not always easy or risk free. After Manuela Urrelo broke off her relationship with Asunción Vásquez, he forced the pregnant woman to walk alongside him one evening, trying to persuade her to resume the relationship. When she continued to refuse, he rammed a knife into her womb, killing both her and the unborn child.[188] For other women it seems as if the violence and persecution began only after they broke off their relationships. Asencia Camacho reported that her former partner had assaulted her and broken into her home several times since she left him, "under the pretext that he had illicit relations with me, which ended some time ago."[189]

Economic dependence tied women to their partners, especially if they had children. Living alone, they usually experienced bleaker poverty than if they had a male partner. María Isabel Ordóñez' experiences exemplify this. She broke off her relationship with Fermín Cerdán following a disagreement, whereupon he stabbed her in the leg. The wound, which was inflicted while she was holding the couple's youngest child, was so serious that she was sent to the hospital, and he to jail. After two weeks Ordóñez wrote to the judge begging that Cerdán be freed, explaining that she and her children depended on his economic support.[190] Clearly, as well as tying women to their partners, economic dependence provided powerful arguments against prosecuting abusers. It is also useful to note that the length of time women endured physical abuse limited their options. At the same time, the fact that some women succeeded in escaping from abusive relationships shows that these limitations were not absolute.

The overview of wife abuse so far, therefore, shows that women frequently regarded domestic violence as inescapable and were likely to continue living in abusive relationships for years. Even when physical abuse led to de facto separation, it rarely produced legal consequences. This happened only in instances of exceptional brutality, or when there were additional reasons for legal action, such as adultery or the failure to provide for the family. Batterers were not the only ones who thought that physical aggression was legitimate; stoic acceptance of violence was widespread. The Astopilco sisters, for instance, explained to the court that Manuela Mestanza had well deserved the blows her husband had dealt her: she drank too much and had a quarrelsome nature.[191] When María Huaccha died, knifed by her husband, her brothers told him, "Malhecho [Evil Deed], you should have hit her, not stabbed her," implying that they thought the use of limited violence was acceptable.[192]

Battered women did receive assistance, however. Families and friends frequently provided moral and practical support as well as outright defense. The example of Simona Paredes, who cried her eyes out while washing clothes with her friends following a beating by her lover during the night, has been mentioned.[193] Jacoba Bermúdez told the court that "people who knew of her life" had intervened and thus saved her when her husband beat her.[194]

In situations of physical danger the limited privacy typical of life in small hamlets, villages, and towns was one of women's principal safeguards.[195] Although the publicizing of marital conflict affected couples' (and especially wives') reputations adversely, women did occasionally resort to this device.[196] There was security in acquainting the public with one's matrimonial squabbles: only by involving family, neighbors, and friends could a woman be certain that somebody would intervene to rescue her in moments of crisis.

Most frequently, help came from close family members. When Antonio Vargas beat his common-law wife, María Castañeda, and attacked her with a sword, it was her brothers, warned by a youth who had run to tell them of their sister's plight, who intervened. Hilario Castañeda recalled that "the youth Gaspar Mendoza arrived and told him that Antonio Vargas had just killed his sister, María Castañeda, and that he thereupon left his field and went to see his sister." Arriving, he saw that Vargas was about to lock himself inside the house and went to search for his sister.[197] When Casimiro Chilcote attacked his wife, María Huaccha, with a knife and realized the probable outcome of the attack, he fled and hid, fearing the arrival of her brothers: "I left the house, fearful that her family [would] blame me [for her wounds]."[198]

The victims' mothers are perhaps the most frequently documented saviors. Thus Melchor Figueroa was incensed when his mother-in-law supported her daughter's refusal to have sex with him.[199] Similarly, the conflict between Calixto Juárez and his wife would not have made its way into court but for the fact that her mother, on hearing the quarrel, came to her daughter's assistance. In the course of the ensuing struggle, the mother was hurt and insulted; within a few days Juárez and his mother-in-law had accused each other of *"agresiones"* (assault).[200] The incident, interesting because of the evident tension between the son- and mother-in-law, was not unique: Johnson reports occurrences from colonial Buenos Aires in which sons-in-laws disciplined their mothers-in-law.[201]

Sometimes relatives seriously wounded the spouses of their daughters, sisters, and nieces. José Sánchez had his leg broken by his brother- and mother-in-law; when a doctor examined Manuel Encarnación Llerena following an assault by various in-laws, he concluded that it would take twenty days for the wounds to heal, and that Llerena would be unable to walk in the meantime.[202]

Historical and anthropological studies note the role of family members, brothers in particular, in protecting female relatives from marital battery. Stavig, discussing seventeenth-century Indian communities in Cuzco, found that women often fought back, frequently aided by their brothers; Harris shows that women in rural Bolivia were beaten more often by their husbands if they had no brothers. In addition, women were, and are, often aided by their children, particularly their adolescent sons, as has been noted by several anthropologists.[203]

Not all assistance came from close family members; occasionally, friends, acquaintances, and outsiders intervened. When Antolino Álvarez beat and tried to stab his common-law wife in the attic of the house in which she worked as a cook, her employer, María Pelaes, climbed the narrow stairs to the attic and fought him off.[204] Gregorio Bringas risked his life trying to stop Elías Arribasplata from using force against his common-law wife. Realizing what was about to take place when Arribasplata forced his partner and her mother to leave a birthday celebration and accompany him, Bringas followed Arribasplata "so as to stop him hitting her."[205] When he heard the blows inside the women's *tienda* (shop, or ground floor room), he intervened and "succeeded in calming him in a friendly way." However, patriarchs in the process of asserting their authority did not welcome such altruistic behavior. Arribasplata responded by pulling out his knife and stabbing Bringas three times.[206]

In some situations, the wish to assist battered wives overrode concern for an individual's own safety—and even allegiance to family members. When Fernanda Rodríguez' husband attacked her by kicking and strangling her and threatening her with her own knife, his sister saved her.[207] Such episodes denote the importance of family and neighborhood networks in women's lives. Geography, architecture, and location and size of family determined the role of the network. Women living in urban and semiurban locations were more likely to obtain assistance than were women living in more remote places. Asunción Ramírez, for instance, decided to leave her husband rather than expose herself to further risk by living with him. She explained that they lived far from her family, exposing her to the full force of her husband's aggression.[208] A great deal went on in the patio, making it easy for neighbors or other outsiders to listen in on arguments and to participate if they thought it appropriate.

As young couples frequently built houses or extensions to existing houses on their parents' property, such interventions were not unusual.[209] A particularly juicy example concerns the trial initiated by Josefa Oyarse against son-in-law Calixto Juárez. Oyarse explained that Juárez and her daughter were engaged in "a tremendous fight" ("una formidable pelea") on the preceding Wednesday, and "when I approached them to find out the reason [for the fight] and to tell them off [for arguing in this way]," her son-in-law started to insult her and proceeded to hit and kick her until she found herself "on the ground with him pulling my hair without letting go." In the interrogation that followed she explained that she had heard her son-in-law call her "an old Indian whore, whore above and whore below" [una india vieja masebada (amancebada) arriba puta y puta abajo], whereupon she "ran to ask him why he talked about me in this fashion." The episode reveals considerable tension between son-in-law and mother-in-law; it also illustrates the lack of privacy and the measure of protection afforded by contemporary building styles.[210]

Witnesses made it clear that they disapproved of violence against women. When Doña Catalina Cáceres saw Andrés Espinoza threatening to beat a young woman with a stick, she scolded him, shouting, "Don't fight with women."[211] Gregorio Bringas called Elías Arribasplata a "maricón" (gay man) for hitting his common-law wife.[212] Another example is the quarrel that developed between Julián Marín Plasencia and his girlfriend, Carmen Ducos, at the *fundición* (smeltery). It seems that the entire village had congregated to watch a local smeltery at work, and that the event had transformed itself into a fiesta with heavy drinking. One of the women reproved Marín Plasencia: "Respect the authorities and other people. . . . If you won't respect anybody, take your woman with you [and hit her in private]."[213] Although she merely objected to the public display of violence, others promptly took more concrete action. A little boy was sent to wake up Marín Plasencia's uncle (also named Julián Marín) so that he could calm his nephew down. According to the uncle, "the child Timoteo Portal came to let him know . . . [and said] he is beating my aunt. . . . Therefore he went to the house where he found his nephew Julián [standing] in the doorway. . . . He had dealt her several blows. . . . Then the deponent said, come here, you won't achieve anything by going on like this." Another witness to the event commented that "he gave her two punches so that she sat down." The irate nephew returned to the celebration, leaving Ducos behind, crying, but accompanied by her mother, her boyfriend's uncle, and the latter's common-law wife.

This incident illuminates a number of issues. While public abuse of one's wife was disapproved of, fear of interfering in marital squabbles dissuaded many from taking action. Instead, they sought the assistance of figures of authority, usually older male relatives of the aggressor, who then tried to defuse the situation.

It is worth noting that, although Julián Marín eventually succeeded in calming his nephew, mothers who intervened in order to protect their daughters from violence did not command as much respect. When Narcisa Mendoza tried to protect her daughter from a former lover, she was killed.[214] Similarly, when Josefa Oyarse interfered in the argument between her daughter and the latter's husband, Calixto Juárez, her interference only exacerbated the situation.[215] In her work on southern Peru, anthropologist Penelope

Harvey notes that "a woman will tend to look to her husband's kin rather than her own for support if she wants the situation to be resolved rather than escalated. Typically, she will turn to an aunt or uncle who have the hierarchical rank to admonish the spouse. . . . If a woman turns to her own kin however, the problem is likely to escalate as her kin have no accepted authority over her husband."[216]

Oyarse's story also echoes another detail of Torre's study of rural Cajamarca in the 1990s. Torre points out the role of children as their mother's allies: when the father becomes violent, the children frequently run to fetch help from senior relatives. Outsiders wishing to prevent violent abuse in nineteenth-century Cajamarca therefore had several options, providing that help was close at hand.[217]

Friends and relatives provided abused women emotional comfort: following the episode related above, Carmen Ducos' mother and other relatives stayed and looked after her. In the same way, Fernanda Rodríguez was taken to her mother's home after her husband's assault on her, partly to aid her recovery, partly for protection.

Both family members and outsiders tried to intervene in fights in order to protect the weaker party and were willing to assist by providing refuge. This demonstrates that there was popular disapproval of wife bashing. As James C. Scott comments (talking about acts of peasant resistance), the intent is inscribed in the acts themselves. He also observes that individual acts of resistance to exploitation are surrounded and "reinforced by a venerable popular culture of resistance."[218] According to Scott, this "style of narrative discourse . . . constitutes a form of resistance that is much more than purely symbolic."[219]

Husbands' authority was not unlimited. Wives consciously sought external assistance in cases of violence and in order to exert moral pressure on adulterous spouses and husbands who failed to provide for their family. Chambers says that it was usually wives who publicized marital conflict. Although wives were more likely to be affected by public censure, Chambers argues that, occasionally, a wife's position in the home was so vulnerable that she opted to submit herself to her neighbors' judgment.[220] In her study of marriage in nineteenth-century Lima, Hünefeldt notes the strength of social networks in the urban barrio, where neighbors occasionally intervened on behalf of abused wives. "Clearly, husbands, despite their many prerogatives, did not have unlimited freedom to beat or cheat their wives," she observes. She also notes that the moral authority of the barrio was far greater than that of church and state.[221]

In the same way, I would argue that widespread support for women who resisted abuse encouraged female resistance to abusive relationships. While such attitudes did not protect them from violent treatment, they provided a more supportive moral climate for female resistance to battery than the officially sanctioned discourse of female submissiveness. The importance of moral support and comfort from relatives and friends should not be underestimated; Torre's work documents the emotional and psychological impact of abuse. By the same token, emotional and psychological support helped victims deal with their experiences.

Both husbands and courts, in particular, objected to the intervention of in-laws. Harvey maintains that even today couples frequently argue over how much contact with her family a woman should be allowed. "In all marital relationships there is a conscious struggle on the part of the husband to get the wife away from the influence and protection of her own kin."[222] Similarly, Hünefeldt records that husbands in nineteenth-century Lima resisted contact between their wives and the latter's parents.[223]

The conflict between Calixto Juárez and his mother-in-law exemplifies official condemnation of intervening in-laws. Although Juárez was sentenced to eight days in jail, the judge made it clear that interference by mothers-in-law would not be tolerated. The judge told Josefa Oyarse, Juárez' mother-in-law, that her behavior was reprehensible: she was not to "meddle in the private disputes of a married couple, which she absolutely should not interfere with." Although she was let off with a warning, she was told that any further offense would result in a jail sentence. The other example referred to above, the forced conciliation between Marcela Montoya and her husband, also displays judges' aversion to the interference of in-laws. The judge in this case assured both partners that neither would be punished, "but any further disorder, or if either of them united with their families, would be punished by immediate arrest."[224] Similarly, Francisca Cotrina's suit for alimony from her womanizing husband did not produce the desired response. The judge sternly admonished both spouses to resume a harmonious married life, "entirely separated and independent of the parents of either spouse, or brothers-in-law, who should not exert the smallest influence in their married life." Clearly the judge had been provoked by Cotrina's decision to quit the marital home and return to her mother's home with her son.[225]

While women certainly received assistance from both men and other women in moments of crisis, I have found no basis for assuming that these gender differences were decisive in determining whom wives called on, or who ultimately intervened. The primary dividing lines seem to run between family members, neighbors, and strangers rather than between the sexes. Obviously, the gender of the intervenor mattered. As I have noted, the presence of brothers meant that husbands were more likely to suffer retaliation, and this threat presumably made them more wary of employing violence. It is worth noting that there are no records of husbands coming into conflict with their fathers-in-law; possibly, paternal protection of daughters (unlike maternal interference) was considered less contentious by husbands, and hence led to fewer conflicts.

Finally, I have found that women rarely sought assistance from the legal authorities, and when they did, there was little help to be had. Nor are there any examples of women seeking new lovers to protect them from abusive spouses. As the examples cited above reveal, such moves were more likely to provoke further tension and violence.

CONCLUSION

My aim in this chapter has been to study marital relations in practice and to compare them with state-sanctioned definitions of gender relations. Despite the explicit condemnation of all informal unions—short- and long-term—by both church and state, consensual unions not only were widely formed, but also were accepted as normal and imbued with a degree of respectability. Many such unions were permanent and were eventually transformed into formal marriages, sometimes on the deathbed of one of the spouses. Others, although permanent, remained informal. Finally, some long-term relationships were eventually dissolved.

Although consensual unions functioned as the virtual equivalent of formal marriage, the latter could imply greater economic security, as the spouses were legally bound to each other. In addition, and just as important, ecclesiastically blessed marriage served as a hallmark of social status, ensuring the legitimacy of any offspring the union produced.

Unlike formal marriage, which state and church regarded as indissoluble, consensual unions allowed unhappy partners to opt out. This was especially important for women who suffered abuse at the hands of their common-law husbands. The courts consistently prevailed on women to return to their husbands and threatened both them and their families with punishment if new challenges to the husband's authority should occur. For the state, therefore, the principles of marital indissolubility—and patriarchal authority—were paramount.

While the state in effect condoned marital violence, the popular classes regarded battery as a regrettable but often unavoidable fact of life. However, records also reveal a plebeian anti-abuse discourse. Relatives and (usually female) friends formed a substantial support network that lent both moral and practical aid to victims, help that occasionally extended to physical protection. They intervened physically and orally in fights, comforted the victim, aided her on the path to recovery, and sought legal recourse on her behalf.

While such networks were not available to all victims and did not prevent abuse, the widely held idea that spousal abuse was not acceptable created a climate that allowed women to take steps to defend themselves. Women chose a variety of strategies, depending on their marital status, economic position, support network, individual temperament, and whether they had children. Some fought back; others bore the abuse indefinitely or for some time before starting to fight back; some developed strategies to minimize violence, such as hiding outside of the house when their drunk husband returned or calling for assistance. Many ended their relationships, although this did not always signify the end of persecution and danger.

Popular and official views of marital relations therefore differed significantly. Whereas women thought themselves entitled to call for assistance and justified in leaving physically abusive relationships, the courts opposed such actions. They particularly objected to the intervention of in-laws or other outsiders. Husbands were quick to exploit official backing once the courts became involved, with the result that the negotiation of matrimonial conflict sometimes included not only the spouses and their relatives, but also lawyers, judges, and numerous witnesses. Husbands resorted to a number of strategies in order to justify their behavior: they denied having laid hands on their wife; they claimed that the fight had been mutual; or they accused their wife of adultery.

Male excuses for abuse are but poor indicators of genuine causes, however. Husbands sought those explanations that were most likely to appeal to judges. Among the immediate factors precipitating violence which do emerge from witness testimonies are alcohol, wives' public challenges to male authority, slander (accusing wives of infidelity), plus genuine cases of adultery by women. The underlying causes of matrimonial tension are more elusive; however, poverty and disputes over the rights and duties of the spouses, including issues such as economic contribution and the provision of domestic and sexual services, were frequent areas of dissension. Male fidelity and female obedience were central points of contention in this context.

Wives and their relatives had their own idea of what constituted acceptable behavior for spouses. As Hünefeldt has pointed out for nineteenth-century Lima, wives were adept at using the arguments offered by the discourse of liberalism. Women displayed an increasing awareness of a husband's duties within a marriage and a growing appreciation of their own contributions. They argued that a husband's failure to fulfill his part of the marriage pact was grounds for divorce, and that their own contribution to conjugal assets entitled them to certain economic returns upon division of the conjugal assets. Although Cajamarcan women appear to have gone to court more rarely than their Lima counterparts, and their arguments were less fully developed, even peasant women manifested similar understandings of conditional rights.

In Lima, wives' demands were countered by more stringent moral standards for women. By the end of the nineteenth century, even extreme circumstances no longer justified divorce; instead, "the ever-forgiving wife became the social standard."[226] In Arequipa, local elites allied themselves with plebeian patriarchs, thereby reinforcing the division between public and private and allowing husbands complete dominion within the latter sphere.[227]

Although my sample is not large enough and the period studied too short to allow conclusions about change over time, my research confirms that the state sought to place a tight lid on wives who openly dared to challenge their husband's authority. Late-nineteenth-century Peruvian legislation and legal practice confirm that the elites sought to protect the institution of marriage from any challenge, whether internal or external. Given the concern for patriarchal authority in a period of growing social change, the insistence on female obedience to husbands matches official policy in a number of other Latin American countries in this period.

CHAPTER 5

Injurias Verbales y Calumnias

SLANDER

A growing literature regarding honor documents its importance in colonial Latin America and during the nineteenth century, as well as some of the changes the definition of honor underwent in this period. Honor was described as all or nothing by contemporaries, a matter as clear-cut and dramatic as life and death. But paradoxically, it was both negotiable and elastic. Twinam has documented how the colonial elite could retain honor by acknowledging transgressions in private, but not in public; in some cases stains on honor could be removed by purchasing *gracias al sacar*, formal legitimation granted by bureaucrats in Spain; illegitimate children could have their status rectified and be legitimized by their parents' subsequent marriage. Contrary to the prevalent rhetoric, then, honor could be regained once lost, and was—as the many applications for *gracias al sacar* in the Cámara de Indias show—subject to negotiation.[1]

Nor was honor necessarily the prerogative of the elite. Despite elite attempts to appropriate honor for themselves, members of the lower classes also saw themselves as possessing honor and staked out their claims to it in a series of arenas, including the legal system. Even men and women of color, women who worked outside of the domestic sphere, and women who had borne children outside of marriage claimed to be honorable and demanded the community's respect—on occasion going to court in order to prove their point. In their arguments, these men and women revealed their own views of honor—views that often differed substantially from the code of honor handed down by their superiors.

As the nineteenth century progressed, these plebeian notions of honor began to color official interpretations. Increasingly, honor was defined as an issue of morality and virtue rather than exclusively a matter of wealth, purity of blood, and social status. Lower-class men had seen themselves as men of honor all along; during the nineteenth century, official discourse, as enunciated in legislation and literature, accorded hard-working patriarchs a degree of recognition as men of honor and citizens. Whether as part of an attempt to co-opt plebeian men in nationalist political projects, or as a re-action to perceived social unrest and miscegenation, notions of honor were redefined, granting patriarchs new rights and increased control over their homes. This transformed discourse of honor affected women by subject-ing them to strengthened patriarchal authority and a stricter moral climate. Sexual virtue and feminine, particularly marital, obedience became even more important criteria in the evaluation of women's worth and, hence, their rights.[2]

Codes of honor were therefore neither inelastic nor static: individuals molded them to fit their behavior, and the codes were transformed over time and space. A series of criminal trials involving, on the one hand, slander and public insults and, on the other, accusations of rape and seduction shed light on how provincial, lower-class citizens dealt with issues of honor, the role it played in their lives, and how they defined and lived with their definitions of honor.

In this chapter I look at trials dealing with charges of public insults and calumny. Public insults, or slander, constituted a powerful slur on a person's reputation and could cause someone to challenge the slanderer informally (usually leading to further arguments and, occasionally, street brawls) or for-mally, in court. The records of such legal encounters reveal the importance of honor, the way in which challenges to it were used consciously to inflict damage on enemies, and the ways in which individuals fought to regain it. A careful reading of the documentation reveals the multiple meanings given to the concept of honor by—and for—individuals of different social status, sex, age, and marital status. Not only did women and men of different walks of life view honor differently, they often successfully used the legal system to propagate and defend their own definition. While the concept of honor had traditionally served to rationalize and legitimize the colonial hierarchy and social discrimination (and has been seen by historians as being imposed from above), by the nineteenth century, lower-class women and men had formed their own understanding of honor and used the legal system in order to ex-plicate their definition while backing their claim to it—often in the face of official opposition.

INJURIAS VERBALES: PICKING A FIGHT

Slander—defined as *injuria* or *calumnia*—constituted a criminal offense,[3] and suits dealing with slanderous insults were filed in the criminal courts.[4] Although the plaintiffs' ostensible motivation was punishment of the slanderer, the underlying aim was to clear the complainant's name of the slanderer's imputations, thus publicly demonstrating the claim to honor. Similarly, charges of rape and seduction, which I deal with in Chapter 6, were also primarily about reestablishing claims to honor, and only secondarily (and, at that, rarely) about punishing the offender.

Between 1862 and 1900 approximately eighty cases of slanderous insults and libel or slander were brought to the provincial court in Cajamarca. I selected all the trials in the third and fourth year of each decade and all trials of obvious interest (for instance, trials involving the same parties in different years); thus I have studied thirty cases in depth. In these thirty cases, forty individuals were accused of slander. In some cases, the defendants were accused of spreading rumors that affected other people's reputations. More frequently, these trials dealt with the outcome of heated arguments in which the parties had flung insults such as *ladrón* (thief), *puta* (whore), or *bruja* (witch) at one another. Usually, such conflicts remained in the realm of informal gossip in the home, at the water fountains, in the plaza or the streets; however, it was only when such exchanges reached the legal arena that they were documented for posterity.

Litigants in slander trials came from a broad social range, but predominantly from the local semiurban petty bourgeoisie. Their social identity is reflected in the everyday concerns described in the trials: complainants, defendants, and witnesses worked the land, worked as carpenters and weavers, sold goods in the market in Cajamarca town, and laundered their children's clothes in nearby streams. They met on their way to and from the fields, often while they were driving domestic animals.

Reflecting the gendered nature of honor, men and women opted for legal proceedings following very different types of insults. Seven of the eight men who defended their reputation in court did so after being called a thief; the most common insult used against women was that of whore. Alternatives were *ramera* (whore), *abandonada* (profligate),[5] *bandida* (outlaw),[6] *chola vandida* [sic] (half-breed outlaw),[7] *adúltera* (adulteress),[8] *prostituta* (prostitute),[9] as well as the more imaginative *par de putas alcahuetas* (pair of pimping whores)[10] and *puta bruja descasada* (unmarried or "dismarried" whore witch).[11] In two cases, women pulled up the dress of an enemy, exposing her publicly and thus seeking to display her shamelessness.[12] Other women were accused of specific incidents of adultery or licentiousness.[13] Words relating to women's sexual mores were the cause for twenty-three of twenty-six cases in which women sought to clear their name.[14]

Although attacks on women's sexual behavior were the insults most frequently recorded in the documentation, they were not the only ones. Five of the women who appeared in the trials had been called "thief."[15] Manuela Chávez was called "witch and thief" by Jacoba Bermúdez;[16] Natividad Arana went to court after Isabel Encalada accused her of stealing five hundred silver soles from her;[17] and Candelaria Arce sued Cayetana Mille after being accused of stealing a hat.[18]

Attacks on female honesty alone, however, were rarely enough to persuade women to go to court. Only two women went to court after being accused solely of theft.[19] Women were more likely to take legal action if their sexual reputation was offended at the same time. The other three women who took legal action following accusations of theft had also been called whores. When María Vigo accused Margarita Hidalgo of stealing a monstrance from the church, Hidalgo's husband remained passive. It was only after Vigo called Hidalgo an adulteress that the latter's husband took legal action.[20] In the course of a dispute between Candelaria Arce and Cayetana Mille concerning a missing hat, Mille also called Arce a whore, aggravating the initial accusation of theft to such an extent that Mille, who called herself a "poor and honorable woman," pressed charges against Arce.[21] Clara Pita called María Chávez "puta, ladrona," with the result that Chávez' husband demanded that his wife be arrested until the charges were proved or disproved, forcing her father to initiate proceedings in order to clear his daughter's name and reestablish her relationship with her husband.[22] Although women were called thieves, it was usually only when this occurred in conjunction with imputations of sexual license that they took incidents of slander to court.[23]

Male sexuality was not debated in the courts at all.[24] The only man to initiate legal proceedings following slander concerning his own sexual behavior was Bonifacio Alvarado. He was accused of engaging in illicit sexual relations with his uncle's wife, Candelaria Alvarado. His opening comment illustrates that his primary concern was reestablishing his aunt's, and supposed mistress', honor rather than his own. He wrote that Micaela Bringas' slander "had treacherously wounded the honor and fidelity of a married woman, as well as my [own] good reputation and integrity." Bringas' apology, which concluded the trial, also underlines the vulnerability of Candelaria's, rather than Bonifacio's reputation: Bringas begged the pardon of Candelaria Alvarado, her husband, and the public for any damage her slander might have done; Bonifacio Alvarado went unmentioned.[25]

Occasionally, the epithet was determined by the subject matter: Natividad Arana was called a thief in connection with a debt she allegedly refused to pay.[26] The fact that Rosario Tirado called her husband's fifteen-year-old mistress "puta" was perhaps understandable; similarly, María Pasión Sumarán's claim that María Linares was having an affair with her brother may have been based on fact, or at least genuine belief. In most cases, however, sexual insults were chosen because of their power to inflict damage rather than for their accuracy. As Pitt-Rivers has noted for Andalusia, the content of the insults often had little to do with the initial dispute: "Every quarrel, once inflamed, leads to imputations of acts and intentions which are totally dishonorable and which may well have nothing to do with the subject of the quarrel."[27]

THE PURSUIT OF HONOR IN COURT: IMPEDIMENTS

Men, frequently on behalf of their wives or daughters, initiated almost half of the trials I studied. However, women initiated fifteen of the twenty-six trials concerning their honor that I found. The fact that these women, most of whom were illiterate and had limited economic resources, went to court at all is a clear indication of how much their reputation meant to them. Only a third of the female initiators of slander trials were literate; for the remainder, engaging with the legal system involved even greater effort, as they could not even read the documents they signed or got others to sign for them. The costs were considerable. For most of the women who engaged in legal action, the cost of a scribe or even a lawyer had to be added to that of the court proceedings themselves. In addition, the court officials were male, white, and educated and rarely sympathetic to complaints brought to them by lower-class women. Some of these issues were valid for male plaintiffs as well.

Going to court was also fraught with potential pitfalls. Judges gave women who involved themselves in unseemly street brawls short shrift and often denied plaintiffs a full hearing; in some cases, the plaintiffs found themselves sentenced to jail along with the defendants. This happened to Manuela Villanueva and Asunción Gamarra, who charged Manuela Abanto and her daughter Carmen Bringas with public slander. The latter two were sentenced to twenty-eight months in jail and a fine of eighty soles, the former two to a "mere" twenty months and fifty soles. Luis Gamarra, husband of the wealthier Manuela Villanueva and father of Asunción, succeeded in overturning this sentence by withdrawing his charges against Manuela Abanto and her daughter and persuading his wife and daughter to do the same. The matter was thus dropped, and the judge dispensed with the punishment.[28]

José Silva y Soto was in for a similar surprise when he accused Jacoba Arbayza and Rosario Ravines of slandering him. Far from being vindicated, he and the defendants were sentenced to two years in jail when both parties were proved guilty.[29] Going to court was thus an option that could easily backfire.

Apart from incurring expense and risking jail time, taking legal action served to publicize the scandal in which litigants were already involved. Litigants were well aware that they were likely to besmirch their reputation further by drawing attention to themselves.

This was not a circumstance peculiar to Latin America. Demos argues that for individuals suspected of witchcraft in New England, actions for slander were in part a delaying tactic, enabling suspected witches to confront their accusers before public sentiment turned against them and they were brought to court. "However," he points out, "the tactic was not without risk. If the case for the defence seemed credible, the court's interest might abruptly reverse itself—with the plaintiff moving over to the prisoner's dock. The decision to file for slander must, therefore, have been a difficult one."[30]

Although nobody in Cajamarca was charged with witchcraft, Demos' reasoning holds true for charges of sex-related slander: going to court might easily turn against the plaintiff.[31] This was presumably the reason why Pedro Horna and José Dolores Jara opted for a settlement rather than provoke more bad press for their families. The trial began with Jara accusing Horna's wife, Rosario Tirado, of publicly beating and insulting his daughter. Tirado apparently "beat the girl with her hands, lifting up the girl's dress in a public manner and in the presence of numerous people trafficking the road," explained Jara. When it emerged that Horna was committing adultery with Jara's daughter, the two men quickly settled their disagreement. There is no record of the private discussion between them, but eventually they both dropped the charges, explaining "that as we are both neighbors of Shirac, and as it is not proper or decent that there should be litigation of this type between us, for as neighbors we should maintain the best harmony, as we also have had in the past, we have decided to make our own arrangements, or rather bury our differences [cortar nuestras diferencias] in order to conclude the ongoing trial." Jara had nothing to gain by publicizing his daughter's dishonor, and Horna no doubt did not enjoy the attention that was being drawn to his affair with the young girl.[32] (It is quite possible, however, that Rosario Tirado, who began as defendant, obtained her objectives: it seems likely that Pedro Horna gave up his affair with Aurora Jara rather than risk further scandal.]³³

In another case, the defendant claimed that the scandal that he was accused of precipitating had in fact been provoked by the complainant herself when she took the matter to court. Although Augusto Krol admitted having commented on the fact that Eusebia Olórtegui was supposedly involved in an adulterous relationship, he claimed that tongues had started wagging only after she drew attention to his comments by filing charges against him. Had she left well alone, he implied, the matter would have attracted no attention.³⁴

Olórtegui's case seems to have been further complicated by a problem also experienced by other litigants: corruption. She claimed that Krol bribed the judge and the scribes so that he would win the case. She told the court that "Krol has said [to me] that the judge and the notary have been paid, and that I will get nowhere with my suit." Regardless of whether he handed over any money, the fact that he was on friendly terms with the court's functionaries made it unlikely that he would be sentenced. According to Olórtegui, "Doctor Vigil was in Krol's shop together with the notaries Rojas and Carmen Vásquez, and their riotous laughter could be heard from the distance of one *cuadra* [one hundred meters]." Clearly, the chance of making headway in the local court, even if one could afford to pay a literate man to write one's letters and the court's fees, were slim when faced with an influential opponent.

THE PURSUIT OF HONOR: INCENTIVES

Suing other people for public insults was therefore an expensive option which could have unforeseen and negative consequences. In the light of such powerful disincentives, what persuaded women and men to go to court in order to clear their names?

The letters that plaintiffs submitted to the court when filing a case supply some answers. In these letters, complainants outlined the motives that brought them to court. All plaintiffs expressed a desire to clear their names. They stated that they regarded going to court as the last resort open to them. Above all, plaintiffs talked of their concern for "honor" and their position in society. Thus, Eusebia Olórtegui stated, "I find myself, then, obliged to defend my abused reputation with the same interest with which I would defend my life."³⁵ José Quevedo declared, with less originality than conviction, "a man's honor is worth more than his life";³⁶ Natividad Arana described reputation as the "most valuable good in any person."³⁷

While repetitive, and redolent of the scribes' regurgitated rhetoric of honor, complainants' opening submissions clearly expressed their concern for how the slander would affect their standing in the eyes of the public, that is, their neighbors and acquaintances. Numerous plaintiffs emphasized that neighbors had witnessed the insults in question. José Silva y Soto complained that Jacoba Arbayza and Rosario Ravines' insults "were uttered . . . in public, in the street, and shouted out loudly. A crowd of people have heard them . . . this whole neighborhood."[38] When Bonifacio Alvarado began proceedings against Micaela Bringas for the accusation of adultery committed by him and his aunt, Candelaria Alvarado, he pointed out that the entire neighborhood had heard these claims.[39] Juan Manuel Vera, who accused members of the Mestanza family of calling him a thief, reported that these words "were heard by a multitude of people."[40] Adelaida Sheen complained that Casimiro Basauri and his entire family were calling her "puta," "not merely in my home, but in the street."[41]

The public nature of the accusations was important because it proved to the court that the insults had a direct impact on the victim's social standing. As Twinam points out, it was the public and notorious (as opposed to private and confidential) knowledge of dishonorable behavior, rather than the behavior itself, which brought dishonor. Indeed, slander damaged honor and thus became an offense only if the plaintiff could document that it had been uttered in public. Thus Juliana Vargas and her daughters got off, because their denunciation of Hermegilda Villavicencio's allegedly promiscuous behavior was made within their own four walls. "Opening the windows of their house, which is situated on the central square of the town of Jesús," Villavicencio declared, "they dishonored me in public, shouting that I was a whore, an adulteress, a witch."[42] Nevertheless, the judge insisted that the nature of the insults was not public enough to warrant a conviction.

Several comments indicate that when it came to scandal or gossip of any kind, the local population formed an eager and receptive audience. Juan Manuel Vera (mentioned above) stated that upon hearing the word *thief* uttered by Leopoldo, Francisca, and Catalina Mestanza and Benito Briones, "crowds of people started to collect, and they all heard the words which were said."[43] Melecio Tirado described how Manuel María Tirado's insults involved a whole crowd: Tirado "slandered me . . . in the presence of many people who listened, and, outraged, the listeners begged him to stop."[44] Similarly, María Centurión's accusations against Emilia Verástegui —which ranged from adultery to theft and murder—quickly drew a crowd: "On hearing these words crowds of people of the neighborhood and passersby [gathered]."[45] Arguments that took place in public spaces, particularly if spiced with juicy accusations of adultery, drew ready crowds, which presumably proceeded to exhaustively discuss the rumors after the fun was over.

Such accusations and the ensuing gossip resulted in loss of respect and status in local society, even social ostracism. Juan Manuel Vera asserted that the rumors that he might be a thief "greatly affect my honor and good reputation as an honorable citizen and artisan," implying that the damage to his reputation might have an impact on his business. Candelaria Arce claimed that, as a result of Cayetana Mille's accusations, she was now considered by the public to be "the woman most unworthy of living in society."[46] Most dramatic was María de los Santos Linares, who lamented that, "with such a defamation I have suffered a moral death in society."[47]

While some of the language was clearly chosen with an eye to effect, honor did determine individuals' social standing: who mixed with whom; who entered into business with whom; who was eligible for marriage. As Twinam observes, "Those with honor recognized it in others and accorded those peers an attention and respect they denied the rest of society. . . . Honor determined who was considered trustworthy, who did favors for whom, who were one's friends, who were invited to parties, who was 'in' and who received greetings on the street."[48] Although Twinam is speaking about the colonial elites, the complainants' and witnesses' comments in Cajamarca reveal that the same held true, to a degree, for provincial life in northern Peru.

Plaintiffs also professed concern for the impact of such accusations on public morality. José Asunción Portilla noted of the Escalante sisters' insults that "it is necessary to repress these crimes which attack the person and the standing of a respectable family."[49] Manuel Luna Leiva pointed out that as a result of the insults to his wife, Melchora Álvarez, "public morality too has been slighted."[50] Similarly, Natividad Arana gave concern for the public as part of the reason behind her suit: "As public justice has been offended . . . by the imputation that has been made . : . I find myself obliged to turn to the court."[51] Even Micaela Bringas in her apology to Candelaria Alvarado asked the public for forgiveness prior to requesting the same from the victim of her insults: "I beg the public, the offended, and her husband for forgiveness."[52]

Most likely, such arguments were chosen for their presumed efficacy vis-à-vis the authorities rather than out of an overriding concern for public morality. As Porter has noted about market women in nineteenth-century Mexico, "while elites knew little about the world of vendors, vendors knew the world of elites."[53] Porter shows how this knowledge of elite gender codes helped Mexican *vendedoras* (sellers) frame their arguments in the jargon most agreeable to the officials with whom they had to contend; similarly, even small-scale shopkeepers and landowners, artisans, and spinners in Cajamarca were familiar enough with official concerns with public morality to use the appropriate formulas, or public transcript.[54]

Underlying these concerns, however, were usually more acute worries. Of the seventeen married women I found who were accused of adulterous relations, four stated that their husbands had left them;[55] others reported that their husbands were threatening to leave them.[56] Several professed to be at risk of violence. Francisca Sifuentes in her introductory letter to the judge wrote, "These words have led to the separation from my husband and to giving me a troubled time [*mala vida*] with him."[57] Sifuentes continued: "Informed of the insults against me, he has acted in such a way that had it not been for the intervention of close friends and family, I might have given up my existence." Jacoba Bermúdez (Francisca Sifuentes' opponent) had similar problems. She claimed that if her case was not dealt with by the court, "I will have to suffer . . . my husband's fury."[58] Emilia Verástegui wrote to the judge that, if her husband were to believe the slander against her, he might "abandon me and cause damage to my person if I fail to defend myself [through legal action]."[59] Petronila Astopilco argued that María Peralta's accusations of adultery were "very serious, considering my status as a married woman, as I could lose my husband and the happiness of my family."[60]

One of the women affected most dramatically by slander was María Chávez from Celendín. On hearing that she had been called an adulteress, her husband demanded that the court look into the accusations and that his wife be placed in custody for the duration of the trial. Such action corresponded to the first step in divorce proceedings: "I charge [the slanderer] so that the defendant prove my wife's thievery and adultery, placing [my wife] under arrest until these charges are proven, for unless light is shed on this matter I will separate from my wife immediately."[61] Despite the court's attempt to reconcile husband and wife, he refused to resume residence with his wife. María Chávez was released from custody only after her father took up her cause and pressed charges against Clara Pita, the woman who had initially slandered her, thus eventually absolving her of all suspicions of misconduct.[62] Candelaria Alvarado was not only abandoned by her husband following slander, but was also expelled from her home: "As the unfortunate [victim] of a hasty calumny, I have had to . . . [flee] to the house of my mother, Doña Hermenegilda Chávez."[63]

While Peruvian law stipulated that fathers retained custody of their children in cases of separation and divorce, in Cajamarca few fathers availed themselves of this option. Jacoba Bermúdez declared that, as a result of the slander of her enemy Manuela Chávez, "[my husband] has left me and his children."[64] Despite having the legal right to remove children from their mother's control, fathers without ready access to servants had little interest in burdening themselves with the practical work associated with child care. If doubtful of his wife's fidelity, a husband may have been (or claimed to be) uncertain of his children's paternity.[65] Usually, therefore, slandered wives who had been abandoned by their husbands found themselves with sole responsibility for their children. Although husbands were expected to assist and protect their wives (Candelaria Alvarado lamented the loss of the "help, and the majestic protection which I had from my good husband and true family father"), a husband's failure to live up to this ideal was not criticized by his wife, the public, or the courts. On the contrary, wives defended their husbands' anger. Jacoba Bermúdez, for instance, asserted that "my husband . . . has been given sufficient reason to believe himself hurt in his honor."[66]

Despite their reserved attitude, it is difficult to believe that these women actually approved of their husbands' actions. After all, they fought to regain their husbands' trust and to reestablish their position in society. While showing outward approval of their husbands' behavior—in accordance with the conduct expected of obedient wives—they nevertheless took drastic steps to change their husbands' minds. By displaying public deference they were helping their husbands restore their public reputation for patriarchal authority, thus paving the way for a reestablishment of the husbands' honor, and hence a reconciliation.

Men who abandoned their spouses were justified in their behavior (and impelled toward it) by contemporary codes of honor that linked their and their wives' honor. First, an adulterous wife betrayed her husband's trust and besmirched his manliness.[67] Second, she made him the laughingstock of the entire community by allowing another man access to his sexual property. Adulterous wives challenged the very idea of their husbands' patriarchal authority over themselves, and thus the very essence of their masculinity.[68] Male honor was linked to the exercise of patriarchal authority in the home, and men asserted themselves by restricting (or at least seeking to restrict) their wives to the domestic sphere. While wives contested such authority, assumptions of patriarchal authority were challenged most dramatically in cases of adultery committed by women, which forced husbands to respond publicly in order to reassert their authority. Violence was one way of doing this; a public—if brief—break from one's wife was another.[69]

Candelaria Alvarado's comments demonstrate her perception of the link between her sexual behavior and her husband's honor. She explained that "this insult has dishonored my good name in my married condition, thus wounding my husband's superiority."[70] Manuel Luna Leiva explained that he was pursuing his case because "both the good name of my wife and my own name deserve that either the accusations be proven, or our names be cleared."[71] Jacoba Bermúdez stated that Manuela Chávez had pronounced "terrible words which affect my honor and that of my husband, Don Manuel Quiroz."[72] Francisco Bringas, Bermúdez' lawyer, explained that his client had initiated her suit "to satisfy her husband that she had received the offenses as [directed against] her husband, as inflicted directly on his marital rights." Hermegilda Villavicencio referred to "my husband's honor, which is mine."[73]

In practice the link between spouses' honor could also work the other way around; occasionally, male sexual behavior was seen to affect women's honor. When Hermegilda Villavicencio was charged by her opponents' lawyer of accusing her enemies, Juliana Vargas' daughters, of having an affair with her husband, she violently denied any such claim: "If [the lawyer] truly believes that one of his clients is engaged in illicit relations with my husband he should have hidden this [fact] out of charity, and not made it public in a document presented to the judicial authorities."[74] Her comment suggests that she tacitly condoned her husband's adultery, providing that it was carried out discreetly.

Villavicencio therefore considered silent acceptance to be less damaging than public protest to her and her husband's honor. Her contemporaries shared this view. Based on a long tradition of colonial law dating to the thirteenth-century's Siete Partidas, Peruvian legislation stated that male adultery was equal to a wife's adulterous affair only if the former was conducted in a scandalous manner.[75] Male infidelity as such was therefore not considered dishonorable or damaging to the wife; honor was affected only by the public airing of such sins. This conclusion is supported by Twinam, who notes that honor was related less to virtue or sin in themselves than to the public knowledge of these attributes.[76]

Women who were abandoned by their husbands turned for help to their parents, as in the case of María Chávez, whose husband wanted her jailed after rumors of adultery reached him. When her husband, José Quevedo, allowed the matter to rest once his wife was placed in custody, Chávez' father stepped in and pursued the proceedings against her detractor. Valerio Chávez told the court that "as a father, desirous of the happiness of my daughter and success in her marriage," he was pursuing her interests in court.[77] Similarly, Candelaria Alvarado's mother could not but welcome her daughter and grandchildren after their husband and father expelled them.[78] Parental feeling, social sanction, and legal obligation probably all played a role in motivating parents to aid their offspring.

Women's and men's responses to slander indicate the cardinal importance of honor even among artisans, small-scale farmers, and petty merchants. Because they lived in small, highly transparent communities where everybody knew everybody else, where neighbors and acquaintances avidly consumed scandal and gossip, rumor could transform social standing overnight. Husbands beat their wives and threatened to abandon them, occasionally carrying out the threat, either in anger or in order to reassert their patriarchal authority. Physical separation was the first step on the legal path to divorce. Although none of the husbands in the trials I have studied went so far as formally initiating divorce proceedings, the implied threat was a way of asserting manliness, and, as important, of protecting husbands from further ridicule and dishonor.

Not every husband left his wife to defend herself alone, however. When Francisco del Campo took his former son-in-law to court for slandering his wife, his conviction of her virtue as well as affection and admiration for her shone through the entire proceedings.[79] When Natividad, Carmen, Dominga, and Mercedes Escalante called José Asunción Portilla's wife a *puta*, he affirmed his faith in her when he stated that her life was "quiet and irreproachable."[80] Manuel Luna Leiva rejected María León's claim that his wife was a whore and asserted his belief that "these weighty charges are made without the smallest basis."[81] Although these men responded differently to rumors spread by José Quevedo and other men who had left their wife, they all acted out of the same motivation, namely, the defense of their honor.

HONOR AND CLASS: MARITAL STATUS AS A MARK OF SOCIAL RESPECTABILITY

Just as honor was gendered, it was also "classed." While less explicitly defined racially than in the colonial period, the post-independence concept of honor continued to privilege the white and wealthy. Historically linked to wealth and nobility, throughout the nineteenth century, honor became increasingly linked to virtuous behavior: premarital virginity and marital fidelity for women, and financial honesty and industriousness for men.

Nevertheless, honor continued to be more easily attainable for the wealthy than the poor. Dependents (including servants and tenants) could not lay claim to honor or citizenship.[82] Only the affluent were seen to be able to protect their daughters and wives from challenges to their virtue. By secluding upper-class women in the private sphere and surrounding them with servants, the wealthier classes could protect them from the pollution of the street and keep them under scrutiny. For most women the ideal that restricted them to the domestic sphere was unattainable, as they had to work in the fields or as servants, run errands for their parents or patrons, or sell foodstuffs or other products in the market. The lower her social status, the greater the probability (it was assumed) that a woman had been contaminated by the loss of sexual virtue, partly because of her exposure to the public sphere, but also, according to the ruling classes, because the popular classes were assumed to be inherently immoral.

Although lower-class women did not, in elite eyes, possess honor, depositions during slander trials show that these women considered themselves honorable and claimed the respect they considered their due. Married women in particular felt entitled to respect. Living in a society where marriage was a far-from-absolute norm, married women sought to differentiate themselves from their unmarried peers. Thus Cayetana Mille declared that Candelaria Arce's offenses "produced a scandal without parallel in society . . . because this [slander], due to my status as a married woman, affects my reputation doubly, exposing me as unworthy of both society and my husband."[83] Petronila Astopilco stated that María Peralta's insults were "all the more serious, as I am married."[84] Candelaria Alvarado complained that "this slander has completely dishonored my good name as a married woman."[85] Francisco Bringas, on behalf of his client Jacoba Bermúdez, also asserted that such insults were "all the more [serious] when directed at a married woman, and one of irreproachable conduct."[86] Being married made it easier for women to demand the respect they considered their due, as Jacoba Arbayza made clear in her suit against José Silva y Soto: "My position as a married woman places me in a position in which I can make my decency be respected."[87] As Lauderdale Graham puts it, "respectability through marriage was a currency worth acquiring."[88] Once acquired, such respectability was considered worth defending, in court if necessary.[89]

The legal system agreed with and fostered this differentiation between married and single women. A clear illustration of this is the suit brought by Jacoba Bermúdez against Manuela Chávez.[90] Bermúdez initiated proceedings following an argument with Chávez *en plaza pública* (in the public realm), in which the latter called her "whore." During the trial it emerged that Bermúdez had replied similarly. Although the insults were identical, consisting of accusations of *faltas de moralidad* (moral shortcomings), the judge considered insulting a married woman more serious than insulting a single woman. "Both of them are criminally responsible," he declared, "with the difference that the concubinage of which Bermúdez was accused constitutes the crime of adultery, which is punishable by law, whereas the slander against Chávez, who is single, is no more than an offense against morality."[91] Bermúdez was sentenced to one year in jail, Chávez to two.

Single women were at a disadvantage in proving their good reputation, since they could not merely point to their civil status as an indicator of respectability. Instead, they presented the testimony of several witnesses in order to corroborate their claim to good character. Citing their witnesses, they all emphasized that their irreproachable conduct entitled them to a good reputation, and that the court was obliged to assist them in the defense of their honor. María de los Santos Linares declared, "With the right given me by the decency and seclusion with which I have lived until this date from my childhood . . . I appear before Your Honor accusing Sumarán [of slander]."[92] Single women, more frequently than married women, felt the need to back up their claims to respectability with the testimony of witnesses. Acting in defense of her and her daughter's reputation, María Encarnación Tirado, for instance, inquired of several witnesses, "How old is my daughter; does she behave modestly, like the daughter of a [respectable] family?"[93]

More exposed to the suspicion of being sexually "loose," single women had to go to greater lengths in order to prove that they and their reputations were eligible for legal protection. As has been noted for other regions, "women of questionable morality had a questionable claim to civil rights,"[94] including the defense of their reputation; in addition to their behavior, women's legal status was defined by their conjugal state.[95]

Single women feared rumors of a promiscuous lifestyle out of fear of how these could affect their chances of obtaining a husband and, hence, the much-coveted status of married woman. Jacoba Bermúdez disclosed the role of her premarital conduct when she told the court that "due to my virtue and my good manners I succeeded in marrying Don Manuel Quiroz, a person well known for his uprightness."[96]

It is telling that mothers who went to court revealed little concern for their own reputations, but all the more for their daughters', even when both had been slandered. Isabel Encalada accused Natividad Arana in court of insulting both her and her daughter, but demonstrated notably more concern over the damage to her daughter's reputation. She declared that Arana had acted "without considering our sex and the courtesy which is owed the virtue which my daughter Tomasa happily maintains to this point."[97]

THE LEGAL SYSTEM AS AN INSTRUMENT OF REDRESS

In what way did the courts help slandered individuals clear their names? Sometimes trials resulted in a public apology. The threat of a lawsuit could be sufficient to produce the desired effect, as happened with Candelaria Alvarado's suit against Micaela Bringas. The latter made a public apology almost as soon as Alvarado filed the case against her: "I have had to beg that I be forgiven the offenses and taunts which I unjustly inflicted on my opponent . . . influenced [as I was] . . . by a fury which made . . . me turn away from common sense." Alvarado accepted the apology, and further proceedings were dropped.[98] After bringing rumors spread by Augusto Krol and Teodoro Fuchs to the attention of the justice of the peace, Eusebia Olórtegui received a letter from Fuchs denying that he had ever slandered her.[99] In total, I found seven trials that ended with apologies and conciliations, thereby clearing the name of the trial's initiator without necessitating the punishment of the accused.

Other cases ended with the conviction of the accused. María León was not given any prison sentence or fine when she was convicted of slandering Melchora Álvarez, but she was obliged to pay costs.[100] When Jacoba Bermúdez sued Manuela Chávez for slanderous insults, the latter was sentenced to jail.[101] Francisca, Catalina, and Leopoldo Mestanza, as well as Benito Briones, were all sentenced to three years in jail and a fine of twenty pesos for having called Juan Manuel Vera a thief in public.[102]

In general, however, the courts were ineffective. Of thirty trials I examined, seven never reached conclusion; for unknown reasons the proceedings were discontinued. Possibly the parties reached an agreement outside the court, or the more powerful party succeeded in shelving the case by exerting pressure on court functionaries. Final outcomes are recorded only for twenty-three of the thirty. Both plaintiffs and defendants frequently complained about the slowness of the courts, and it was not unusual for several months to elapse between the presentation of questions for witnesses and interviews of the same witnesses.

In ten cases the defendant was acquitted. Of the six trials that ended in convictions, three resulted in the conviction of both parties, understandably pleasing neither. Two of the other three convictions were overturned on appeal. In only one case, therefore, did the plaintiff succeed in obtaining the desired punishment without detriment to him- or herself.[103] If we include the seven conciliations, only eight cases were therefore concluded to the satisfaction of the plaintiff. Complainants, in other words, rarely achieved vindication through the legal system.

Despite the frequent failure of the courts to resolve cases, women who sued their enemies in order to persuade their husbands to return home seem to have been successful. In most cases in which rumors of adultery led to separation or the threat of separation, the husbands appear to have returned to their wives before the conclusion of the trial. This is not stated explicitly, but emerges from the fact that husbands took over the proceedings, started to sign their wives' statements and letters, or appeared before the judge together with their wives. Such was the case with Eusebia Olórtegui, whose husband, claiming to be busy with work, initially provided her with a *licencia judicial* and left her to defend her name in court. Toward the end of the trial he stood by his wife's side and signed documents, implying that he fully supported her legal steps.[104]

Candelaria Alvarado's husband behaved similarly. Although her husband left her upon hearing of the rumor that she had had an affair with his nephew, he was at her side when the slanderer delivered her apology to the court.[105] Petronila Astopilco's and Emilia Verástegui's husbands, who had both threatened separation and failed to support their wives in the early stages of the court proceedings, backed them as the trials neared conclusion.[106] Neither Verástegui's nor Olórtegui's trials were ever concluded; nevertheless, their husbands returned. José Quevedo also eventually returned to his wife; although the defendant, Clara Pita, was absolved of slander, his wife's reputation had been publicly defended.[107]

It therefore seems as if the act of going to court was seen as so significant that it removed further suspicion from the women concerned. The mere act of initiating legal proceedings was regarded as a public assertion of innocence that possessed a symbolic value independent of the trial's outcome. The significance of such acts is easier to comprehend if we bear in mind the cost involved, as well as the social distance between those who initiated these proceedings and court officials. In general, slandered women and men went to court only if they thought they stood a fair chance of winning.[108]

The language used by the women who initiated proceedings confirms that going to court was regarded as a step toward clearing their names. Jacoba Bermúdez, for instance, stated, "I am forced to satisfy him [my husband] by taking action . . . against Manuela Chávez."[109] In a later lawsuit, against Francisca Sifuentes, she explained, "Allowing an act of such significance to pass without taking action would make society look upon me as the most unworthy person living within it. . . . [Therefore] I am forced to resort to the only legal instrument [at my disposition]."[110] Emilia Verástegui declared, "If I remain silent, [my husband] might believe that what the Centurión woman says is true, therefore I turn to the legal system with these charges."[111] Natividad Arana's comment is illuminating: "As public justice has been violated by such accusations . . . I find myself obliged to resort to the court in order to satisfy [my honor], recover the esteem of the public in whose eyes I have been dishonored, and obtain the punishment of the delinquents."[112] The order of priority is revealing: she mentions her private sense of honor first, and the punishment of the accused last.

In this sense Arana's statement may well reflect the priorities of many women who went to court: their main objective was to clear their names; punishment of the accused was secondary. Husbands returning and plaintiffs dropping charges following more or less official apologies show that the courts did fulfill a useful function, although not necessarily the most obvious one—finding and convicting culprits.

The courts influenced local opinion by publicizing the personal conflict that had led to the slander. The accusations of adultery and theft were thus explained and plaintiffs' reputations cleared. The courts thereby served as an official arena for the negotiation of honor and respectability.

LIVING WITH, BETWEEN, AND OUTSIDE CODES OF HONOR

Apart from functioning as an official arena in which victims of slander could prosecute their detractors and prove the slander false, courts were also used by complainants as a venue for explicating their own definitions of honor. Among the women who defended their reputation in court were several who had challenged established norms. By their assumption that they, too, had the right to defend their reputation, they asserted their claim to honor and redefined the concept to suit their individual cases.

Twinam has likened honor to a bank account, with elite women being given a certain deposit at birth. This could be soundly invested by marrying respectably and bearing legitimate children. Alternatively, the balance might decrease if virginity was lost or illegitimate children were produced.[113] Unlike elite women, women of the lower classes received at best a small deposit of honor at birth, depending on their family's social status and behavior. To expand on Twinam's metaphor, one might say that they were much more likely than elite women to end up overdrawing their "honor account." Whereas elite women who might be suspected of dishonorable conduct were usually given the benefit of the doubt—promises of marriage, engagements, and even formal marriages were assumed to exist where there were none— this was not true for women of the lower and intermediate classes. Behavior that detracted from honor, such as excessive circulation in the public sphere for reasons of work or otherwise, immediately placed plebeian women under suspicion of dishonorable conduct. Lower-class women who bore children out of wedlock were not automatically assumed to have been lured by their lovers, but were regarded as morally flawed. Victims of rape were assumed to be complicit in their loss of honor and were usually suspected of trying to trap the accused into compensating them.

Although plebeian women who incurred public censure through conduct judged dishonorable were treated harshly, they, too, could recoup lost honor if they went on to make wise social "investments." Ideal investments included marriage, but leading an otherwise respectable life could also shore up a dwindling honor account. Over time, they could reaccumulate respect. Once regained, such respect was worth defending, and well worth going to court for, for it was there that these women could put forth their own arguments for why they should be accorded public esteem.

Carolina Montoya lived in consensual union for fifteen years before formalizing the union on her deathbed. The publication of her obituary in the department's newspaper, *El Ferrocarril*, testifies that her reputation was unimpaired (or at least reparable), despite her ostensibly immoral lifestyle. The newspaper described her as worthy, and her fifteen years of common-law union as "an intimate and virtuous marriage."[114]

Although honor need not be permanently lost, despite transgressions against the code women who once exposed themselves to suspicion continued vulnerable to attacks on their reputation. One such woman was Francisca Ramírez, who as a young woman in Lima had been seduced and promised marriage by Pedro Ambuldequi, a man several years her senior. Ramírez and her lover moved to Cajamarca. There she lived with him for a few years in common-law union and had several illegitimate children by him. Her second, formal, husband, Francisco del Campo, explained thirty years later that "she was forced to leave . . . her partner due to the bad behavior she observed in him." Three years after this separation, del Campo added, "Captivated by her good conduct, [I] asked for her hand" and married her.[115] In 1862 the couple came into conflict with the husband of Ramírez' recently deceased daughter over an inheritance. Manuel Espantoso, the son-in-law, offended both his parents-in-law and physically abused del Campo. He called Ramírez "*una puta adúltera*" (an adulterous whore). This insult, based on her history of common-law marriage, came twenty-nine years after her relationship with Ambuldequi had ended. The (rather flimsy) basis for Espantoso's claim that Ramírez was an adulteress was the fact that she had entered a second relationship while her common-law husband was still alive. According to Espantoso, "Mr. Campo took her away from Mr. Ambuldequi and took her with him to live in the Cinco Esquinas barrio." He also blamed her for being involved with Francisco del Campo while her common-law husband was alive. In a sense he was equating common-law marriage with formal marriage. The fact that Espantoso implicitly recognized the quasi-marriage character of such relationships at the same time as he regarded nonmarital relationships as immoral (for women) shows that different codes of conduct could be acceptable to one person at the same time.

The incident illustrates both how vulnerable a woman's honor could be several decades after any transgressions of the moral code, and how her subsequent respectability could be used to defend her reputation. A single offense made public in anger could threaten decades of "passing."[116] Ramírez' husband, who pressed charges in order to clear his and his wife's reputation, opted to recount his wife's entire life history. By laying it open to scrutiny he enabled both the court and the public to judge whether the slander was accurate or not. He attempted to demonstrate that Ramírez had lost her virtue as a result of seduction and betrayal rather than immorality; that she had retained some respectability throughout her relationship with her seducer; and that she had eventually obtained the status of a virtuous and respectable wife. He emphasized the fact that Ramírez had lived in an honorable household with her godmother until the time of her seduction. He pointed out that her seducer had promised marriage, albeit only orally, and subsequently failed to fulfill this promise. Her intentions had therefore been entirely honorable. In justifying her relationship with him and their subsequent marriage, he underlined that three years had elapsed between the end of her first relationship and her subsequent marriage, and that Ambuldequi was already engaged in another relationship by the time Ramírez married del Campo. By laying the responsibility for past misdemeanors at the door of her lover or common-law partner and focusing on her honorable behavior throughout her life, her husband was arguing that past transgressions should be condoned, as Ramírez had proven her honor through her subsequent good behavior. He was in effect rephrasing the definition of honor.

In early-twentieth-century Andalusia, by way of comparison, Pitt-Rivers notes that, although the disgrace of unmarried mothers was recognized, "they are not treated as shameless. Their status is somewhat similar to that of a young widow. Their prospects of remarriage are poor . . . yet if their conduct gives no cause for scandal, they are distinguishable from the loose women who are sometimes described by the word *deshonradas*."[117] If this parallel can be extended to Cajamarca—as the monologue of Francisca Ramírez' husband in defense of her honor seems to allow—blaming the seducer and subsequently displaying virtuous behavior could salvage honor.

As is clear from del Campo's long exposition and Manuel Espantoso's incoherent and self-contradictory logic, slander was regarded as a large enough threat to require the public airing of Francisca Ramírez' entire past. The lengthy and complicated nature of the trial testifies to the fact that defending her good name was more complicated for her than for a woman who had never engaged in a consensual union or had illegitimate children. Certainly no other woman engaged in slanderous insult trials had her entire history recounted before the courts in such detail that I could find.

Other women in a similarly vulnerable position chose different strategies. Several produced witnesses who were willing to testify to their good conduct. Adelaida Sheen, the only woman of means among those involved in slander trials, was exposed to criticism and slander. She and her husband, Manuel Ruiz, were separated. She claimed he had abandoned her, but whatever the reason, her relations with his family were acrimonious. It is not surprising that, following an incident in which her nephew bad-mouthed her in the street, she asked witnesses to confirm that her behavior was respectable. Sheen asked her witnesses whether they had "observed also that her conduct has always been restricted to the duties imposed by social morality, matrimonial honor, and that her conduct has been irreproachable to the present day." Although separation was not socially acceptable (and even less so for a woman of the upper classes), Sheen demanded to have her reputation defended in a court of law and succeeded at least in bringing her suit to court and getting several witnesses to confirm that her conduct so far had been unimpeachable.[118]

In the same way, Manuela Abanto and her daughter Carmen Bringas, who were disdainfully called "beer makers and market women" by the plaintiff, Luis Gamarra, tried to defend themselves from accusations of slander by pointing out that their honor, too, had been attacked. Like Sheen, Abanto produced a series of witnesses who could testify to her daughter's and her honor. Despite their profession, which laid them open to charges of immorality, they succeeded. Although Abanto and Bringas were themselves condemned to jail for having insulted Manuela Villanueva and her daughter, the latter two were also sentenced to jail for the same offense. The courts therefore backed Abanto's claim, despite the evident disapproval of Gamarra, who exclaimed that such women, being mere *vivanderas*, could not be expected to behave in a decent fashion.[119] Whatever the truth of Abanto's morality, she was able to use legal institutions to her own advantage.

Above all it was women who lived "in between" codes of honor—women who had previously transgressed against them but who could, for various reasons, claim to have regained their honor—who opted for legal action. Adelaida Sheen and Manuela Abanto are two cases in point: the former lived scandalously separated from her husband; the latter had borne an illegitimate daughter who worked with her in the market. Sheen had fallen from her former glory of being a moderately wealthy but respectable matron; Abanto had clearly obtained enough economic resources and social status since giving birth to an illegitimate child to make it worth her while to defend their reputation. To return to the analogy of the bank account, for Abanto, legal action was a way of defending the social investments of the last fifteen years and her and her daughter's current honor balance.

While these women were upwardly mobile in the sense that they could at least aspire to formal recognition of their reputations, a much larger group of women never even approached the legal arena. Lower-class women, especially if they lived in consensual unions or had children by several men, rarely engaged in legal proceedings to clear their reputation. Most of them knew that they had no claim to honor in the eyes of the ruling classes, and hence little to gain from legal action.[120] Instead, plebeian women and men asserted their own sense of honor in different arenas. A number of the street brawls that I deal with in Chapter 7 were the product of arguments in which insults had been flung, thereby challenging integrity. Women and men retaliated with more insults, the spreading of gossip, and outright violence.[121]

From the perspective of the ruling classes, any woman who was willing to engage in street brawls had forfeited all claims to honor, as such behavior was by its very nature not respectable and hence dishonorable. In terms of their own class' definition of respectability, however, such concrete and violent defense of their status was essential for their social survival. As Stern has commented about colonial Mexico, the imperative of maintaining decorum and avoiding gossip, scandalmongering, and "unfeminine" resort to physical force did not necessarily make sense to lower-class women. Accepting male negligence, sexual improprieties, or the imputation that they were guilty of such transgressions could all imply the risk of abandonment and hence destitution. They therefore rejected, or failed to adhere to, elite norms of female submissiveness and reticence and defended their own honor and controlled their husband's behavior in loud-mouthed and occasionally violent fashion.[122] Similarly, plebeian men in colonial Buenos Aires defended themselves from insults and slights by resorting to violence or, occasionally, the courts. "A man who failed to defend himself and the challenges of his peers found life intolerable," Johnson notes.[123]

Honor was experienced at a multitude of levels, and defended in multifarious ways, only a few of which have been documented and preserved. It is therefore important not to be blinded to lower-class women's subjective experience of honor because of their near absence from the records. The fact that market women such as Manuela Abanto and Asunción Gamarra made it into the legal arena at all, and with them the scandalmongers Francisca Sifuentes and Jacoba Bermúdez, is testament to the existence of many, many more women of their ilk.

CONCLUSION

While not an efficient arbiter of justice by any standards, the local courts were an important arena for the negotiation of honor for Cajamarcans from nearly all social spheres. A notary, market women, servants, artisans, smallholders, and petty merchants all entered the legal system in defense of their honor, revealing the importance of reputation to individuals from all walks of life.

The motives which impelled these people to take on their opponents in a medium that was unfamiliar and often hostile to them were, of necessity, powerful. Most of the women were illiterate or only partially literate; most complainants had to fork over considerable sums for their various depositions; and many found that the judges and their interpretation of the legal texts did not facilitate legal action. Only rarely did the courts supply plaintiffs with the desired outcome; sentences for offenses against honor were rare and legal proceedings were known to backfire. Honor was an important commodity, however. It determined who mixed with whom and who conducted business with whom, and it shaped marriage prospects. Indeed, the presence or absence of honor could make or break a marriage. While an attack on a wife's honor could create a fissure in a marriage, a similar attack could kindle public manifestations of conjugal loyalty and affection.

Honor was debated and negotiated in a number of arenas, most commonly in the form of small, mundane exchanges and gossip on street corners, the plaza, or in the home. While the regional elites did not usually have to lower themselves to defending their reputation in court, the lower classes did not enter the legal arena. Official prejudice against lower-class morality meant that women who defied the elites' code of honor in their daily life by working in the public sphere or living in common-law unions were well aware that they had little to gain from going to court. Instead, plebeian notions of honor and respect were dealt with outside of the legal arena, with gossip, public arguments, and, not infrequently, street brawls.

It was those women and men who lived in between codes of honor who aspired to official recognition of their social standing, but who were by no means secure in their position, who opted for legal proceedings. Those who qualified for at least a modicum of respect, or who had risked their good name earlier in their life by behaving dishonorably, were the most likely to go to court. Although legal action did not always promise a conviction, going to court was in itself an assertion of innocence, and therefore had an impact on the plaintiff's standing in the community. Moreover, the legal proceedings themselves offered an opportunity for defending one's good name and unfolding a less stringent definition of honor that made allowances for past transgressions. Complainants who sought to defend their name thus illustrated that honor, once lost, could be regained through subsequent virtuous behavior.

Occasionally, the victims of slander were backed by judges; in other cases, it seems that the interface between legal proceedings and public esteem produced its own results—as can be seen from the fact that estranged husbands usually returned to their wives' sides before the conclusion of legal proceedings, regardless of the outcome. The courts were not, in other words, the exclusive arbiters of honor. Instead, they functioned as a space in which slandered women and men could publicize their grievances and defend their reputation. Plaintiffs did not wish to sway only the judge, but, more important, the community at large.

While honor, once lost or threatened, could be renegotiated and defended, the trials also indicate what a fragile commodity it could be. Once a person had transgressed against the code of honor, past misdemeanors might come back to haunt him or her in the form of slander concerning past or new misconduct.

CHAPTER 6

Rapto, Seducción, Violación, *and* Estupro

MOVING BEYOND THE LOSS OF HONOR

This chapter addresses questions of sexuality and how women and men of the lower orders reconciled their actions with their concern for reputation and honor. To this end I analyze trial transcripts catalogued under the labels of *"rapto," "seducción," "violación,"* and *"estupro"*—abduction, seduction, and rape.

Legally, the terms overlapped and partially contradicted one another;[1] nevertheless, most plaintiffs used them interchangeably and apparently indiscriminately. Thus Bartolomé Gálvez complained that his niece had suffered *estupro, violación,* and *seducción,* but he did not differentiate among the mutually exclusive meanings of these terms. Marcos Paz sought to force his daughter's recalcitrant fiancé to the altar by accusing him of *rapto y estupro,* and Pedro Chavarri charged his stepdaughter's abductor and lover with both *rapto* and *violación,* adding later that *seducción* had been involved as well.[2] In reality, only a few of these cases dealt with rape or sexual violence; most transcripts, in order to rescue the reputations of the young women concerned, relate tales of consensual relationships described as forced intercourse or seduction resulting from deceit.

Both in terms of legal definition and in the eyes of the litigants, the trials were about honor rather than personal suffering. However brutally carried out, rape was punished only if the victim could prove herself to have possessed honor prior to it. "The abduction of a married woman, a virgin, or a chaste widow, if carried out with violence, is to be punished with prison to the fifth degree," observed García Calderón. If the victim did not fit the above description, the sentence was reduced.[3] Although the law stipulated a prison sentence for the rape of women without honor (i.e., an adulterous wife or a never-married woman who had given up her maidenhead), in practice, such cases did not result in prosecution.

In the thirty-eight years of legal documentation I studied, I found only sixteen cases of sexual crime;[4] of these, only five dealt with genuine incidents of rape (as opposed to cases of seduction camouflaged as rape by plaintiffs).[5] In addition, there were three accusations of attempted rape; however, all three plaintiffs desisted from further proceedings after filing their complaints.[6] The sample of sex-related crime includes seven charges of rape,[7] four of attempted rape,[8] two of breach of promise,[9] and two of seduction.[10]

We can assume that fifteen cases of sex-related crime represent only a fraction of the total number of such crimes that took place in the province of Cajamarca between 1862 and 1900. Confirming that the underreporting of rape was evident to contemporaries, an article from 1862 in *La Opinión*, a Cajamarcan newspaper, complained that the authorities had failed to take any action in the matter of the rape of a young girl, even though the crime had been reported forty days earlier.[11] Instances of rape of peasant and other lower-class women, including servants and other dependents, are totally absent from the criminal court records.[12]

Unlike slander trials, trials dealing with sex-related crime could not deflect suspicions of sexual misconduct; instead, they were intended to oblige the defendant to marry or monetarily compensate his victim for her loss of honor, or (failing that) to sway public opinion in favor of the victim. Although virginity might be indisputably lost, plaintiffs sought to demonstrate to the public that the woman in question was the victim of violence or *engaño* (deceit), and hence not responsible for the misfortune that had befallen her. In this way, a woman could be represented as the victim of a man's designs, rather than being herself considered morally flawed, and, in Pitt-Rivers' words, lacking in shame.[13] The trials were therefore essentially about shifting the blame from the female to the male.

In addition to illuminating how honor, once damaged, was redefined and, where possible, restored, these trials shed light on the differences and tensions between lower-class sexual practice and elite definitions of female sexual behavior. Between the two extremes—the elite ideal of feminine seclusion and chastity, and the cohabitation and serial monogamy practiced by the uneducated and poor of color—we find gradations of socially differentiated gender practice. The intermediate social groups (including artisans, small-scale tradesmen, and well-to-do peasants) between these two extremes frequently aspired to upper-class codes of sexual conduct, although not always conforming to them in practice. Women who left the domestic sphere to work nevertheless considered themselves honorable; similarly, women who had had sex outside of marriage retained (or, more often, recovered) their community's respect. Part of the explanation for this can be found in the trials dealing with cases of sexual transgression, including transcripts relating to *rapto, estupro,* and *violación.*

While ecclesiastically blessed marriage was the ideal, among the lower classes, including Cajamarca's middle sectors, premarital sex was condoned, providing that it led to marriage. Even when unions were not formalized, their permanence gave couples respectability. The lower-class code of honor was openly challenged only when young women who had given in to their suitor's courtship and given up their virginity were jilted. Such events usually caused some furor. Even if the period of courtship had escaped the public's notice (as it often did the parents'), either the couple's romantic escape to a remote location where the union was consummated or the subsequent casting off of the mistress attracted public attention.

Although women in such predicaments had clearly breached the code of honor, they, with the help of their family, asserted their respectability. Some opted for a tranquil life out of the public eye; in the course of time their dishonorable behavior might be forgotten, or at least fade. Other families took a more active course and entered the legal arena, accusing the faithless lover of *rapto.* Criminal trials dealing with the rape or seduction of young women therefore served as a device for mediating the tensions between everyday sexual practice and professed gender norms. As I show in a later section, parents of dishonored women therefore often used the concept of *rapto* (abduction and elopement) as a means of bridging the tension between sexual practice and sexual ideals.

DEFENDING HONOR IN COURT: OBJECTIVES AND STRATEGIES

Complainants' concern with honor was reflected in their initial depositions; much ink was spent lamenting the loss of virginity. Following the rape of Catalina Pájares, her uncle (the local priest) told the court that her virginity had been "her most prized possession."[14] In the same vein Cayetano Sánchez was accused of having "done away with the most brilliant object with which a young girl is adorned" when he seduced Marcelina Paz, a peasant's daughter.[15] In young, unmarried women, virginity was regarded as the guarantee of *honestidad,* honorable behavior. Thus, when Rosario Villacorta accused a local merchant of abducting and raping her daughter, she denounced "the infamy he has committed violating my daughter's chastity after having dishonored her before society."[16] Josefa Alcántara, a single mother and shoemaker living and working in Cajamarca, had similar high-flown ideas about honor:

"The violent corruption of a virgin," she wrote, "[is one of the] gravest crimes, as it kills the most precious part of the rational person, which is honor."[17] Clearly, poverty and low social position were no impediment to a concern with honor. Marcos Paz, a peasant from San Marcos and Marcelina's father, pointed out that "even if I am a poor wretch lacking in resources, I am not so ignorant as not to understand that honor is the life of the spirit, and that compared to honor material goods or pleasures are worthless."[18]

Plaintiffs also pointed out that their entire family's honor was compromised. Pedro Chavarri, for instance, described his stepdaughter's seducer, Juan Esteban Cabrera, as "the author of my daughter's, my own, and my family's dishonor."[19] In order to describe the impact which the loss of family honor had on him and his wife, he referred to the girl's "poor mother . . . , whose heart [has been] lacerated by the loss of her daughter's virtue and her and the whole family's honor, the entire neighborhood has pitied and pities her."[20]

Like Chavarri, Francisco de las Llagas Ruiz stressed that his honor had been damaged by his daughter's seduction. He declared that "Don Vicente Noriega has . . . with promises of marriage managed to seduce the innocence of my daughter . . . thus affecting . . . my honor and reputation."[21] Josefa Alcántara explained that the attack on a woman's honor affected "not only the damaged person, but the entire family."[22]

While the rhetoric of honor can to some extent be viewed as part of a public discourse designed to appeal to judges,[23] the depositions nevertheless shed light on what litigants hoped to achieve through legal action. How did plaintiffs think going to court would aid them in their quest for honor? Were there other reasons for pressing charges?

Francisco de las Llagas Ruiz made it clear that his concern went beyond defending reputation. "Regardless of the great care I haven taken with my daughter . . . the plans a father makes for his daughter should not be ridiculed," he told the court. His aim with this trial—which followed Vicente Noriega's prolonged courtship of his daughter Clemencia, involving premarital sex—was to oblige Noriega to fulfill his promise of marriage. Failing that, de las Llagas Ruiz demanded that Noriega at least provide Clemencia with a dowry and child support for the son who was born a few months after the trial.[24]

Other parents shared de las Llagas Ruiz' preoccupation with a daughter's marital prospects: Andrea Sánchez commented that her daughter's rape might "cause the misery of a poor girl and have grave consequences for her future" by affecting her chances of marriage.[25] María Resurrección Julcamoro, who charged Lisandro Altamirano with raping her daughter Rosario

Sichas, settled for marriage as the best compensation for her daughter's sufferings. Despite the acrimonious tone that the mother maintained during the proceedings—assuring the court that she did not "believe that Altamirano possesses any seductive gifts to captivate the affection of the female sex"[26]—the mother acquiesced to the defendant's offer of marriage. Disappointingly for Julcamoro (but maybe fortunately for her daughter), it turned out that Altamirano's offer was not made in good faith. He had already married another cast-off mistress whom he had abandoned shortly after the marriage, and could therefore not "repair" the damage done to his latest victim.[27]

Although marriage was a common way of resolving the damage done to women by robbing them of their virginity,[28] not all plaintiffs regarded it as the ideal solution. Pedro Chavarri stubbornly resisted Juan Esteban Cabrera's desperate attempts at avoiding jail by offering to marry Chavarri's stepdaughter Rosaura Carbajal. Far from being opposed to the idea of marriage as such, Chavarri expressed concern that Cabrera would prove a poor husband. He described Cabrera as "this lazy youth [without] any occupation but loafing about, believing himself an important personage."[29] As Chavarri pointed out, Cabrera had already left his mistress stranded once: "After he took her from her home in her virgin state, he abandoned her completely." Chavarri was convinced that Cabrera, once married, would fail to fulfill his obligations as a husband. "As soon as the union has taken place in order to liberate him from his punishment, . . . he will abandon her to greater risks and dishonor, something which we as parents will not be able to bear with equanimity," he wrote. Chavarri maintained this stand, despite Cabrera's lawyer's surprised statement that "a woman refuses tenaciously to comply with the acts which society respects . . . preferring instead to prostitute herself."[30] Although Rosaura's good name could have been restored by marriage to her seducer, her stepfather was persuaded that she would be better off single. However, the option of rejecting a potentially risky marriage following public dishonor was open only to women from relatively well off families, as was Carbajal.

Pedro Chavarri's decision concerning Rosaura's suitor may well have been a sensible one. The example of Lisandro Altamirano shows that it was not unusual for rapists and seducers to marry their victims in order to get out of serving their sentence, only to abandon them as soon as they were freed. Even if Rosaura Carbajal was no longer a virgin, she was still single and might hope in a few years, when the brouhaha surrounding her three dramatic escapes had settled down, to capture another suitor. Her mother, Candelaria Carbajal, had in her youth succeeded in marrying Pedro Chavarri—a notary, and thus fairly respectable—despite being encumbered by an illegitimate daughter, Rosaura. Given that Chavarri was directly opposed to the repair of his stepdaughter's honor by marriage, the question of what he hoped to obtain with his suit becomes all the more intriguing. By pursuing legal proceedings he may have sought to demonstrate to the local community that (despite the misfortune which had befallen it) his family remained respectable. If nothing else, harping on the family's claim to respect might assure his remaining daughters of the opportunity to make a successful match.

Several trials, including that involving Rosaura Carbajal, were launched in order to force the local authorities to assist the parents in the hunt for an errant daughter. Thus Rosaura was returned to her parents' home only after the local authorities had initiated a search for her. Similarly, María Rosario Villacorta informed the judge that her daughter had been abducted from her home during the night and kept prisoner in Manuel Estevan Rocha's house for two days. The girl was found only after Villacorta got the local authorities to search the premises.[31]

Trials dealing with elopement and seduction could be about exerting authority as much as about honor. Like the parents referred to above, María Natividad Chavarri went to court to force her niece Beatriz, whom she had reared from the age of one, to return to her home. When the girl disappeared one night, Chavarri told the court, she searched Beatriz' trunk and found a number of love letters written by Capt. Manuel Ortega. The aunt's letters demanding the return of her niece punctuate the proceedings, indicating her keen interest in Beatriz' prompt return. Beatriz' reply to the judge's questions more than insinuated that her aunt was acting out of self-interest rather than altruism. According to Beatriz, she had acted as her aunt's servant. According to her, she had not been seduced by Ortega at all, but had asked him to help her get away from her aunt, following "an argument with her *señora* aunt, who had offended her."[32]

Other young women also claimed to have been exploited as servants. Rosaura Carbajal affirmed that she had escaped her stepfather's home in order to get away from the "yoke of servitude and slavery under which I have found myself."[33] Pedro Chavarri gave some credence to his stepdaughter's allegation that she had lived the life of a servant when he complained that he had lost "the service of his daughter in all the time she has been out of her paternal house" as a result of her elopement. In addition to claiming to defend a ward's honor, plaintiffs wished to reestablish patriarchal (or, in Natividad Chavarri's case, matriarchal) control over their dependents.

In these cases, the arguments between plaintiff and defendant had a bearing on the extent and legitimacy of paternal authority. Chavarri legitimated his claim to paternal authority by emphasizing the protection Rosaura had experienced under his *abrigo* (shelter), contrasting that situation with the poverty and dishonor to which her lover had exposed her. By way of emphasis, he asked witnesses to confirm that he had maintained his family, including Rosaura, "with the daily sustenance and usual decency, using honorable means." Cabrera, on the other hand, had abandoned the girl, "giving her the greatest ill-treatment, and without supplying her with . . . nourishment for life, . . . not even a pair of shoes, or garments, or dress with which to keep herself warm." By pointing out that Cabrera had failed to provide materially for Rosaura after taking her from her parents, Chavarri was trying to demonstrate that it was he, not Cabrera, who could legitimately claim to represent Rosaura. Cabrera on the other hand accused Chavarri of despotic behavior, in particular, neglecting Rosaura's education. This criticism reflects the increasing access to education in the region, and the developing expectations that the younger generation had—expectations which, at least in this case, were not shared by the older generation.[34]

Despite Rosaura Carbajal's claim that her stepfather merely wanted to exploit her domestic labor, he persuaded the court that he was motivated by parental concern. Arguing for Cabrera's arrest, he pointed to "the painful situation of my wife, who goes from house to house and field to field searching for her daughter."[35] Asking that the search for the girl be intensified, he again sought compassion for his wife's suffering: "I seek a way to quiet the moans of my wife, dry her inconsolable weeping and give . . . her intense pain the [consolation] of seeing her daughter."[36]

Similarly, when Loreto León accused Gerónimo Miranda of attempted murder, assault, and *estupro* of his young daughter, he stated that such crimes could not but "affect humanity deeply."[37] Josefa Alcántara insisted that her accusation against Manuel María Alcántara be taken seriously by the court, partly because her daughter Zoila was a minor, but even more because of the crime's brutality: "The rape . . . has been perpetrated . . . under the grave threat of taking her life."[38] While plaintiffs clearly had strategic motivations for underlining the victim's suffering, genuine parental concern and worry also shine through in the court documents.

Plaintiffs consistently pointed to the victim's defenselessness and vulnerability. The motivation, clearly, was to absolve them of any suspicion of complicity in their loss of honor. Bartolomé Gálvez, for instance, pointed out that the rape of his niece was committed "with the aggravating circumstance of covering her mouth so that she would not call for help."[39] Similarly, Pedro Chavarri argued that the seduction of his stepdaughter had been made possible only through the use of alcohol: "The young girl . . . has been intoxicated with liquor by the said Cabrera in order to carry out the abduction."[40]

In trials involving *rapto*, the fact of imprisonment was underlined by plaintiffs. In the case of Rosaura Carbajal—who had joined her lover willingly—her stepfather's insistence that she had been restrained forcibly made her appear an unwilling victim rather than a consenting adult. When he finally found her after searching for several hours, Chavarri told the court, he found her "locked up in a room in the upper floor of the house of Doña Gertrudes Pita."[41] Similarly, Josefa Alcántara pointed out that Manuel María Alcántara, after raping her daughter, detained the girl for four hours in a house on the outskirts of the town of Cajamarca.[42]

Plaintiffs also portrayed the victim as younger than she actually was. The law stated that sexual intercourse with girls under the age of twelve was to be punished with greater severity than rape or seduction of girls above that age. In such cases, whether the girl had agreed to sex or not was irrelevant, as "she, due to her young age, may lend her consent without knowing what she consents to."[43] When María Resurrección Julcamoro accused Lisandro Altamirano of abducting and raping her daughter, she falsely claimed that the girl was eleven years and five months old. In fact, Rosario Sichas was at least twelve years old at the time. Loreto León claimed that his daughter María Asencia León was only eleven years old; her baptismal certificate revealed that she was in fact fifteen.[44]

The purpose of reducing a girl's age and highlighting the use of force or imprisonment was obviously to remove any shadow of personal responsibility from the victim herself. The legal battles were thus attempts to shift the responsibility for the loss of honor to the male participant in both consensual and violently obtained sex. Although the stain of improper sexual activity was described by plaintiffs as irreparable, vestiges of honor could be recovered by demonstrating that the girl in question had been an innocent victim of violence, or a near-innocent dupe of an ill-intentioned seducer. Given certain conditions, the legal apparatus and public opinion could, therefore, excuse what was perceived as female sexual misconduct. Plaintiffs who brought charges of seduction and breach of promise tried to avail themselves of those spaces within the existing gender code which permitted female sexual activity. As Boyer shows in his analysis of a trial dealing with the alleged rape of a young woman in 1696 in Mexico, these tactics were not specific to either the region or the period being studied. The victim's brothers, who pressed her suit, "invoked all the right elements common to pleas for damages," he notes, "stealth, treachery, force, deflowering, and . . . the cynical use of a promise to marry."[45]

Although women who had lost their virginity through illicit sex, whether voluntarily or not, were regarded as diminished, they were also pitied. Chavarri invoked public sympathy when he lamented, "There you see the loss of virginity and good name which Rosaura enjoyed, now infamously seduced by Cabrera."[46]

Twinam points out that in the colonial period, "the loss of virginity was not considered evidence of a fatal moral flaw"; despite expectations of sexual control, a recognition that women might be "fragile" existed.[47] Plaintiffs and defendants were in a sense engaged in an argument about which code of honor women should be judged by: the multilayered code outlined by Twinam for the colonial elites, or the monodimensional, all-or-nothing view espoused by defendants accused of rape, who tried to prove that their mistresses had not lost honor, as they had not possessed any prior to the rape.

As in slander trials, plaintiffs appealed to the court's concern for public morality. Pedro Chavarri declared that Rosaura Carbajal's seducer had acted "in a way that caused outrage to all local society. . . . There is no father of a family who is safe, regardless of how high his social position might be, from somebody like Cabrera . . . , a man without shame or respect."[48] María Rosario Villacorta informed the court that she had pressed charges because "morality has been offended, and so that the public's wish for punishment can be avenged."[49] Bartolomé Gálvez described Simón Alegría's crime first as an attack on *la moral* (morality), and only second as an act which robbed his niece of her virginity. By calling attention to the public's shock at the crime, plaintiffs thus sought to underscore its seriousness and align themselves with the authorities.

Legal channels were not the only option open to families that wanted to defend a female dependent's honor. Francisco de las Llagas Ruiz threatened his daughter's former fiancé, Vicente Noriega, with forced conscription if the latter did not make good his promise to marry Clemencia Ruiz. However, the option of exerting this type of informal pressure was available only to those with local influence, as appears to have been the case with de las Llagas Ruiz.[50] When such attempts failed, individuals sought redress in the courts. Seen in conjunction with the report of the violent encounter between the various members of the Alcántara family, de las Llagas Ruiz' threat confirms that the legal arena was but one of several where conflicts were played out.[51]

Fear of notoriety persuaded those who could to use alternative means of exerting influence on faithless lovers. I have already shown how legal action could be risky in cases of slander, as it might well lead to further publication of the insult and hence embarrassment for the recipient of the insult. The same applied to rape victims, as Boyer has noted for colonial Mexico: "Litigation fueled the gossip network, adding insults to injuries and thus bringing dishonor; for honor, after all, was a thing of appearances."[52] As a rape case described by Johnson indicates, it was the public knowledge of the dishonor rather than the assault itself that was considered problematic by the victim's husband. In Johnson's case, taken from late colonial Buenos Aires, charges were initiated only after the rapist began to taunt the victim and her husband.[53] My conclusions about the public nature of insults and slander also indicate that the degree to which suspicions of sexual misconduct were known publicly played a significant role in determining their seriousness, in the eyes of both the population at large and the court.

COUNTERING ACCUSATIONS: THE DEFENDANT'S VERSION

Like the plaintiffs, defendants considered honor the central issue in cases of rape and seduction. If the plaintiffs sought to blame them for the rape or seduction, they in turn described the women as morally flawed. Seed has described these as cynical male "strategies" designed to avoid the contract implied by the promise to marry.[54] The term captures the defense strategies used by the accused in Cajamarca well. As all legal proceedings were premised on the value of virginity, four defendants claimed that their victims, having lost their virginity much earlier, had no honor to defend. Following such countercharges, fear of further damaging the victim's reputation drove several plaintiffs to drop charges.

Capt. Manuel Ortega claimed that Beatriz Chavarri, whom he was accused of abducting, had told him that she was not a virgin.[55] The justice of the peace of Chetilla, Simón Alegría, claimed that his alleged victim, Catalina Pájares, had been engaged in an illicit relationship with another man for several months prior to the alleged rape, which he denied had taken place. According to Alegría, this man had even taken her along to several "parties and other public occasions without anybody accompanying them or telling them off."[56] Lisandro Altamirano, accused of raping Rosario Sichas, claimed that the girl was "known as a mere prostitute in the military quarters [no pasa de la esfera de prostituida en los cuarteles]."[57] Least convincing of all was Baltazar Ramos. Given that the midwives confirmed that the girl (who was younger than twelve) had indeed been subjected to a brutal and bloody sexual assault, but found that the rape had not been completed due to the girl's resistance and that she was still technically a virgin, it is not surprising that Ramos' lawyer did not get far with his ploy.[58]

The line of argument pursued by Cayetano Sánchez in the proceedings with Marcos Paz is particularly illuminating. Not content with merely besmirching his former fiancée's reputation, he opted for a full-scale character assassination. Sánchez was charged with *rapto y estupro* of Marcelina Paz after he seduced then dumped her.[59] As the relationship between Paz and Sánchez had included elopement, a three-month absence from her family home, and pregnancy, her father was anxious to persuade the young man to keep his promise of marriage.

Sánchez did not deny his elopement with Paz, nor the initial seriousness of his intentions. On the contrary, he admitted that he had "stolen [her] from her parents' bosom, and . . . taken her to another house." When asked by a friend "where he was taking this girl to leave her in strange territory . . . he answered that he was . . . taking her to meet his parents and hers in order to get married." His parents "treated her as a daughter-in-law." The couple's parents even went as far as exchanging ritual gifts, the usual preliminary to formalizing a union.[60]

Everything changed, explained Sánchez, when his brother told him that Paz was not a virgin, but had had sexual relations with several men before him. Following this revelation, Sánchez abandoned her—literally—at the altar. "When the talk [*habladurías*] began," he explained, "and I was told of this by my brother, I got rid of her." He accused Paz of having been a *rabona* (a woman who followed the Peruvian army and guerrilla troops and cooked and washed for them) during the War of the Pacific. "Doña María Marcelina Paz," Sánchez declared, "has been a woman of the world, for she has been a camp follower with the *montoneras* (bands of guerrilla fighters usually united under a common leader by clientage bonds) and went along with them from San Marcos to Cajabamba and Huamachuco." He concluded that, given her history, she could not possibly have been a virgin when he eloped with her. "What virginity can there be in a woman who has been around, who has met up with guerrillas?" he asked. "She who is said to be a virgin and a minor has thus been a woman of the world, and above the age of majority [twenty-one],"[61] he added. He concluded that "it is ridiculous chicanery to affirm that there has been rape of a virgin girl and the abduction of a vulgar and willing [*corriente y voluntariosa*] woman."

His statements demonstrate an understanding that promises of marriages made to sexually experienced women were worthless, and that women who had already lost their virginity—such as Marcelina Paz—could not hope for redress in the courts. The sheer number of accusations he leveled against her made it difficult for Paz and her father to defend her moral character, with the result that, after seven months and 126 pages of legal transcripts, they eventually gave up.

Not all defendants claimed that their alleged victims led immoral lives; some simply asserted that the victims had been willing partners in the act, and had even made the first sexual overtures. Thus Manuel Alcántara, accused of raping Zoila Alcántara at knifepoint and fathering her child, testified, "The truth of the matter is the following: on the said date . . . Zoila Alcántara took him with deception and at her will . . . to the foot of the hill of Santa Polonia, and there made him commit sinful acts."[62] Juan Esteban Cabrera denied having seduced Rosaura Carbajal, stating that Carbajal and her sister had invited his attentions by playfully taking his hat and inviting him for a cup of wine.[63] Similarly, Vicente Noriega and Manuel Ortega declared that their alleged victims had entered relations with them willingly.[64]

In some cases, defendants spoke the truth. Gerónimo Miranda, accused of raping Asencia León, explained that he had no need to rape the girl, as he "had had illicit relations with the said María Asencia for a long time of their own free will." Although no one believed him at the time, León later exonerated him. Fearing punishment when her mother discovered her with Miranda, she told her mother that he had assaulted and raped her, she explained some months later.[65] When Cayetano Sánchez stated that the agreement with Marcelina Paz "to contract marriage [had been made] in a voluntary manner between the parties,"[66] there is no doubt that he spoke the truth.

Although plaintiffs, in an attempt to garner the judge's sympathy, portrayed the victims as sexually passive, this image of passive female sexuality did not always reflect reality. While several defendants grossly exaggerated their victim's or former lover's sexual activities, women willingly entered sexual relationships—usually following a promise of marriage, as evidenced by the cases of Marcelina Paz and Clemencia Ruiz.

Another common strategy defendants used was straight denial, accompanied by more or less persuasive alibis. Simón Alegría, Chetilla's justice of the peace, procured an alibi for the time when he was in fact forcing Catalina Pájares into the local jail and raping her brutally.[67] Juan Esteban Cabrera also made a weak attempt to establish an alibi for the night during which Rosaura Carbajal was abducted. He soon abandoned this attempt, however, as his opponent had more than enough witnesses to prove Cabrera's complicity in Carbajal's disappearance.[68]

Instead of, or sometimes in addition to, attacking the victim's sexual mores, defendants might question her entire family's honor. If the family could be shown to lack honor, its daughter could not be assumed to be a virgin and thus was unworthy of legal redress.

Manuel Estevan Rocha, who was accused by Rosario Villacorta of raping her daughter Andrea del Aguilar, tried several lines of defense. First, he denied having raped the girl at all and claimed that she, fearing a beating from her mother, had fled and hidden in his home. Second, he accused Aguilar of having had relationships with several other men prior to the alleged abduction and rape. Most important, however, he told the court that Villacorta had already proven her and her family's lack of honor by neglecting to take any legal action when her other two daughters were seduced. Having failed to defend her family's name on previous occasions, she should not be believed when she now claimed to be acting to safeguard her family's reputation. He declared that he had been charged at the instigation of the local priest, who bore him a grudge—and in order to force money out of him, as he was a respectable and well-to-do man.[69] Like Manuel Estevan Rocha, Cayetano Sánchez supplemented his imputations of Marcelina Paz's sexual incontinence by asserting that "the father, far from impeding this, showed himself indifferent."[70]

Rocha's reasoning also helps explain why some parents chose to press charges even when they had little to gain from a trial. By going to court they at least publicly demonstrated the family's concern with public esteem. This may explain Pedro Chavarri's persistence in pursuing his stepdaughter's seducer. Carbajal had little to lose with regard to her reputation; by hounding her seducer, her stepfather could at least advertise his own concern for honor and thus reestablish his and the rest of his family's honor.

Other defendants attacked their victim's employment, thus making social class an obvious criterion for the possession of honor. Lisandro Altamirano pointed out that Rosario Sichas was a servant, and therefore continually exposed to damaging influences. "The virginity of a girl is assured," he claimed, "by the fact that she has maintained modesty in her conduct; and not frequented the businesses and squares at all times on errands for her employer."[71] He equated honor with a secluded lifestyle unobtainable for Rosario Sichas and most women of her social background.

Women of lower social status were more exposed to suspicions of sexual misconduct than were women of higher social standing. Cayetano Sánchez's claim that his fiancée had a history as a camp follower illustrates this. As her father explained, Marcelina Paz accompanied her mother in an attempt to obtain compensation for two horses taken by the Peruvian forces. "Three years ago," Marcos Paz told the court, "Colonel Puga's forces took two of my horses, and out of fear that they might recruit me I did not go to retrieve them. For that reason and no other dishonorable [motive] my wife went to retrieve them . . . with a child she was breast-feeding; my daughter Marcelina Paz accompanied her in order to help her."[72] Whether Sánchez' accusation that Paz had been a *rabona* was true or not, the case shows how poverty exposed young women to situations in which their virtue could be questioned.

As can be seen from the distrust of Luisa Cabanillas, women who had previously deviated from the path of sexual morality were assumed to be inherently morally flawed. The mother of three illegitimate children, Cabanillas lived in common-law union with Nicolás Malca. She initially accused him of raping her eight-year-old daughter, Mercedes Velesmoro, but withdrew the charges on being told by the midwives that they found no sign of penetration. The judge suspected that her decision to drop charges was the result of "collusion between lover and mistress," thinking that "these illicit relations may have impaired [*desvirtuado*] motherly love."[73] In the end, the court-appointed prosecutor dropped the case after hearing the midwives' evidence.

In addition to meeting distrust based on assumed moral flaws, poor plaintiffs struggled with the cost of lawsuits. When the proceedings against his daughter's rapist dragged on, Catalino Saucedo Silva asked the prosecutor to take over the case, as his "absolute poverty" made it impossible for him to pursue the matter further.[74] Only a few days after Beatriz Chavarri's aunt accused Manuel Ortega of abducting her niece, the girl's father withdrew the accusation, explaining, "It is not possible for me to continue this suit as I lack the necessary means."[75] Apolinario Chavarri, Beatriz' father, also feared "fresh slanderous attacks against the . . . reputation of my family."

Lower-class plaintiffs discovered that judges did not take their complaints seriously. When Andrea Sánchez reported her daughter's rape, the judge refused to order the midwife to examine the girl, as the incident had taken place during a court holiday. The delay made it impossible to document the rape, with the result that the charges were dismissed.[76]

Some defendants tried to intimidate the plaintiffs into withdrawing charges. Zoila Alcántara's rape by her cousin is a case in point. The book of verbal settlements, where minor offenses and conflicts were dealt with by the justice of the peace, records an assault by the rapist and his father on Zoila Alcántara and her mother, Josefa. The encounter may have been the natural result of enmity between the two halves of the family, but was probably also intended to intimidate Josefa into giving up her legal challenge.[77]

OFFICIAL RESPONSES: THE RESULT OF STRATEGY

Legal action on behalf of young women who had been dishonored by rape or seduction provided no guarantee of vindication. Three of the sixteen defendants were absolved by the court, some of them on rather dubious grounds.[78] Six trials were never concluded. In some, the accusations were formally withdrawn, such as happened following the elopement of Beatriz Chavarri; in four other cases the proceedings were discontinued, but no reason is given in the records. It seems likely that the plaintiffs tired of lengthy legal proceedings, the public notoriety which accompanied them, and the associated costs.

The court was inadequate for several reasons, related both to the slowness of the legal system and the state's lack of coercive power. In Cajamarca, three of the four defendants who were sentenced escaped the law simply by leaving the province. Charged with rape and seduction, Juan Esteban Cabrera shrugged off the matter and said that "if [he] lost the lawsuit, he would saddle a horse and leave and there we would have . . . Rosaura [*si perdía el pleito, ensillaría un caballo y se iría y que allí nos quedaba . . . Rosaura*]," the girl's stepfather reported.[79] This was a promise which Cabrera did, at least temporarily, keep. María Jamina Guevara's rapist, José Uriarte, was never sentenced; he fled immediately after raping the girl in 1886. In 1932 charges were formally dropped by the authorities, as Uriarte had not been seen since charges were filed.[80] In other cases the defendant's absence merely delayed proceedings by a matter of months. Nevertheless, such delays helped exhaust complainants.

Corruption also played a role. When Simona Malaver accused Benedicto Llanos, Juan Pérez, and Manuel Ruiz of breaking into her home, stealing money, and attempting to "rape [*violar*] [her] married daughter and rape [*estuprar*] the other one," the case dragged on for three months, only to be dismissed by the judge.[81] Despite the fact that numerous neighbors witnessed the attempted rape of the two young women, the judge concluded that Malaver had failed to substantiate her charges. More likely, the judge favored the three men because they constituted a semiofficial recruitment force and could therefore count on support from local power holders.

The main reason so few charges of sexual crime were brought in the first place, and so few of them met with success in the courts, lay in the very definition of the categories of rape and abduction. Unless the plaintiffs could convincingly portray the victim as a virgin prior to the alleged crime, they were unlikely to win the case. As Lisandro Altamirano—himself accused of rape—pointed out, proving that the woman in question had actually been a virgin prior to her supposed deflowering was no easy matter. According to him, "It would be necessary . . . for the midwives to have verified virginity before the events, in order for the consequences of the rape [*estupro*] to be proved."[82]

Instead, reputation became the principal issue. Only women who could prove that they had an honorable reputation—something which could best be proved by their family's status and their own decorous lifestyle—were likely to be assumed to have been bona fide virgins prior to the sexual encounter in question.

The degree to which young women were active in the public sphere thus became an important focal point, and complainants sought to prove that a ward had led a secluded life. When Bartolomé Gálvez tried to redeem his niece's honor following her rape by Simón Alegría, he pointed out that the girl had been working in the home, "dedicated exclusively to service in domestic matters and under my own vigilance, and that of a virtuous lady, Doña Patricia Días."[83] Those women who did not meet the criteria of respectability and seclusion were in effect denied any legal protection in cases of sexual crime. Kuznesof, working on nineteenth-century Brazil, has observed that women who had illegitimate children, frequented the street, and consorted with men were not afforded any legal protection in cases of rape, as their behavior was seen to have invited male attention and even assault.[84] In her work on Rio de Janeiro in the same period, Lauderdale Graham observes that "simply being on the street unescorted was sufficient to raise questions about a woman's purpose and morals."[85] Such a narrow definition of feminine honor in practice prevented women of low social status from seeking legal redress.

A comparison of the courts' treatment of women from different social backgrounds further illustrates this point. Despite the fact that Rosaura Carbajal was evidently a willing party in her relationship with Juan Esteban Cabrera, the court was persuaded that she had been seduced *con engaño* (deceitfully), as the law required, and sentenced him to jail. It is likely that Pedro Chavarri's social position and his employment as a notary all worked in his and his stepdaughter's favor.[86] This was not the case for Zoila Alcántara. Although her cousin admitted to the court that he had had sexual intercourse with her and boasted to his friends that he had "raped . . . Zoila last August, and that she was pregnant,"[87] he was acquitted of raping her at knifepoint. In both cases, young women lost their virginity, one voluntarily, the other when threatened with a knife. Alcántara even became pregnant, further reducing both her chances of marrying and of finding employment. Nevertheless, the trial on Carbajal's behalf was brought to a successful conclusion, whereas Alcántara failed to obtain any support from the legal system. Clearly, a very different value was assessed on the virginity of a relatively respectable young woman such as Rosaura Carbajal and that of Zoila Alcántara, whose mother was single and who worked as a shoemaker.

As Twinam has found in cases in which elite women bore illegitimate children in colonial Spanish America, they, unlike their lower-class counterparts, received "the benefit of the doubt even in questionable situations where marriage may not have been promised, for witnesses assumed that a woman of honor would never have engaged in intercourse without such assurance."[88] Such assumptions did not, however, extend to women from the popular classes.

Married women who were raped or nearly raped also found that there was little help to be obtained from the courts. The only case involving the attempted rape of a married woman, Rosario Rodríguez, was withdrawn six months after it was initiated—six months during which the court took no action at all. Although Rodríguez, a respected and literate widow, produced several witnesses to the incident (witnesses who had also been instrumental in stopping the rape from being completed), the court took no action.[89]

Even though the courts rarely assisted married rape victims, married women sometimes took legal action in order to defend themselves from intimations of having acquiesced and hence having engaged in dishonorable behavior.[90] Although the bias in the legal system focused almost exclusively on honor, leaving aside the victim's suffering as being only marginal, there were exceptions. The available sample contains two examples in which the legal apparatus appeared to take the suffering of a rape victim seriously. Both cases deal with the sexual abuse of children.[91] In neither of them did the parents of the victim or the representatives of the legal system mention the word *honor* in relation to the crime committed; they focused exclusively on the suffering of the girls.

Returning from putting out a fire in her father's sugarcane field, nine-year-old María Jamina Guevara was raped by José Uriarte. "From shame," as she explained to her aunt the following day, she did not tell anybody until her aunt discovered the girl's severe vaginal bleeding. Guevara died a few hours later of hemorrhage. The midwife examined the child's body twice, once alone and once in the presence of the alleged perpetrator's mother, and stated that "his mother . . . at seeing the state of the girl remained silent and wept." It should be noted that the girl had internalized the notions of shame and dishonor to such an extent that she chose to remain silent until a trail of blood alerted her aunt to the fact that there was something amiss.[92]

The other case is less clear-cut. When eight-year-old Mercedes Velesmoro ran to find her mother and told her she had been raped by her stepfather, Nicolás Malca, Luisa Cabanillas, the mother, immediately reported the crime to the subprefect and had her common-law husband arrested. As the midwives' examination of the girl showed that her hymen was still intact, the court concluded that no deflowering had taken place.[93]

Whatever the truth of Mercedes Velesmoro's accusations—and they may well have been accurate, as sexual abuse might well have taken place without penetration—the fact remains that the legal apparatus did react to the rape of children in a more serious and direct fashion than to that of sexually mature women. When sex-related crime concerned children, it was regarded as a crime against the individual, not against honor.

The actual events underlying criminal charges were sometimes obscured by the overriding emphasis on honor. It is, for instance, impossible to know what transpired in Zoila Alcántara's case. Although she gave birth to a child fathered by her cousin, we do not know whether this was the result of a single instance of rape, as she told her mother, consensual sex (as claimed by the defendant), or sexual abuse over time. The same applies to Marcelina Paz. Although both sides agreed on the nature and the seriousness of her relationship with Cayetano Sánchez, we cannot know whether this was her first relationship, or whether she had, as Sánchez claimed, already had one or more relationships. In the trial initiated on behalf of María Asencia León, the truth emerged only a year after the charges were brought.

The cases of both María Asencia León and Zoila Alcántara illustrate a further reason why sexual encounters were misrepresented when brought into public view. Both girls feared punishment at the hands of their parents and hence seem to have told them rather less than the full truth. Zoila Alcántara's sister reported that Zoila had told her about the rape by Manuel María Alcántara some time earlier. "As my mother beat her a lot, [my sister] did not want to tell her anything, but she confessed everything to me," Manuela Alcántara declared.[94] As a result of this delay, Zoila's mother learned of the rape only when the girl's pregnancy was well advanced. Similarly, María Asencia León was motivated by fear of her mother when she claimed to have been raped; only on her deathbed—and presumably safe from parental punishment—did she tell her father that "for fear that her mother would beat her she had said that Miranda had ill-treated her."[95]

The most elusive character in the legal proceedings was usually the victim herself. The principal protagonists were the plaintiff, usually a parent or guardian of the victim, and the defendant, as well as, in some cases, lawyers. The testimony given by the young woman at the center of the issue was often the only source that might reveal her state of mind. In several cases even this was lacking.[96] Rosaura Carbajal's stepfather portrayed her as a respectable young woman who had been led astray by the wiles of an ill-intentioned seducer and who ended up bitterly regretting her mistake. Following her discovery and liberation from the room in which, according to Chavarri, her seducer had locked her, her stepfather quoted her as saying, "Do not blame me as party to this [*a mí no me culpen de consentidora*]." Cabrera asserted that it was Carbajal who had flirted with him first. He said that she and her sisters tried to persuade him to enter their home while they were "chatting . . . in the doorway of their house as is their habit." Concerning

Carbajal's second escape, he claimed that she had "left her parents' home . . . after showering them with insults." Carbajal's version remains obscure. On the one hand, she behaved submissively and repeated her stepfather's version when interviewed by the judge; on the other hand, she escaped from her parental home on three occasions and refused to return for months at a time.[97]

The confusion concerning Rosaura Carbajal's personal wishes is augmented by an exchange of letters between her parents and her lover, both claiming to speak on her behalf. As Carbajal was illiterate, Cabrera could with impunity present letters allegedly written with her authorization and in which he claimed that she had left the Chavarri family home of her own volition, and that she wished that all charges against Cabrera be withdrawn. Pedro Chavarri, on the other hand, obtained witnesses who declared that Carbajal had said that she had never "made such an appeal nor had any part in it." The confusion concerning Carbajal's wishes reached its climax when Cabrera (hoping to escape a three-year jail sentence) proposed to marry her. Her stepfather angrily refused the proposal, stating that the girl "refuses absolutely to give her hand to the said Cabrera," a refusal which the court accepted as valid, since the girl was only eighteen, and hence a minor. When asked in person, in her father's presence, she replied, "Under no circumstances [will I] consent to contract the matrimony which said Cabrera desires." Needless to say, Cabrera contested the validity of Carbajal's reply, claiming that "the timid youth Rosaura, faced with her stepfather's whims, has had to go against her own wishes and labor against pressures which are insurmountable for a woman who lives in the house of her parents."[98] Whatever Carbajal's true wishes may have been, the suggestion that she feared to oppose her parents openly is plausible.

Although Cabrera presented a letter, supposedly authored by Carbajal, in which she accepted the offer of marriage, the court refused to accept this as valid. Despite Carbajal's apparent acceptance of the proposal, the legal system decided to uphold her stepfather's authority and insisted that Cabrera serve his three-year sentence.

RECONCILING SEXUAL PRACTICE WITH NOTIONS OF HONOR

Given that the individual at the heart of the dispute, her personality, her views, and her wishes often remain elusive, any conclusions about the issue of female sexuality can be only tentative. What does emerge is that women's reputations could be endangered by a multitude of factors. These included their actions, male behavior toward them, their social position, and their occupation. When Simón Alegría claimed that defending Catalina Pájares' honor was meaningless as she had been seen going about the town in the company of another young man, he did not tell us anything about Pájares' sexual mores. His assertion was no more believable than that of other defendants wishing to incriminate their former mistresses. He did, however, tell us that such behavior was not considered acceptable and could do much to undermine a young woman's reputation. Similarly, Cayetano Sánchez' claim that his former fiancée, Marcelina Paz, had followed the Peruvian troops as a *rabona* cannot be verified; his claims and the girl's father's counterclaims do, however, give us an idea of how war could affect women's lives far beyond the cessation of military action.

The same was not true for men. Contemporary gender values allowed men considerable sexual freedom and viewed the display of male virility as a positive thing. Whereas women lost their "honor" when they gave up their virginity, men's reputations were enhanced by sexual conquest.[99] The status associated with the display of male virility increased male motivation for sexual conquest, and thus placed women at greater risk from sexual aggressors.

The rape of virgins was associated with a particular status. When three men broke into Simona Malaver's house one night, they inquired of her daughters whether they were married. Hearing that the eldest was married, they ignored her and instead concentrated their attentions on the youngest, who, her sister told them, was "single and modest [*recogida*]." One of them shouted, "Let's go" [*Arriba compañeros*] and, grabbing a machete, tried to pull the girl with him onto the bed.[100] After raping his cousin Zoila Alcántara, Manuel María Alcántara boasted of the event to several friends.[101] Manuela Dilas Chalán had every reason to be fearful when Manuel Chalán (no relation), intoxicated after a collective work party, "invited her repeatedly to go and drink *chicha*."[102] Her refusal resulted in an assault (causing her to lose three toes) and attempted rape.

As I have shown, common-law unions and premarital sex were the norm in the rural areas, and far from unusual in the urban centers. Sex outside marriage also occurred among the more educated and wealthier social groups. Rosaura Carbajal's mother had one illegitimate daughter, but went on to marry a notary and lead a respectable life; Francisca Ramírez, who was seduced when young, married Francisco del Campo some years later and remained at his side for at least thirty years, enjoying the esteem of her neighbors.[103] The relationships of Marcelina Paz and Cayetano Sánchez and of Clemencia Ruiz and Vicente Noriega provide further examples. Although neither liaison led to marriage, the way these young women engaged in sexual relations with their fiancés shows that their behavior was common. Had the unions not been broken off, both Ruiz and Paz could have gone on to lead honorable lives.[104] In Ruiz' case the affair was even conducted with her mother's approval. The judge stated "that the mother of said Doña Clemencia, be it for weakness or because she wished for her daughter to marry said Noriega, . . . allowed [him] access to her house."[105] Although defying the official gender code could be risky, especially for women, this did not mean that gender rules were immutable: deviations occurred and were sanctioned.[106]

This gap between norm and practice challenged official gender culture and created tensions which needed to be negotiated and resolved. One of the ways in which such contradictions were unraveled was through the concept of *rapto*. Literally meaning "abduction," it was usually taken to mean the elopement of young couples who wished to force a marriage regardless of their parents' desires. Although *rapto* has often been considered an Andean custom,[107] it was not restricted to the Indian parts of the population, nor to Peru. In the face of parental opposition, elopement was a common way of forcing parents to accede to a daughter's romantic intentions; once virginity was lost, even marrying a man of lesser means or darker pigmentation was preferable to spinsterhood.[108]

Elopement also occurred among more moneyed and educated segments of the population. Capt. Manuel Ortega's love letters are a case in point. The fact that both he and Beatriz Chavarri were literate indicates that they were, if not part of the local upper class, at least of some social standing. In his letters the captain tried to persuade Beatriz to elope with him, explaining that they could "in this way trouble your parents so that they will give in to our desire."[109]

Thus most charges of *rapto* brought before the Cajamarcan courts were the result of consensual relationships between young women and men. Some of these had developed gradually, such as that between Gerónimo Miranda and María Asencia León, who had met regularly when she was out pasturing her parents' cows. Their rendezvous included visits to friends, and sometimes a little alcohol, "*unas copas de huarapo*," as Miranda told the judge.[110] Alcohol also played a role in other liaisons, such as that of Rosaura Carbajal and Juan Esteban Cabrera. Chavarri claimed that Cabrera got the girl drunk before abducting her; whatever the truth of this statement, some wine was drunk before her escape from home.

Occasionally, women eloped for other than purely romantic reasons. Several wished to escape their domestic situation. Such, at least, was Manuel Ortega's defense when he was accused of seducing and abducting Beatriz Chavarri. Beatriz lived in her aunt's house; Ortega implied that hers was the life of an unremunerated servant. He claimed that Chavarri had approached him and reminded him of "their romance about two months ago and begged him . . . to take her away."[111] She seconded his version and asserted that she had left her aunt's house of her own free will following a spat.

Although the legal definition of *rapto* presupposed that it was men who incited women to illicit sexual behavior, female volition was often at the center of events. For obvious reasons (if indeed they knew of the relationship), however, plaintiffs did their best to gloss over this.

The trials analyzed in this chapter were the result of women and men living according to mutually contradictory gender codes. Given certain conditions, including an otherwise unblemished sexual history and the promise of marriage, young women who gave in to their yearning for romance and to sexual desire could be forgiven. A subsequent marriage would redeem their honor and legitimize any children. In cases of male default, however, these women found themselves with a besmirched sexual record and deprived of honor. While this was common enough among the peasantry and plebeian urban population not to cause great uproar, women of semirespectable family resisted being classified alongside the former. Instead, their families rallied around them and pursued various strategies in order to reestablish the family's honor. If the matter could not be hushed up, or the groom forced to the altar by other means, legal proceedings offered some promise of recovering honor. While the courts rarely succeeded in turning reluctant fiancés into model husbands, they did function as a public arena for the airing of such disputes.

Plaintiffs used the opportunity these debates provided to present the seduced or raped woman's actions in the most favorable light. They sought to shift the blame for the dishonor which had befallen them from themselves and their no-longer-virgin daughter or dependent to the sexually aggressive male who had seduced the woman in question.

This conciliatory approach to illicit sexuality had a legal foundation. The law recognized the custom of abduction and elopement followed by more permanent union. Provided that women could prove themselves to be honorable, the law displayed a sympathetic attitude toward them. Proving honor after the fact was no simple matter, however, and the trials revolved principally around the victim's reputation rather than the "crimes" they were meant to judge. Although the legislation effectively excluded the majority of women, and although it belittled the suffering of women who had experienced sexual abuse or rape, such provisions did open space for maneuver within an otherwise rigid legislative framework.

CONCLUSION

As in the slander trials, the social range represented in the rape and seduction trials underscores the vital role honor played in the life of individuals from all walks of life. While much of the flowery rhetoric employed by plaintiffs in their depositions was designed to appeal to the judge (and was usually authored by a scribe rather than the plaintiffs themselves), the very fact that smallholders, servant women, and notaries went to court on behalf of daughters, wards, and relatives illustrates the importance of honor in the lives of a relatively broad cross section of the population. Although charges were submitted under labels of *rapto, violación,* or *estupro,* most trials dealt with consensual sex. Rape of plebeian women in particular was rarely reported, and reached the legal arena only in exceptional circumstances, such as when a child was involved. Most cases were the result of romantic liaisons, several of which resulted in elopement and which were deliberately misrepresented in court. By claiming that the woman in question had been the victim of force or deceit, complainants sought to free her from blame and shift responsibility to her seducer. In order to achieve this they altered the victim's age and spread elaborate tales of deceit, drugging, and imprisonment. Such accusations enhanced the chance of obtaining a conviction and demonstrated to the public the victim's irreproachable character. A modicum of honor could be regained and the family's preoccupation with honor publicly demonstrated.

The real course of events was, consequently, obscured. The actions, thoughts, and intentions of the principal actors in these dramas, the women themselves, remain elusive. Although many were clearly active parties to their seduction, their voices were rarely heard. Instead, plaintiffs and defendants, usually coming up with highly divergent versions of events, both claimed to speak on their behalf.

Despite these challenges, it is clear that young women were far from always the passive creatures they were described as. Many engaged willingly in romance; some consciously exploited a relationship to escape their homes. Defendants were often well aware of their mistress' multiple motives for entering a relationship. In several trials defendants entered into lengthy debates with plaintiffs over the legitimacy of paternal and patriarchal authority. Although the trials rarely resolved these issues, and the price the young women paid for their escape from patriarchal (or, in some cases, matriarchal) authority was exorbitant (in the form of protracted and possibly lifelong dishonor), these trials allow us to guess at some of the motives which propelled women into such relationships. Despite their guardians' attempts at portraying them as hapless victims of wily seducers, it is evident that young women had to maintain a balance between patriarchal control, on the one side, and retaining their reputation, on the other.

The plaintiffs' objectives thus included the defense of family honor and the reestablishment of patriarchal authority (especially in those cases which were filed before the victim had been returned to her parents' home). Honor could be restored by portraying the victims as entirely innocent of any complicity; a sentence for the accused evidently gave such claims legal authority. This, however, was rarely achieved. Few trials resulted in convictions, and sentences were rarely served if they did. A far better alternative was forcing the perpetrator to marry his victim; in this way honor could be reinstituted —and in those cases in which the background was a romantic affair rather than physical violence, formalizing the union was clearly a desirable solution for all parties, possibly excepting the fickle lover who had already demonstrated his commitment angst by abandoning his mistress one or more times.

Although the courts were inefficient arbiters of justice, relatives of seduced maidens nevertheless used them as an arena for debating these women's reputations. Plaintiffs and defendants exchanged versions of events, alleging male duplicity or female wantonness. While giving their own version of their daughter's, niece's, or ward's behavior, complainants also explicated their own understanding of honor, and why the woman in question should still be considered honorable. In doing so, they unfolded their own, alternative, codes of honor, codes which allowed women and men of the lower classes to depart from the formal code yet retain some honor, and often recoup it when it had been lost. Plebeian definitions of honor were thus clarified and publicized on an official platform, openly manifesting the existence of separate, and occasionally conflicting, sets of gender norms. Wealth, virginity, and female seclusion were not absolute requisites (although they enhanced and were seen to guarantee honor); faithfulness once one was in a long-term union was.[112] Codes of honor can best be described as layered and allowing for flexibility and negotiation between different definitions of honor. The legal system served as an important arena for negotiation.

Despite the repeated rhetorical descriptions of honor as a fragile treasure, the disputes dealing with its negotiation illustrate its durability and elasticity. Whereas the willingness of the slandered husbands' wives to abandon their families (see Chapter 5) confirms that a mere imputation of dishonorable behavior could be sufficient to destroy the reputation of a woman and her family, the subsequent legal action and its results indicate that honor could be regained. Similarly, the efforts made by the victims of rape and seduction—or rather, the efforts of their senior family members—reveal that something was to be gained from legal action. In some cases "honor" was repaired by marriage—which, in turn, was achieved only through the pressure exercised through a number of channels, including the legal apparatus. In others, the trial was used to air the victim's version of events, contributing to a diminishing of responsibility for her fall. While the loss of virginity could not be undone, at least the blame could be placed somewhere else and the deflowered woman placed in the category of victim rather than wanton prostitute.

While honor could therefore not be entirely regained, it could at least be renegotiated and partially reachieved. However, as shown by the example of Francisca Ramírez, who appears to have led a respectable life for thirty or more years as a married woman after producing two illegitimate daughters, the crack in the reputation was likely to remain. Although such a woman might "pass" (in Twinam's words) for decades, she—and her family—might still be exposed to reminders of a less respectable past at any moment, making her permanently vulnerable to such challenges.

CHAPTER 7

Conflict and Cooperation
among Women

This chapter begins with the story of Remigia Bermúdes and her former employer, Isabel Basauri, who came to blows in 1862. The incident sheds light on this chapter's theme—conflict and solidarity among women—and highlights the issue of illegitimacy, the plight of single mothers, the complexity of patron-client relations, and the prevalence of violence in Cajamarcan society.

Remigia Bermúdes and her five illegitimate children lived in poverty, and evidently in a client relationship with the Basauri-Cabanillas household. Bermúdes was employed as a servant by the Basauri household, and Isabel Basauri's brother had fathered several of her children. An assault on Bermúdes and, more important, her decision to take legal action must have shaken her relations with the Basauri family.

The immediate background for the quarrel was the disappearance of two eggs, which Isabel Basauri blamed on Remigia Bermúdes' son. Fearing that Basauri would chastise her son, José Trinidad, Bermúdes sent one of her children to borrow a whip and then went to tell Basauri that she had already dealt with José Trinidad. Unwisely, she also blamed Basauri's daughter, Sebastiana Cabanillas, for the theft of the two eggs, thus provoking the girl's mother. Infuriated, Basauri and Cabanillas attacked Bermúdes with a heavy stick and sicced a fierce dog [perro bravo] on her. She was blinded in one eye and knocked unconscious. The incident ended when Basauri's husband, Pedro Cabanillas, returned home for his midday meal and stopped his wife and daughter from inflicting any further injuries on their prostrate victim.[1]

Several of the details of this case are typical of a number of the incidences of interfemale conflict that I have come across in the trial records. The sudden eruption of aggression and the brutality of the attack on Bermúdes were recurring features in those fights among women that found their way to court. As in many other cases, the women in question were related, albeit informally. The tensions that the clash between Bermúdes and Basauri revealed clearly predated the assault and were not, as was the case in many other suits dealing with similar subject matter, elucidated during the proceedings. As in the case of the marital disputes analyzed in Chapter 6, it is more difficult to understand the causes than the nature of these conflicts, as plaintiffs, defendants, and witnesses did not always tell the judge the entire truth, and judges had little patience in dealing with women's quarrels.

The way in which this particular incident started was not atypical, as several of the trials dealing with exclusively female fights originated in women's defense of their children. Other causes of conflict were rivalry over men and disputes over property. Unequal social status—and a relationship, either past or present, between employer and servant, especially—was a frequent component of female conflict as represented in trial records. As we shall see, oral insults were often chosen by lower-class women as a weapon against their social superiors; violence was more likely to be initiated by women who had the advantage of greater economic and human resources to back them up.

The other side of the coin, as in this case, is seen in acts of support and cooperation. Isabel Basauri's daughter assisted her in her assault on the hapless Remigia Bermúdes; the latter's daughter, in turn, returned to the Basauri-Cabanillas household in order to demand an explanation for the treatment her mother had received. Neighbors and acquaintances demonstrated their solidarity by testifying in favor of one or the other of them.

This trial therefore allows a glimpse at another of this chapter's themes, namely, female solidarity and support networks. In many instances female solidarity was strongest among close relatives, such as sisters and mothers and daughters, but more distant relations and neighbors also offered help. Support could manifest itself in the form of assistance in a physical fight, as demonstrated by Isabel Basauri and Sebastiana Cabanillas, or by encouraging women to refrain from fighting. In many cases older relatives, both female and male, tried to calm a daughter or niece in order to keep heated arguments from exploding into violence. Other forms of help were entirely unrelated to conflict and took the form of care for sick or injured friends and relatives, assistance at the time of birth (including miscarriages and abortions), the sharing of household tasks, and simple conversation.

I have found forty-nine trials that refer to conflict among women. In a further six instances, tensions among women were revealed as I investigated unrelated matters. The abuse of female servants by their mistresses, for instance, did not usually produce legal consequences; unless it led to the death of the servant, it was likely to be of only passing interest during the investigation of other issues.[2] In three other cases, dealing with unexplained illness and death[3] and suspected arson,[4] women were accused of having harmed their enemies, but were proved innocent of causing them any damage. But most of the trials which refer to hostility among women deal with concrete episodes of conflict. Twenty conflicts resulted in oral altercations, many of these involving public insults and slander, and twenty-two included physical fights, resulting in three deaths. One trial dealt with alleged fraud. Although the disputes that ended in court were clearly serious matters, the underlying motive was not always revealed. In fifteen of the trials dealing with conflict among women, none of the plaintiffs, defendants, or witnesses provided an explanation for their antagonism.

VENTING AGGRESSION:
EXCHANGING WORDS, BLOWS—AND POISON

While only the most extreme episodes resulted in legal proceedings, the degree of brutality in interfemale conflict is striking. Clashes resulted in serious injuries, miscarriages, and, in several cases, death. On at least two occasions infants died as a direct result of combat between women.[5]

A woman who witnessed the brawl between Manuela Mestanza and Gregoria and María Jesús Astopilco explained how she, "believing there to be a fight, . . . approached [them], and as there was plenty of moonlight, [saw] Manuela Mestanza with Gregoria Astopilco lying on top of her, pulling each other's hair; and [María] Jesús Astopilco kicked the said Mestanza. . . . When Mestanza got up we saw that her face was bathed in blood, and the wound on her forehead looked as if they had torn a piece of flesh from it."[6]

Not all fights among women were as gruesome as the above description implies. Many lesser conflicts never made their way into the records of criminal trials;[7] in other cases, women resorted to magic, slander, and gossip.

Certain weapons and techniques recur in accounts of struggles between females. The number of references to women pulling each other's hair seems to indicate that this was common[8] and, given that most lower-class women wore their hair in braids,[9] an effective one. Sticks were another effective weapon and universally available; to judge from the damage that some women managed to inflict with their sticks, they were expert in wielding *palos*.[10] Stones seem to have been a dreaded weapon, used by women against both men and other women.[11] In 1865 a crowd of five hundred women armed with sticks and stones threatened a military post in Bambamarca and secured the release of husbands and sons who had been forcibly recruited by the authorities.[12] Some women used knives, with occasionally fatal consequences for their opponents.[13]

Anthropological evidence from contemporary Cajamarca confirms that women continue to rely on these same methods. Torre notes that women pull each other's hair and scratch each other's faces when they fight; some hit their adversary's vagina.[14]

Women often united against each other's enemies and preyed on victims in groups. Thus, Bernardina Sáenz was (according to her statement and that of several witnesses) attacked by at least four women and, depending on the witnesses one chooses to rely on, possibly two men.[15] Manuela Mestanza had to pit her strength against both María Jesús and Gregoria Astopilco,[16] and Martina Marreros was found "gravely injured among many drunken women" who had attacked her with their bare hands, sticks, and a knife.[17]

Sometimes the trading of insults and threats heralded the use of physical violence, as in the conflict between Jacoba Bermúdez and Francisca Sifuentes. Sifuentes reported that Bermúdez called her "a whore and a witch," [adding] 'you have killed a daughter of mine with poison, but don't even think of killing me, for I have a good knife here,' which she then pulled out of her bosom and threatened me with, even throwing herself upon me."[18] Similarly, oral offenses preceded violence when three of Juana Miranda's enemies broke into her home and, after insulting her ("whore, witch, spinster [*descasada*] . . . thief") and threatening her ("we will drink your blood"), "took stones and started attacking [Miranda] with them." Miranda retaliated by throwing a number of stones, hitting the infant daughter of one of her assailants.[19] In much the same way, the no-holds-barred fight involving Manuela Mestanza, described above, began with Mestanza's insulting María Jesús and Gregoria Astopilco, accusing them of adultery with her husband, and threatening to cut their faces.[20]

In some cases, oral sparring served as a warning, as when Elena Cruzado fled her enemy, Tadeo Terán. He had first insulted her with the words *prostituta, hechicera* (prostitute, witch); when Elena saw more men appearing in the company of her adversary, she feared for her life and fled.[21]

Frequently, therefore, oral insults led merely to physical aggression. Sometimes, however, insults were considered to weigh more heavily than physical injury. José Asunción Portilla, for example, accused two local women of insulting and attacking his wife and daughter. The blows they received, he argued, were "not grave crimes, but the fact of calling my wife and daughter . . . whores is punishable by the law."[22]

Insults and slander were powerful weapons in their own right, as I showed earlier, and many used them consciously in order to harm enemies. Juliana

Vargas and her three daughters clearly stated their intentions when they propagated rumors about Hermegilda Villavicencio's disreputable behavior before and during her marriage: "We inform the public . . . so that the devil may take her marriage."[23]

Anthropologists and historians confirm the forcefulness of slander as a weapon. Romanucci-Ross, working on 1970s Morelos, Mexico, notes that "the verbal component of the morality contest [among women] is even more destructive than the physical violence that is . . . occasionally involved."[24] Stern describes "the weapon of scandal, the loud venting of information and accusation in a manner that forced public resolution of a matter heretofore private or discreet" as one of the most powerful weapons available to women.[25] While slander was among the most potent weapons deployed by women, we should note that it was used not only in the battle between the sexes, but also among women, belying notions of female solidarity.

Women who wished to challenge their social betters were wise to avoid open confrontation, as Remigia Bermúdes and Matea Gallardo learned to their cost. When Gallardo tried to free her daughter from the domestic servitude in which her employer, Prudencia Chávez, kept the girl against her will, she was beaten by Chávez' dependents and locked up for several days. After charging Chávez with the assault and unlawful arrest, Gallardo was herself sentenced to jail for four years. Although both Bermúdes and Gallardo denied having physically attacked their enemies and social betters, their tales demonstrate the possible consequences of open opposition to more influential women.[26]

Given the limitations of the legal system and the dangers of openly challenging more influential enemies, gossip and slander, as I have noted, could be attractive alternatives. As Lipsett-Rivera has observed for colonial Mexico, individual women chose their strategies in accordance with their relative social status. The upper class was free to use violence when attacking social inferiors, whereas lower-class women's only hope of retaliation against women of higher social standing was legal action, and even then, as we have seen, they had little chance of success.[27] Spreading gossip about a powerful enemy might be a way of seeking revenge for mistreatment.

The oral mudslinging between Manuela Villanueva and Manuela Abanto and their daughters is a case in point. Abanto called the respectable Villanueva and her daughter *"putas, cholas, vandidas [bandidas]"* (whores, halfcastes, thieves); Villanueva's husband explained that the defendant and her daughter were "beer brewers and market women" who, because of their low social station, "have little or no respect for people."[28] The social differences are marked in this case. While Manuela Villanueva and her husband, Luis

Gamarra, gave their profession as *propietarios* (landowners), were literate, and were formally married, Manuela Abanto was a market woman, illiterate, and had an illegitimate daughter. Judging from Gamarra's prompt legal response to Abanto's insults, they had found their mark and proven a public embarrassment to him and his family.

All the examples I found of violence among women of different social status deal with employers abusing their clients or servants. Thus Manuela Soto de Rodríguez struck María Isabel Araujo when the latter announced that she was unable to honor her debts;[29] and Matea Gallardo was, as recounted above, beaten and locked up for wanting to reclaim her daughter from the girl's employer, Jesús del Campo.[30]

Violence was most likely to occur in relationships in which both employer and servant were female. Having past experience of her employer's temper, Bernabé Cabrera attempted to escape when her employer threatened to wring her neck;[31] Zoila Maita was whipped regularly by her sister-in-law, in whose house she lived as a dependent and servant. Maita eventually died as a result of violence, malnutrition, and overwork, or a combination.[32] Finally, several witnesses confirmed that Lorenza Cabrera both beat and in other ways abused a girl who lived in her care and acted as her servant.[33]

Another, less overt, weapon was witchcraft. Although the late-nineteenth-century courts had little patience with charges of witchcraft, the three trials I found dealing with accusations of poisoning reveal a powerful local belief in the phenomenon. Six women were prosecuted for poisoning enemies, and although the courts substantiated none of these charges and acquitted all of the defendants, the fear of witchcraft is palpable in the witness depositions. Mariana Montenegro was charged "for the brew she has given Francisca Marín." Marín's mother reported that she had heard "from the talk of the people of Cajamarca that the Montenegro woman had given my daughter the *chicha* which drove her mad. . . . I do not know why that woman would wish to harm my daughter, but they say that she hates her."[34]

All the references to witchcraft and poisoning which I have found are associated with the ingestion of poison, and thus linked to women's role as providers of food and, particularly, as brewers of *chicha*. As Fairchilds argues for prerevolutionary France, it seems that "poison was the standard explanation for any sudden and unexpected death which the medical profession could not otherwise account for; in this way it played the role that witchcraft had in earlier periods."[35]

Women were suspected of witchcraft or poisoning for different reasons. Some were assumed to have had a motive for harming a woman who was taken unexpectedly and inexplicably ill or who died. Others were vulnerable to suspicions of witchcraft because of their medical or herbal expertise. When Jacoba Bermúdez insulted Francisca Sifuentes, claiming that the latter had murdered her daughter, the claim was linked to Sifuentes' assistance as a midwife when Bermúdez' daughter was in labor.[36] Three of the women formally accused of poisoning made a living from making and selling *chicha*; one of them had at various times occupied herself as a midwife, and two of them (including one of the beer brewers) laid themselves open to suspicion when they took an active part in trying to cure their supposed victims. Andrea Camacho, who was accused of having poisoned Juana Chávez with *chicha*, succeeded in restoring the girl with herbs. She further fueled local gossip by telling the court that, had she given the girl poison, the effect would have been instant, and not crept up on her during the night. Instead, she explained to the judge, Chávez' recent pregnancy was the likely cause of her temporary illness. Her employment as beer brewer, her knowledge of herbs, which enabled her to cure the girl, and her knowledge of a pregnancy (terminated possibly with her assistance?) that nobody knew of (or admitted knowledge of) all indicate that Camacho was a *curiosa* (wise woman, i.e., someone with a knowledge of female health, midwifery, etc.), as some witnesses said. Certainly, she possessed skills that also made her feared, and a prime suspect in this case of inexplicable illness.[37]

In much the same way, Andrea Cerdán was suspected because of her well-known skills with herbs. When Francisca Marín apparently went mad, she was locked up in the hospital and Cerdán placed in charge of curing her. Marín's mother was understandably shocked upon her arrival in Cajamarca when she found her daughter locked up in a room in the town's hospital, "restrained, despairing, tearing apart mattresses and pillows," and Cerdán trying to cure her with a potion concocted of (among other ingredients) the head of a dog.[38]

Although not all women possessed the know-how to make a threat of poisoning believable, they could ally themselves with women who did: Andrea Cerdán was believed to have acted in association with Mariana Montenegro, whose common-law husband had left her for Francisca Marín, their alleged victim. Similarly, Agustina de la Cruz, a beer brewer who was blamed for the death of Melchora Azañero, had no motive for killing the girl. But wagging tongues claimed that Rosa Culqui, who had been deserted by the father of her three children for the young Azañero, had persuaded de la Cruz to poison her rival.[39]

In general, however, information on the uses of poison and witchcraft is scarce. As Stern has pointed out, there is little evidence for the weapon of "magic," as its use was usually hidden from the local community and, even more so, from the authorities.[40]

To sum up, tensions among women erupted in a number of forms. These ranged from oral disparagement to physical, occasionally (albeit in an impromptu fashion) armed, conflict. Insults and threats were often precursors of more direct action and could serve as a warning; in other cases, public offenses and slander were used as weapons in their own right. Public concern with interfemale hatred was so strong that women who were thought to be hostile toward victims of sudden, inexplicable death were jailed on suspicions of poisoning. Very likely, several had made themselves vulnerable to mistrust by threatening their alleged victims. The palette of weapons was large, the choice of instrument determined by the women's social status, their networks, and the circumstances.

FEMALE HOSTILITY: CAUSES

The extreme nature of such conflicts and their rapid progression from oral exchanges to physical injury is symptomatic of the prevalence of violence in Cajamarca's society and culture in this period. More pertinent, however, the rapid escalation of conflict among females uncovers underlying tensions among them. If such antagonistic relationships were in many ways self-perpetuating, there was usually a reason for their inception. In most cases, the motives for the squabbles that produced legal proceedings remain obscure; judges showed little interest in resolving disagreements, and litigants rarely confided the cause of their resentment to court officials. Nevertheless, it seems as if the most frequent points of conflict were property, the treatment of children, and rivalry over men, as noted earlier.

Several of the incidents that culminated in criminal proceedings were the result of long-standing antagonism. In most of the trials, the precipitating incident was only the latest and most extreme in a long series of hostile encounters. When José Asunción Portilla accused Natividad and María Mercedes Escalante of hitting and insulting his wife and daughter, he pointed out that this was not the first time his family had been victimized by the defendants.[41] The persecution and abuse of María de los Santos Díaz by María Emilia Carrero and her mother drew official attention only after Carrero's husband tried to shoot de los Santos Díaz.[42] Feuds among women persisted for years and resulted in repeated trials, as the protagonists offended again and again.[43] After serving a twelve-day sentence for assault and battery of Juana Miranda, Micaela Galarretea and Zoila Sorogéstua gleefully informed their victim that their imprisonment "had seemed to last a mere twelve hours—no time at all, in fact, . . . as it had not caused them any discomfort." Two years later Miranda charged them with assault again, revealing that loathing continued unabated.[44]

Such long-term enemies were commonly called *enemigas capitales* or *enemigas implacables* (deadly enemies).[45] The incidents that ensnared the court's attention were therefore rarely isolated events, but the product of long-term, and presumably mounting, tensions.

In some cases, people fought because of long-standing antagonisms between entire families. Thus Emilia Verástegui claimed that María Centurión had called her "a whore, . . . thief and murderess [merely] because [she says] I am the sister of the murderer and assassin Agustín Verástegui."[46] Andrés Mestanza became involved in a major brawl with Simona Toculi's family involving at least ten people because the Toculi family was suing his mother-in-law over some property.[47]

Sometimes individuals were exposed to violence as a result of political turmoil and feuds. Carolina Infante reported that a group of men belonging to the *banda de los colorados* (red gang) attacked her nephew, who sought refuge in her home. As a result, Infante, her mother, and her brother, all of whom denied any allegiance to either of the dominant local factions, suffered injuries.[48]

Even when individuals were not directly involved in feuds and conflict, they could nevertheless become embroiled in them as a result of their connection to more or less distant relations. Nor were they always involved as victims. In Celendín, the disputes between the Silva and Horna families, involving competition over political office and the allotment of irrigation water, simmered for years. When the tension finally culminated in the assault on and death of Juan Silva, his widow charged Lorenzo, Tomás, and Micaela Horna, as well as their mother, Doña María Silva, and two other women (Doña Gregoria Araujo and Pascuala Araujo) with the assault. Witness statements confirmed that the women in question had not been passive onlookers, but had participated actively in the fatal beating.[49] In Cajamarca today, Torre notes that women participate actively in violent conflicts between families that disagree about borders, water sources, canalization, and cattle theft. As happens in intrafamily disputes over inheritance, she traces women's active and occasionally violent involvement to the fear of losing material resources that their families depend on.[50]

More frequently, in the nineteenth century, female conflict seems to have occurred among women only and to have had its origins in issues intimately related to gender roles. The trial dealing with María Jesús Salazar's miscarriage, for instance, involved only women, with the exception of the husband of one of the defendants, who represented his wife in court.[51] The same applied to a number of other confrontations.[52]

In some cases, men were far from enthusiastic about their womenfolk's disposition to quarrel. When María Rosario Tirado beat and publicly offended her husband's young mistress, the girl's father and Tirado's husband agreed to a quiet settlement, ostensibly in the interest of good neighborliness, but perhaps also in order to avoid further embarrassment.[53]

As the set-to between Fidela Vargas and María Vásquez shows, close family ties did not preclude conflict. During the investigation of the fight it emerged that the defendant was Vásquez' niece by marriage.[54] Close kinship also existed in other conflicts between women. Natividad Bardoles, accused of assaulting María Jesús Salazar, said that they were related "*carnal y espiritualmente*" (by blood and spiritually, i.e., related through *compadrazgo*).[55] Felipa Álvarez and her sister Manuela Viscende were heard to insult each other in the street;[56] and sisters Gregoria and Francisca Bustamante ended up in court over an inheritance dispute.[57] In other cases, family relationships were implied, but not outlined clearly. Ana y Cruz Campos' and Tomasa Tirado's oral contests were serious enough to lead to legal action, although Campos' mother shared Tomasa Tirado's surname.[58] María Josefa Calderón and Jacoba Concepción Castillo, who accused each other of assault, were sisters-in-law.[59]

Neighborly relations were no impediment to suspiciousness and quarrels, either. When one of Casimira Rubio's sons died, an old friend and neighbor, Melchora Martos, attended the wake and contributed half a bottle of *resaque* (strong liquor) that she had made. When another one of Rubio's children fell ill shortly after the wake, Martos was accused of having poisoned the girl. Although the court acquitted her, the story demonstrates how erstwhile friends could turn enemies.[60] In his work on plebeian honor and violence in colonial Buenos Aires, Johnson confirms that "even among friends and kinsmen, jests, pranks, and roughhousing could provoke violence."[61]

Given that many of the women who bore each other grudges lived in small communities, or were close relatives, avoiding conflict could become difficult, especially if the wrangling was protracted. Evasion was a common and accepted way of minimizing confrontation, but one that, sooner or later, was destined to fail. Thus Estefania Espinoza explained that she and her sisters had gone to visit their uncle Remigio Puerta, "whom they called on out of family obligation, despite the fact that his *muger* [common-law wife], María Díaz, and his daughter Baltazara Puerta were their *enemigas implacables*."[62] Predictably, the Espinoza sisters bumped into their enemies, and a fight ensued.[63]

In those cases in which the cause of conflict was more immediately visible, women often clashed over men. The example of María Rosario Tirado, who tried to end her husband's relationship with the pubescent Aurora Jara by shaming and beating her in public, was mentioned above.[64] Like Tirado, Cayetana Salazar hoped to get rid of her husband's mistress by assaulting her.[65] Not only formally married wives staked out a claim to exclusive proprietorship: Carmen Ducos berated another woman for daring to invite Ducos' common-law husband for a drink.[66] Nor was female rivalry always based on certain knowledge of infidelity; mere suspicion was often enough to provoke a confrontation. María Jesús Salazar claimed that Natividad Bardoles had attacked her merely because gossipmongers had "persuaded her that I [was] having an affair with her husband."[67] Manuela Correa said that three generations of Burgos women attacked her for no reason other than that "their quarrelsome character [makes María Jesús] jealous of my sister, as she is of almost all women in San Pablo."[68] In another case the relationship had ended years ago. Asunción Medina complained that "the women Zoila y María Peralta [*a. las sacapapas*] have accused me of having an affair with José María Briones, with whom I broke off relations three years ago." The women had persecuted and threatened her for some time before attacking her in her own home, prompting Medina to petition the departmental prefect to warn the aggressors off.[69]

Popular opinion recognized conflict over men as a potent motive for struggles among females. In cases where other motives for conflict remained absent, witnesses speculated that jealousy played a role. As outlined above, several women were falsely accused of poisoning because their jealousy provided them with a plausible motive. When Melchora Azañero, a young woman who had eloped with a man who already had a family, died unexpectedly after a brief illness, his common-law wife, Rosa Culqui, was suspected of getting somebody to poison her.[70] Carmen Ducos was suspected of arson when a barn owned by Isidora Paico (the woman who had presumed to offer Ducos' partner a drink during a fiesta) burned down later in the evening.[71]

In all these instances, the charges proved groundless. However, the suits show how prevalent jealousy and rivalry were as causes of conflict. This pervasiveness continues to the present: the *tablas de Sarhua*, painted panels from the department of Ayacucho from the 1960s depicting Andean practices surrounding marriage and courtship and traditionally given to newlyweds, contain a picture of two women fighting over a man. The wife, already injured and with her baby on her back, is pictured attacking her husband's mistress and trying to cut off her braids.[72] Torre confirms that women continued to take revenge on their rivals by means of physical assault in 1990s rural Cajamarca.[73]

Whereas cuckolded men battered their wives, wives who were cheated on opted to attack their rivals rather than confront their husbands. Research from other regions and periods confirms that rivalry was a typical response to male infidelity, with conflicts often staged with an eye to maximum public impact.[74]

Why did competition over men assume such proportions, and why did women channel their resentment into woman-on-woman aggression? The first question is probably best explained in material terms. In addition to the emotional impact of betrayal and the public humiliation of abandonment, single women, especially those with children, faced poverty. As Deere has described, subsistence for peasants depended on the participation of both male and female partners. On the haciendas, plots were rented to men, so landless tenants could obtain access to land only through a man. Because their labor was valued more highly, men were paid higher wages. Even for those women who owned land, obtaining labor could prove difficult, as they were not seen to be able to reciprocate in kind.[75] Some single mothers were reduced to stealing in order to feed their children;[76] others were forced to send their daughters (e.g., Matea Gallardo) to work as servants.[77]

Faced with such hardship, it is not surprising that women went to great lengths to assert claims on their husbands and to frighten off rivals. As Stern has pointed out, confronting their partners would only exacerbate conflict; by going after rivals, women retained the possibility of a somewhat amicable reunion with their partners.[78] In addition, extreme violence toward potential rivals may well have been an effective means of warning off possible challengers.

Labor migration intensified competition over men. Beginning in the 1860s a growing number of men migrated to the coastal sugar plantations.[79] Although most of the migration was seasonal, many men failed to return. Some became caught up in a never-ending spiral of debt to contractors; others were prevented from returning by illness or death; some chose to remain on the coast. As for those who were free to return, some formed liaisons with other women in the meantime; others lost their sense of attachment to their partner or saw a convenient chance to extricate themselves from a burdensome relationship with heavy economic duties. The frequency of the different responses is impossible to ascertain, but traveling to the coast was a common way of escaping problems at home, including prosecution or impending sentences[80] and, presumably, women.

The resultant shortage of men must have affected the nature of male-female relationships, with informal marriage arrangements being particularly vulnerable. Certainly, by the time the 1876 census was conducted (some years before seasonal labor migration reached its height), the statistical imbalance between the sexes was marked. Although boys tended to outnumber girls in the towns and villages in the province of Cajamarca up to the age of fifteen, the balance between the sexes changed in the fifteen- to twenty-year-old age group. In the district of Cajamarca (including the town of Cajamarca and its surrounding villages), there were 481 boys aged fifteen to twenty compared to 642 girls in the same age group; in the age group twenty to twenty-five, there were 629 young men to 944 women. Only 43 percent of the fifteen- to twenty-year-olds and 40 percent of the twenty- to twenty-five-year-olds were male. The figures for the other districts in the region were comparable, with only 32 percent of fifteen- to twenty-year-olds being male in Chetilla, for example.[81]

These regional factors intensified the situation in Cajamarca, but studies of other areas indicate that female rivalry over men was not unique to Cajamarca. In her study of a village in Morelos, Mexico, Romanucci-Ross observes that women, despite the cultural emphasis on female chastity and fidelity, "make more of a spouse's adultery than do men . . . , but they do not regard it as a basis for separation unless it leads to non-support." Further, she notes that women faced with abandonment usually fight their rivals rather than holding their partners responsible for the breach of faith.[82] In his study of gender in colonial Mexico, also based on evidence from criminal trials, Stern found that female jealousy—rather than male claims on female sexuality—was central in 51.5 percent of jealousy cases. He argues that material considerations were central in female battles over men and claims that the link between sexuality and economic obligation explains the female contestation of male sexual freedom.[83] As these studies confirm, female rivalry over men and hence female conflict was—and is—prevalent to a greater degree than has traditionally been recognized by feminist, or gender-oriented, historians and anthropologists.

Another common cause of conflict between women (and between women and men) was property. Disputes relating to property accounted for thirteen of the twenty-eight trials in which the background to the conflict was provided. In some cases the issue at hand was debt or damage to borrowed items.[84] Isabel Encalada and Natividad Arana exchanged words over Arana's failure to pay rent;[85] similarly, Manuela Soto's attack on María Isabel Araujo followed on the latter's falling in arrears with debt repayments.[86]

Inheritance and border disputes were also frequent points of conflict that resulted in lawsuits and face-to-face fights. Francisca and Gregoria Busta-mante tried to settle their disagreements concerning the division of their father's estate in court—only to be told that the court would not adjudicate between sisters.[87]

Sometimes unsatisfactory legal solutions led to physical challenges: when the justice of the peace adjudicated in favor of Juana Jara over a *chacra* (field) which she had inherited jointly with María Manuela Casas, the latter and her family attacked both Jara and the judge during a visit to the field in question.[88] Manuela Quiroz, who lost a suit over a piece of land, repeat-edly orally abused her opponent, Virginia Barba, resulting in further court proceedings.[89]

As caring for domestic animals was primarily a female task, it was women rather than men who were blamed for damage done by their animals. A num-ber of women quarreled because their crops had been destroyed by other women's animals. Thus Gertrudis Azañero and Leandra Álvarez y Narro—who were closely related—had a vociferous argument in Azañero's cornfield after Álvarez y Narro's pigs wrought havoc in it;[90] a similar argument be-tween Magdalena Díaz and Juana Peralta precipitated an exchange which ultimately led to the former's death.[91] Even when women were not held di-rectly responsible, they became targets of anger: Clara Pita, angered by a foray by Valerio Chávez' pigs into her field, feared to challenge the man him-self and instead insulted his daughter.[92]

Anthropologists have pointed out how women resort to violence, both in inheritance and other property disputes, in order to defend their family's patrimony. Torre states that women employ force against relatives, most fre-quently in inheritance disputes, and against other family groups, typically, in the modern day, in disagreements over borders and water rights. "It is in defense of the rural family's essential . . . resources that we can [most clearly] discern the determination and strength of rural women," she writes.[93] Lapie-dra, researching southern Peru, writes that women are usually the most out-spoken in protesting damage caused by animals in fields and even assume the principal role in defending family property, such as land, in court.[94]

Finally, women entered into conflict with other women in order to pro-tect their children. Those mothers who backed daughters in disputes with rivals have been dealt with above; in addition, mothers who lived as depen-dents or whose children were servants confronted patrons when these dealt harshly with their offspring.[95] Remigia Bermúdes, who interposed herself be-tween her son and Isabel Basauri, is an example.[96] An equally unjust outcome can be seen in the Gallardo case. Poverty had forced Matea Gallardo to send her daughter into service in the home of Jesús del Campo. When del Campo beat the girl and had her locked up, Gallardo interceded on her daughter's behalf. The plea was not well received, however, and ended in a belligerent argument, in the course of which del Campo had Gallardo beaten and subsequently jailed.[97]

Gaining a clear sense of the causes of interfemale conflict is not easy. In some trials, no explanation—apart from vintage hostility—was given.[98] In others, the explanations provided by the opposing parties were multiple, diffuse, and contradictory, as in the case between Jacoba Bermúdez and Francisca Sifuentes. These women charged each other with threats, insults that injured their honor, and physical abuse. According to Sifuentes, who did not elaborate or explain in further detail, Bermúdez was motivated by "jealousy of past matters." Whatever the precise reason for the hatred between these two, it may have been related to the fact that Jacoba Bermúdez was married to Manuel Quiroz, the former common-law husband of Francisca Sifuentes and the father of her daughter. Either from resentment against her rival, or in a desperate attempt to make sense of the loss of her daughter, Sifuentes blamed Bermúdez for murdering her daughter, who died in childbirth. Clearly, these two women were bound together by multiple threads of history, resentment, and former friendship and assistance, as can be guessed from the fact that Bermúdez actually acted as midwife to Sifuentes' daughter.[99] The conflict between Jacoba Bermúdez and Francisca Sifuentes therefore provides an example of how conflict could develop because of rivalry over a man—competition which was tinged with resentment at the economic loss which his breach of faith signified. This resentment was exacerbated in this particular case when Sifuentes sought the explanation for her daughter's death in Bermúdez' alleged evildoing.

Physical violence seems, on the basis of the criminal court records, to have been a frequent result of female conflict: half of the trials involving conflict among women involved the use of violence. In this respect Cajamarca seems to have differed from modern Morelos, Mexico, where, Romanucci-Ross writes, "physical violence is only occasionally involved."[100]

LEGAL ENCOUNTERS

Many of the causes of female conflict remained obscure during the official investigation of the complaint. Eighteen of the trials dealing with incidents of female conflict contained no explanation for the hatred these women bore each other.

Both defendants' and initiators' reticence vis-à-vis officialdom was justified. While judges showed some sympathy for the dead victims of lower-class struggle, little was shown for living participants. Judges only reluctantly accepted charges of *agresiones* among women,[101] and rarely considered it necessary to punish misbehavior by the lower classes: twenty-seven of forty-three trials led to acquittals; in a further six cases the proceedings were never concluded. Only five of the forty-three trials led to sentences, and in two of these both plaintiff and defendant were sent to jail—possibly indicating the judge's exasperation.[102]

The implication that female conflict was irrelevant was made clear to Agueda Sorogéstua when she reported one of numerous scuffles with her longtime enemy Juana Miranda. After concluding that no crime had been committed, the judge threatened the complainant with a hefty fine if she should dare attract his attention again.[103]

In some cases the court's inefficiency can be attributed to corruption. Gregoria and María Jesús Astopilco were acquitted, despite numerous witnesses to their brutal assault on Manuela Mestanza. No doubt their brother, who was the local *teniente gobernador*, encouraged the judge to treat them leniently. In addition, the family's position of power influenced the witnesses' testimony. When questioned, a number of women who were initially named as having watched the fracas denied having witnessed the fight. Alvina Campos, one of the women who had actually helped separate the brawling women, later claimed that she had been asleep in her house and only found Mestanza much later, stained with blood, on the ground. Another deponent claimed to have been too drunk to recall anything.[104]

In another case, the court's bias was even more blatant. When Máxima, Matilde, Estefania, and Baltazara Espinoza fell upon Bernardina Sáenz and her baby daughter, injuring the infant badly enough that she died the next day, all witnesses who could have helped Sáenz' case were studiously ignored by the judge. According to the bereaved mother, her assailants even went as far as to unearth the baby's corpse some weeks after the event, smashing its head in order to further destroy the evidence. Her claims were supported in a public letter written to the authorities by several of the village's citizens. Predictably, however, the charges against the assailants were dropped, after the doctors who were to conduct an autopsy stated that too much time had elapsed and that the body was rotting, leaving only "a shapeless mass."[105] In other cases, the influential position of powerful enemies made it difficult to file a suit against them; there is at least one example of several judges refusing to accept a complaint on the grounds that they were related to the defendant's husband.[106]

Even where corruption did not play an obvious role, legal proceedings moved slowly, as noted earlier, so that pursuing a denunciation could become a time-consuming and costly matter. A number of trials were therefore never concluded: charges were dropped or proceedings were simply discontinued, either because the litigants lost interest or the courts moved too slowly.[107] Social class undoubtedly played a role in determining the court's willingness to accept and process charges: Remigia Bermúdes stated that not a single judge in the town of Cajamarca would accept her case, because of her poverty.[108]

The inefficiency of the courts was further accentuated—and excused—by the low level of medical knowledge. Autopsies and examinations of wounds often produced inaccurate results. In cases such as that of Ricardina Sáenz (the infant hurt in the set-to between her mother and the Espinoza sisters) the inconclusiveness of the initial medical examination of a corpse necessitated exhumation. Conflicting medical opinions were common. When María Jesús Salazar was reported to have miscarried following a hand-to-hand clash with two other women, the professionally qualified midwife confirmed that the miscarriage was the result of a blow. Andrea Glebara, a local woman who had attended Salazar during her miscarriage, disagreed; according to her, Salazar had "taken something in order to abort the infant." In this case, the traditional midwife's opinion was supported by Salazar's admission that she had gone to the fair of San Antonio specifically to obtain something to induce an abortion.[109]

In addition to the dubious techniques used by medical experts, in some cases considerable time was allowed to elapse between the assault and the medical examination. Following an assault in their own home during the night, José Dolores Olivares and his wife, Paula Saucedo, suffered several injuries and Saucedo miscarried—almost dying in the process. Twenty days were allowed to pass before they were examined. Not surprisingly, the wounds had healed, and the doctor found no trace of them. The foetus, which had been placed in a jar of alcohol for the purposes of conservation, had (far from being preserved) disintegrated completely. The doctor found himself unable to confirm that a miscarriage had taken place. "The pains which Saucedo claims to have felt are subjective symptoms, whose existence cannot be proven," he argued, despite the fact that the woman in question was a mother of several children and well acquainted with the symptoms of labor.[110] Contemporary medical science was therefore imprecise, to say the least, and often a poor basis for conducting investigations into the seriousness of injuries or cause of death. It could also serve as a convenient excuse for not pursuing charges of assault.

Women who engaged in public brawling broke with the establishment's gender norms and automatically disqualified themselves from claims to respectability—thus losing any right to legal redress. Even Manuela Villanueva, a literate woman married to a landowner, found that she was not treated with the lenience usually accorded women of her social class following a noisy altercation with two market women. Her opponents were sentenced to twenty-eight months in jail each, and she and her daughter were sentenced to twenty months. While some consideration had been given to her social status, the message was clear: by involving herself and her daughter in a noisy public argument she had placed them on the same level as the market women they despised.[111]

Although the legal apparatus was at best an imperfect means of obtaining redress for women who had suffered assault at the hands of other women, individuals tried to involve the authorities in their personal vendettas and inflict damage on their adversaries through legal action. There are several cases in which the charges that were leveled against women were trumped up. In addition to employing slander, public insults, and violence, women engaged in legal action—not in order to obtain vindication, but as a further weapon in their struggle against their enemies. María Jesús Salazar's supposed miscarriage is an example. Her sister Manuela, well aware that Salazar's quarrel with Natividad Bardoles could not have caused the miscarriage, nevertheless hastened to the authorities and tried to lay the blame on Bardoles.

Although obtaining a conviction was extremely difficult—in part because responsibility for the confrontation was usually evenly divided—legal action brought its own rewards. Discomfiting one's antagonist, possibly including a brief spell in prison, could be sufficiently galling to the defendant. Thus Isabel Encalada complained that Natividad Arana had got "the police to put us in jail, causing a great stir, without regarding our sex and the consideration which my daughter's virtue deserves."[112]

ALLIANCES AND NETWORKS

So far I have focused on the various dimensions of female conflict: the forms which struggle among women took; some of the causes of interfemale tensions; and the responses women met in court when they brought their complaints into the formal legal arena. The trials that deal with women's conflicts also reveal other aspects of social relations among women, however, namely, solidarity and cooperation between the sexes and among women. Examples range from assistance in physical fights to more everyday instances of joint action, such as gifts of food from a cook to a hungry servant girl. I look first at examples of assistance and solidarity in moments of crisis.

Many, but far from all, of these examples will be drawn from the same trials dealing with female conflict to which I have already referred. After looking at instances of support directly connected to female and female-male conflict, I look at other examples of—largely, but not exclusively—female support networks.

As we have seen, women frequently allied themselves with other women—and occasionally with men—when confronting opponents in fights. In most cases such allies were closely related. As we saw earlier, both Manuela Mestanza and Bernardina Sáenz had to contend with sisters.[113] When Sebastián Ortega assaulted his former girlfriend, Narcisa Mendoza, he had to deal not only with her, but also with her mother, Lorenza.[114] Manuela Correa claimed that she and her sister were attacked by no fewer than three generations of Burgos women: allegedly, María Jesús Burgos was assisted by both her daughter and her mother.[115]

Sisters and mothers or daughters were therefore the most likely allies in violent encounters with enemies. In some cases relationships were more tenuous: the woman who tried to extricate Bernardina Sáenz' baby daughter from the fight in which Sáenz became engaged was Bernardina's mother's stepdaughter (i.e., Bernardina's stepsister).[116]

Male relatives also sided with their mothers and sisters against their enemies and tried to defend them from violent abuse when they were present.[117] But as many of the violent incidents of which women were a part were not premeditated but the result of sudden eruptions of animosity, their most likely allies were those who shared their tasks and happened to be present—in other words, other women.[118]

If brothers, fathers, uncles, and brothers-in-law were rarely present when their female relatives were at physical risk, they did bring offenses against family members to the attention of the courts. Juan Álvarez, for instance, was absent from home when his sister Felipa Álvarez was assaulted by several women from the neighborhood; unable to defend her physically and believing the blows to have caused her miscarriage, he pressed charges against the alleged culprits.[119]

Because married women and minors were placed under male tutelage and most women were illiterate, we might expect most disputes with female victims to be reported by men; in fact, most crimes committed against women were reported by the victims themselves. Of forty-three trials dealing with physical or oral conflict between females, twenty (47 percent) were initiated at the behest of the victims themselves. Four trials were the result of official investigations. Twenty of the trials (44 percent) were pursued following complaints by relatives: fifteen of these (79 percent) were male and five (26 percent) female. When relatives represented women before the authorities, the relatives were usually male; in most other cases, however, women represented themselves.

In the context of potentially violent confrontation, older relatives frequently expressed their commitment to a daughter or niece by defusing a developing situation. Thus Narcisa Tejada claimed that her mother had come and taken her home "in order to avoid problems even though . . . Felipa continued offending me."[120] In much the same way, Andrea Chávez led her niece Natividad Bardoles away from an argument with María Jesús Salazar.[121]

Intervention in order to calm volatile encounters was not a role reserved exclusively for women: Cecilio Espinoza tried to recall his daughters from their fight with Bernardina Sáenz, albeit with little success.[122] The case of Julián Plasencia Marín, who was called to desist by his uncle while beating up his common-law wife, shows that, like women, violent men could be curbed by the authority of elders.[123] As María Asunción Portal's comment shows, respect for age was crucial in such situations: she explained how, when Don Dionisio Terán told her not to let Andrés Espinoza provoke her to physical aggression, she obeyed him, out of respect for Terán's seniority.[124] By the authority they commanded, older relatives may well have provided angry younger women with something of an alibi for leaving an explosive social situation without losing too much face.

In situations in which individuals were reluctant to engage in open conflict, peers might fulfill the same function. Stern notes how, in colonial Mexico, men tended to "enter . . . the arena of informal masculine sociability in the company of a friend or two. If joustings of manhood began to spin out of control, a man relied on his companions to help him escape the trap. They might deflect the verbal sparring and innuendo in another direction."[125]

Another way in which women assisted each other in moments of conflict was by looking after their allies' children, thus protecting the child from the blows of opponents and freeing the mother to retaliate.[126]

Assistance and solidarity were not restricted to moments of conflict. Social visits; moral support; loans of domestic or agricultural instruments, money, food, or even a place to stay; help in looking after children or preparing food (especially for fiestas) were among the ways in which women assisted their friends and neighbors. One woman described her relationship with her neighbor in the following terms: "We have had a good friendship as we are neighbors, and have done each other different favors."[127] A number of the acrimonious disputes in court began as amicable exchanges of favors. The dispute between Natividad Arana and Isabel Encalada followed a period in which the former and her husband resided in Isabel Encalada's home, shared domestic tasks—including the feeding of the three pigs they later quarreled about.[128] Neighborliness and friendship also implied support in difficult moments: Melchora Azañero explained how she attended a wake at the house of Casimira Rubio, "as a little son of hers had died, and by way of a present I brought along half a bottle of liquor which I make."[129] In another case, a woman told the court how she had provided medication for the malnourished and seriously ill servant girl of a woman who resided on the same hacienda; when her mistress failed to provide her with treatment, the girl turned to neighbors.[130]

Such concrete acts of friendship and solidarity were recorded in part because they were practical and relevant to the events described by witnesses. Female friendship for its own sake was not viewed as something positive. Miller, who has interviewed working-class women from Lima who were young in the early decades of the twentieth century, observes that young women were taught to avoid friendship with each other because of the danger this might pose to their reputation.[131] Streicker notes much the same for contemporary Cartagena, Colombia: women who visit each other in their homes or—worse—gossip in the street are frowned upon. Women therefore refrain from socializing with each other and mask their social encounters as shopping.[132]

While these restrictions presumably did not inform the lives of lower-class women in nineteenth-century Cajamarca (who manifested their lack of concern for respectable norms by public brawling), it is possible that friendship among women was closely linked to chores to avoid gossip and for the simple reason that these women had little leisure time in which to socialize. Sharing labor, socializing during work, and assisting each other in moments of illness or grief were socially acceptable acts as well as practical ways of meeting.

The commitment to friends and relatives was evident in the care of the sick and injured, as is particularly clear in those trials that deal with miscarriages. When María Jesús Salazar sought to hide from her father and stepmother her pregnancy and the abortion she provoked by ingesting herbs, she depended on her sister Manuela. Sensing that labor had begun some days after taking an herbal remedy in order to provoke an abortion, Salazar went to the stream, ostensibly to wash maize. Her sister covered for her. While Salazar rested in the grass as best she could, her sister did the work. For the final stages of her labor Salazar went to the house of Andrea Glebara, a local woman and experienced midwife, who assisted her, and where she remained for several days.[133] Another woman who availed herself of the services of a midwife widely recognized for her skills was Gertrudis Azañero.

After being knocked down by a bull she "suffered for a week" before going to see Doña Joaquina Díaz, whom she begged to cure her.[134] Trial records concerning births, miscarriages, and illness illustrate both the concern of close family members and the existence of a wider network that provided access to individuals with some medical expertise. Mannarelli, writing about colonial Lima, confirms the importance of women's networks and the role played in these by midwives in regard to matters of birth and reproductive health.[135]

Although the first part of this chapter, with its focus on tension and discord, may have presented an image of conflictual relations among women, this is only part of the picture. The very cases that illustrate tension between women also contain examples of female solidarity and commitment. As I have shown, allies who were willing to risk life and limb and to take on the burden of reporting abuse to the authorities were primarily relatives. Whereas women were most likely to be present, and hence to assist female relatives in physical confrontations, provide moral support, and care for the sick and injured, male relatives—where such existed—usually represented daughters, sisters, and wives in dealings with the authorities. In most cases a wider network of friends and acquaintances in the community interlinked with this primary ring of allies. Examples range from attempts to find homes for orphaned children to passing on messages about where the best fruit could be bought. My aim is not to list specific types of cooperation, but to outline how the networks of mutual assistance functioned and how a shared set of values among lower-class women can be detected.

The story of Manuela Chávez describes how the concern of close relatives interacted with that of a larger social circle in caring for an individual, albeit not always to that individual's satisfaction. Chávez' mother, Estefania Chávez, died in childbirth, leaving the girl an orphan. No father or paternal relations showed any concern for the baby, so her maternal uncles and aunt ensured that she was christened, given godparents, and placed in the care of a wet nurse. Tadea Casas, the half-sister of Manuela Chávez' maternal uncle, explained that, "having just lost an infant, I was ready [*espedita*] to nurse [another one]." It is possible that she was paid; however, no such payment is mentioned, and she was forced to return the girl to her godmother when she reached the age of two, as Casas was too poor to keep her. If she was paid, the sum was probably symbolic, and certainly not enough for the girl's upkeep. Francisca García, the godmother, promised to "educate and love her a lot," and took Chávez into her home. So far the story illustrates how a network of relatives, friends, and acquaintances provided for an orphaned child, but the story also reflects the deficiencies of such loose networks.[136] As several witnesses later told the court, Lorenza Cabrera—García's daughter, who got the girl after García's death—was known to beat the girl regularly and cruelly. Although these facts were well known and Chávez often sought refuge with her former foster mother, Tadea Casas, nothing was—or could—be done to protect the girl from ill treatment. When she reached the age of eleven, she begged her uncle and her former foster mother to arrange for her escape from Cabrera and to help her find a situation in a distant town. Chávez' story made its way into the records of criminal trials when this plan was implemented. With the assistance of a well-to-do military man temporarily stationed in Cajamarca, she was successfully sent to Lima—much to the outrage of Cabrera, who considered the girl's services her due after having kept her for nine years, and accused the captain, Tadea Casas, and Chávez' uncle of kidnapping the girl.[137]

This account illustrates how a variety of solutions—none of them wholly satisfactory—were employed in order to provide for a destitute orphan. The first option in this case, placing Manuela Chávez with her wet nurse and foster mother, Tadea Casas, probably also alleviated the latter's grief at losing her own child.[138] The strength of her commitment to the girl—compelling her to commit a criminal act in an attempt to secure a better future for Chávez—is testament to the strength of her attachment. Casas' inability to keep Chávez in her own home also testifies to the poverty of unattached women, single mothers in particular, and the emotional dilemmas poverty-stricken women experienced.

If Chávez' first foster home demonstrates the potential for kindness in such undertakings, her second foster home reveals the (often unequal) reciprocity of such apparently charitable arrangements. Chávez was expected to provide labor and endure ill treatment in return for her upkeep. Her example therefore also points to the vulnerability of female dependents to abuse at the hands of patrons, as well as the social acceptance of child abuse. Lorenza Cabrera's assumption that she had a claim on Chávez' labor in return for having kept her for a number of years also shows that not all fostering of orphans was based on charity or affection: Cabrera expected her investment in the girl to pay off now that she had attained an age when she could be useful. At the same time that Chávez' local community was suffused with values of solidary action and cooperation, poverty placed her in a position in which she was exploited and abused.

Chávez' uncle and Tadea Casas were bound to the girl through close ties of blood and affection; however, it did not always take such close ties for women to show solidarity with girls in similar situations. Jacoba Sánchez, a cook working in the house of a well-off market woman, Juana Cabanillas, took in a servant girl from a nearby household who complained of abuse at the hands of her employer. Sánchez explained that she had known the girl, Bernabé Cabrera, from when Sánchez had worked as a cook in the same household from which the girl now wished to escape. Combined with the bond of shared origin—both women were from Celendín—this proved sufficient to persuade Sánchez to assist Cabrera. She hid her alternately in the house's attic and the kitchen, supplied her with food, and tried to find somebody who could take the girl to Celendín, where she thought she would be safe from her former employers. Sánchez' employer, Juana Cabanillas, did not know about her scheme, but Cabanillas' daughters did. They, the cook, and Cabrera were all busy kneading bread dough when Cabrera's employer burst in with several soldiers in order to reclaim her. Cabanillas had earlier been arrested on suspicion of complicity in Cabrera's escape. When she returned home in the company of the soldiers who were looking for the girl, she was livid at having been implicated in the plot and swore to dismiss her cook. A passerby explained that he had listened in on the argument, "believing some friend of mine might be involved in a fight." He heard both Cabanillas' threat and how she relented when her "little grandchildren cried and would not let go of the cook."[139]

If the first example, of the so-called kidnapping of Manuela Chávez, reveals the concern of relatives for an orphaned niece and the ties of affection which could grow out of nursing and fostering a child—or not—the story of Jacoba Sánchez tells us that on other occasions a less intimate acquaintance could lead to solidary action. Sánchez took in a young paisana and former colleague out of pity, risking—like Tadea Casas—a jail sentence, but also unemployment. Finally, the account provided by the two witnesses to the argument between Juana Cabanillas and her cook demonstrates their readiness to inform themselves of gossip and be of assistance to friends who might be in trouble.

Although women were most likely to assist people to whom they had close ties, or at least whom they knew fairly well, occasionally women intervened on behalf of relative strangers. There are numerous examples of men and women assisting their neighbors or mere acquaintances who were in distress.[140] However, bystanders, too, acted. Viviana Villavicencio was one of them. She described how, seeing that a group of women had collected to watch a fight, she went to see what was happening. She found two women begging Gregoria and María Jesús Astopilco to desist from kicking and pounding their victim, Manuela Mestanza, and a man—known to her by name—trying to restrain María Jesús Astopilco. After taking in the situation,

Villavicencio and another woman, Alvina Campos, set about separating the women and berated the onlookers (apparently all women) for "watching the brawl without separating the brawlers." The example demonstrates the willingness of women and men to intervene in a fight and to protect an acquaintance from further harm, and the reluctance of the majority of onlookers to become involved.[141]

María Isabel Ordóñez' former partner slashed her in the leg and cut up her face with a knife. In another example of relative strangers stepping into a dangerous situation to assist a victim, "several women—among them an elderly woman known as *la valerosa* [the brave one] . . . approached her and took her to Telemaco Battistini," a doctor.[142] The willingness of some women to separate brawling enemies and to assist victims was, in other words, not restricted to close family members or friends. A certain code of behavior existed, a code which induced some women—and men—to intervene in potentially dangerous situations in order to assist victims of violence. As the reluctance of most of the onlookers of the Mestanza-Astopilco conflict indicates, adherence to the code was not universal, but depended on individual women's evaluation of the circumstances, on their strength, and on their command of allies in the vicinity. It seems more than likely that the passivity of onlookers to the Mestanza-Astopilco argument was motivated not only by fear of immediate physical harm, but also by fear of crossing the Astopilco family. Helping their victim would inevitably be construed as an act of enmity by Gregoria and María Jesús, and might precipitate their hostility. Onlookers, in other words, reacted to contradictory logic: the desire to assist victims of violence, on the one hand, and fear of becoming involved in a long-term enmity with the victim's foe, on the other. In this case, onlookers' fear was compounded by the fact that the Astopilco family wielded considerable power and influence.

On some occasions the adherence to a code of fairness prevailed over tension and overt conflict. When Felipa Álvarez' brother reported two women with whom she had quarreled the previous day for causing her to miscarry, she saw that the charges were dropped. Despite the tension in her relationship with her neighbors, Felipa had no desire to see them taken to court over something of which she believed them innocent.[143] In much the same way Gertrudis Azañero, who initially blamed Leandra Álvarez y Narro for her miscarriage, gradually realized that an encounter with a bull some weeks previous to the oral quarrel with Álvarez y Narro was the more likely cause. Following the first shock of grief, she was able to reconsider the situation and did her best—through her own statements—to free Álvarez y Narro from further suspicion.[144]

The intervention of mere acquaintances in fights in order to avert fatal consequences, as well as the example of Felipa Álvarez' retraction of her initial statement to her brother, hint at a common code of fairness and solidarity which formed a basis for social relations among the lower classes. This code was not sufficient to motivate all members of the local communities we are looking at to do what was considered the right thing, and it certainly failed to prevent the violent escalations of feminine conflict.

Certain routines, meeting places, and rituals recur in the accounts of female relations. Most sites where females met were linked to their daily chores. Many encounters—both amicable and conflictual—centered on the *pileta*, where women collected to fetch water and wash clothes.[145] The *piletas* were meeting places, where women who came to fetch water chatted, exchanged gossip, confided in—and sometimes confronted each other. The buildup to the controversy between Natividad Bardoles and María Jesús Salazar illustrates this perfectly. Having met at the *pileta*, Simona Paredes told her friend Bardoles how her lover had beaten her during the night "for jealous reasons." Her confidences were interrupted when Salazar appeared and started to exchange insults with Bardoles. Andrea Chávez, Bardoles' aunt, discovered the incipient conflict when she came to fetch water and led her niece away.

In much the same way, the trial involving Felipa Álvarez and Narcisa Tejada revolved around the local water fountain. According to Álvarez' brother, she was "washing some baby clothes" at the channel alongside the road when Tejada fell upon her. Tejada's version differs somewhat, but confirms the centrality of water sources: "When I went to fetch water at the town's *pileta* I was surprised by Felipa, who started to insult me." According to Tejada she did not return Álvarez' blows "because [her] hands were occupied [with carrying buckets]."[146]

Other frequent meeting points—which could quickly be transformed into conflict zones—were the fields. I have described how numerous fights between women took place following arguments over damage done by animals, most commonly, pigs. These oral skirmishes took place in the fields themselves, which could be both a private and a public arena, depending on the timing. The fields, and the channels providing them with water, were also arenas for shared work and conversation. The argument between Ana Quiroz and Manuel María Cabrera illustrates this. Quiroz sued Cabrera after he insulted her in the fields between the town of Cajamarca and the nearby village of Baños. She claimed that the insult was public, as all the people engaged in repairing the channel heard him. He stated that the offenses could not be labeled "public," as they had taken place in a field and had only three witnesses.[147] Thus fields could be considered both isolated and public, depending on the timing and location as much as the interpretation of the individuals involved in an incident.

Like the *pileta*, where women met to gossip, the marketplace was an urban rather than a rural meeting place. As several historians have pointed out, going to the market could provide a welcome break from the isolation experienced by women tied to the home by domestic tasks,[148] especially for servants.[149] The marketplace was clearly a site for the propagation of gossip. When Hermegilda Villavicencio accused Juliana Vargas and her daughters of purposely insulting her in a public manner in order to spread gossip, she complained that "all the market women who were in the main square at this hour and on this day" heard them.[150]

Market women were clearly held in low regard by the educated classes, as Luis Gamarra's contemptuous comment concerning Manuela Abanto implied: "Abanto and her daughter Carmen are beer makers and market women who have little respect for people."[151] His perception was accurate: the conflict between a market woman, Manuela Alcántara, and a municipal officer, Aurelio Barrena, illustrates how market women obeyed their own code of social conduct—a code which clashed dramatically with that laid down by the upper classes. When Barrena approached Alcántara and charged her one centavo for the right to sell in the marketplace, she refused to pay. She pointed out that all she had for sale was two centavos' worth of potatoes. When he insisted, she replied, "Eat it, then, wretch" [*Comelo ambriento*]. According to his uncle she also threw stones at him. The response to her challenge to the officer's authority was violent: she was hit and kicked with *vofetones y puntapies* (slaps in the face and kicks) and beaten with a stick by the two men. According to the doctor who examined her for the court, she would be incapable of work for one month due to her injuries. Unusually, in this case, she managed to get her own back, however: after some vacillation, the judge sentenced Barrena to sixty days in jail.[152] The outcome of this trial is an indication of the potential resourcefulness of market women such as Manuela Alcántara, who, although poor, was well versed in dealing with officials and probably—in this case—possessed contacts that swayed the judgment her way. Her initial refusal to pay the sum demanded by the municipal authorities and her contemptuous comment when she finally handed over the money also indicate a self-assurance that grated on her social betters.[153] The judge was certainly perplexed by the fact that neither Alcántara nor any of her colleagues knew the name of the municipal tax collector. Their ignorance revealed something about the relationship between the market women and the municipal official which accorded poorly with the women's view of their position: "Strange indeed that the victim does not know the name of the man who wounded her, as all the market people should know the name of the tax collectors, as even the least of the soldiers knows the name of his boss."

We can only speculate about where Alcántara's self-confidence came from, but it seems likely that some of it was developed as a result of her experience as a market woman, her exposure to the public arena of the marketplace, and her daily work of selling goods. Likewise, it seems probable that her sense of security was enhanced by the presence of other women of her class and profession, whom she might expect to assist her in case of conflict.[154] James Scott, in discussing the development of "hidden transcripts," points out that the existence of social sites where the offstage transcript can grow is crucial for its development: "The hidden transcript exists only to the extent that it is practiced, articulated, enacted, and disseminated within these offstage social sites."[155] Although the concepts of public and hidden transcripts cannot be simply transferred from class to gender relations, the importance of sites where women could socialize, develop solidary and cooperation, and—for that matter—fight, should be noted.

CONCLUSION

As my analysis of female tension and confrontation, their nature and causes, shows, conflict among women was common and could assume dramatic proportions. The extreme nature of the physical—and oral—violence that was used is a testament both to the prevalence of violence in Cajamarca's lower-class society and to the strength of interfemale tensions. Moreover, it demonstrates the complete disregard in which lower-class women held official gender norms. While women were ostensibly categorized according to their sexual virtue and decorum, lower-class women in practice expressed little concern for such evaluations. For them other considerations were paramount. These included such fundamental issues as economic survival for themselves and their children, and—hence—defense of their material property and male partners. As Stern points out, "for poor women, keeping up such appearances [of respectability] posed added dangers: tolerance of male negligence and sexual improprieties implied the added risk of destitution."[156] Given these alternatives, women did not shy from confronting rivals, or from arguing vociferously and coming to blows over material goods.

No doubt concern for their and their family's material welfare was not the only factor motivating women to defend a claim to a lover or husband. Emotional attachment and the fear of public humiliation as a result of abandonment should not be disregarded. Even when women's aggression toward alleged rivals was premature—as it seems to have been in a number of cases —it nevertheless served to stake a claim to sole "ownership" of their partner and served to warn off other women from even trying to seduce their partner. In practice, therefore, a reputation for being aggressively jealous and a ruthless fighter was therefore likely to serve lower-class women better than a reputation for decorum.

Although Stern's findings agree with mine in that we both point to the frequency of female competition for and aggression with regard to men, I differ with his conclusion that "this larger contestation belies the simple notions of female acceptance of a double sexual standard."[157] Although women clearly expressed their anger at male infidelity by attacking rivals, this need not imply that they fundamentally contested men's culturally accepted "right" to philander. Instead, they attacked other women's attempts to occupy their own sexual "territory." I do not think that "male sexual rights and freedoms" were necessarily rendered "contingent rather than innate." Rather, the "right" of other women to seduce someone else's partner was thus contested; the prospect of purloining another woman's partner was made substantially less attractive once this became tantamount to losing one or several teeth, receiving a black eye, or losing several handfuls of hair. In the material I examined, women's motives were often only hinted at, and rarely described explicitly. Thus, the men who were at the center of the conflict remained conspicuously absent from the trial.

Although jealousy was a frequent cause of conflict among women, it was not the only one. Defense of property and retribution for damaged property were also recurring themes in female struggle. The other—although, it would seem, less frequent—cause of dispute among women was children. This could express itself in a number of ways, but the most frequently documented context for maternal protectiveness was situations in which children, especially daughters, had been sent into domestic service. In other words, most of the concrete causes for female aggression I have been able to uncover are directly related to poverty and the dilemmas women faced as a result of it. As far as I have been able to make out women fought for what was most precious to them—their partners and their children—and in defense of the material resources that enabled them to maintain themselves and their families. This existential aspect—the threat of destitution—may go some way toward explaining the extreme nature of the resentment women felt toward each other.

As the instances of patron-client and mistress-servant abuse show, violent behavior was not merely the product of poverty or a feature of female relations among equals. Unlike the causes of violence outlined above, mistreatment of dependents should be seen as a result of a context, namely, that of everyday proximity and familiarity and extreme social inequality. In such a context the cause of the violent act is not necessarily found in the relationship between participants; violence often might have been the result of frustration vented on social subordinates. It is intriguing that I have found only incidents of violent female employers and none of abusive male patrons. This may be related to the intimate relationship between female servants and employers and the amount of time spent together; on the other hand, it may also be a reflection of the greater cultural legitimacy of male chastisement.

For a variety of reasons it is often difficult to understand precisely the causes of the tension among women. For one thing, the courts were not overly interested in the details of such incidents, and the participants— although desirous of using the legal system to settle their personal vendettas—did not volunteer much accurate information. In addition, female conflict, much like the family and political feuds between the different client groups that pervaded the region, was in many ways self-perpetuating. Injuries from past confrontations were recalled and formed the basis for further conflict. In this way resentment and hatred grew, and—although contained much of the time—were volatile enough to produce occasional eruptions of violence. In cases of long-term female hostility, the initial cause might well be buried under a growing mound of mutual offenses.

Despite their—often confusing—complexity and the limited interest of the court in the details of hostile encounters among females, the trials nevertheless tell us much about the gendered tensions among women. Gender or women's history often focuses on the relationship between the sexes; relationships among women may be equally relevant for understanding the nature of women's lives and the prevailing gender system.

Despite potential tensions—which could invert friendship and turn it into conflict—a study of lower-class women's lives and their conflicts also reveals the ways in which women built up alliances. The strongest and most natural bonds were those within the family context—both immediate and extended—particularly with female relatives. Family was, however, a flexible concept and could include common-law partners or even the families of the common-law partners of close relations. On other occasions, the neighborhood, and the mutual assistance and sharing of work which proximity favored, could be an equally fertile ground for the development of friendship. The focal sites for casual—and potentially threatening—encounters included the water fountain, particularly in the towns and villages, communal work on the channels in the fields, or even work in the fields themselves, could also provide opportunity for socializing.

In addition to a network of family members and close friends who were likely to succor each other in moments of distress, a certain ethos of mutual assistance and protection existed among lower-class women. This occasionally compelled mere acquaintances to act on behalf of women who were being victimized by other women or by men, risking both involvement in the ongoing brawl—and hence severe injury—and the long-term resentment of the principal aggressor. Because of the dangers involved in intervention in scuffles between other women, far from all women adhered to this moral code, but preferred instead to remain onlookers. Nevertheless, it seems that certain ideas of "sisterhood" or mutual solidarity existed.

CHAPTER 8

Conclusion

DEALING WITH THE SOURCES

The trial transcripts I used as sources for this study contain a wealth of stories and record moments of both high tension and everyday banality. They offer insights into how gender worked in provincial towns and hamlets in northern Peru in the nineteenth century. Honor mattered to both the poor and the rich. People lived according to multiple, overlapping, and, above all, potentially conflicting definitions of honor. Despite the importance of honor, many couples defied the norms, opting for consensual unions rather than formal marriage. In contradiction of official norms, spouses involved in-laws in their battles, usually—but not always—to the advantage of the wife. Young women willingly engaged in premarital sex, risking their and their family's honor. The families, in turn, exploited rhetorical and legal means to defend young women's reputations. Finally, understandings of gender shaped not only relations between the sexes, but also among women. Relations among men influenced relations among women; similarly, the degree of support women gave each other positioned them differently vis-à-vis men.

As well as documenting the past, this book tests the potential and limitations of judicial sources. As sources, criminal trials are fraught with challenge. Events outside the courtroom—of particular importance in slander trials, where reputation was, ultimately, arbitrated outside of the legal arena —remain undocumented. The truth of slanderous rumors is difficult to ascertain over a hundred years later; the social sphere to which litigants pertained is difficult to pinpoint; the background for quarrels remains uncertain. Only part of the complicated process of negotiating reputation can thus be traced.

Homicide and assault trials differ from honor trials. Charges were initiated by the public prosecutor rather than the plaintiff and were aimed at securing retribution as opposed to reestablishing reputation. Overall, there is less reason to question plaintiffs' motivation. However, charges of assault, too, abound with conundrums. Apart from the obvious problem of faulty documentation and the conflicting evidence presented by victim, witnesses, and defendant, the researcher's inevitable focus on conflict and violence can easily distort perceptions of marital relations and relations among women. Needless to say, not all wives were battered to within an inch of their lives or, indeed, murdered; nor did all relations among women consist of aggressive and volatile encounters. As in the honor trials, litigants sought to dramatize their experiences and tried to emulate elite views on appropriate behavior, which tends to obscure lower-class gender practice. The stories often go into considerable detail and in many cases give the protagonists, most of whom were peasants, laborers, petty merchants, market women, domestic servants, and artisans, a direct voice. However, the sample remains small and cannot be assumed to be wholly representative, thus making it difficult to generalize.

At the same time as telling stories, then, these documents pose new questions and fail to answer others. While a few must remain unanswered for the moment, some of these questions may serve as inspiration for further research. Their passionate rhetoric notwithstanding, how much and how seriously did plebeian women and men covet honor as defined by the elite? Was legal action primarily about negotiating for acceptance by their social betters or by their peers? What differentiated all those cases of slander that did not result in legal proceedings from those that did? What was the long-term impact on reputation of slander and rape trials?

What other sources can we access in order to glean even more of everyday interaction between official and lower-class discourses of honor and of gender? Regarding marital conflict, although we know that mothers-in-law and siblings were well informed of daughters' and sisters' marital experiences and opted to interfere in cases of serious abuse, we do not know how fathers responded to such violence. Were women perhaps less likely to be abused if they had a father and brothers in the vicinity? What other factors favored or discouraged abuse, and how did plebeian men discuss violence among themselves, as opposed to how they justified their actions to the court? How did both wives and husbands define their spousal and parental duties?[1]

Apart from intervening in cases of intense violence, how else did family members respond to conjugal tension? Where no clear answer can be identified, I have chosen to include the legal process and the rationales presented by litigants in my analysis rather than to venture any guesses. By taking into account the ways in which plaintiffs and defendants adapted to the judge's values and looking for evidence hinting at litigants' norms in their acts and statements, a picture of the contradictions in gender norms can be pieced together.

As well as addressing the challenges posed by the sources, this approach offers a partial resolution of the dilemma formulated by Klubock. In his overview of the historiography of women in Chile he notes the tension between the study of gender politics and the everyday history of subaltern women. He argues that understanding the various discourses that underlie attempts at social discipline is pivotal to understanding the context in which lower-class women and men lived their lives. "The history of women of the *bajo pueblo* [common people] is defined by the process of state formation and by the disciplinary apparatuses that constitute both women and men as subjects," he notes.[2] At the same time, he points out, those studies which have analyzed legislative evolution, feminist movements, the politics of social reform, and the ideologies of labor movements in Latin America have tended to overlook how subaltern women and men *lived* gender relations every day. In particular, the ability of state, church, and other institutions to regulate popular gender practices and plebeian responses to attempts at reform require further exploration. By taking judicial documents as my point of departure, I have sought to identify everyday gender practice through the medium of a regulatory apparatus, thus forcing myself continually to compare official attempts to structure gender with evidence of subaltern practice. In this way, the interplay between official efforts to police lower-class social practice and everyday practice remain at the heart of my analysis. I focus, in the words of Trazegnies, on the very "battlefield where different social interests confronted each other." While the national elite defined the laws, Trazegnies argues, the legal process itself opened up to continued argument about the exact interpretation of the law.[3] By looking at how plebeians used the legal apparatus, some of their social practice of gender can be uncovered, as can the encounter between official and plebeian norms.

Klubock further suggests that reliance on judicial records in the study of subaltern history (combined with the use of patriarchy as a category of historical analysis) contributes to an overemphasis on men's and women's contests over social power. This reliance can "flatten out the experience of sexuality and gender, reducing them to contests over social power and to predetermined conflicts between men and women."[4] While legal records are indeed imperfect sources for a conclusive study of how sexuality and labor shaped patriarchy (and also one of the richest sources available), they document much more than conflict. Behind the trials' principal stories a wealth of subplots and details are recorded. Thus the trial dealing with the supposed rape of Asencia León and the very real and repeated rape of Zoila Alcántara also tell of the girls' fear of their parents, none of whom were told about their daughters' sexual experiences. The story of Clemencia Ruiz' seduction, on the other hand, tells of a mother and daughter sharing secrets concerning the latter's love life. The incident in which Isabel Basauri beat her former servant, Remigia Bermúdes, senseless details years of dependency on the part of the illegitimate mother and informal dependent of the family and reveals the patron family's custom of chastising Bermúdes' family at will; it also exposes Bermúdes' ploys to keep such punishment from being visited on her children. The documents therefore contain sketches of individuals' lives, sometimes spanning years. Contained either within the longer stretches of time described, or inscribed into the events leading up to prosecution, are accounts of friendship and mutual assistance and examples of solidarity. Although details about how plebeians lived are rarely to be found in the forefront of the "action," the sources abound with examples of solidarity, support, and cooperation and uncover as many relationships between women as between the sexes.

LIVING BETWEEN HONOR CODES: PLEBEIAN ATTEMPTS AT (RE) ESTABLISHING HONOR

If litigants' behavior is not always revealed in court records, at least their attempts to portray their actions in a favorable light is recorded. The sources confirm that no simple code of gender behavior existed. Despite institutional attempts to impose a single, Catholic, and state-sanctioned understanding of appropriate behavior for women and men, the plebeian classes deviated from such norms by failing to formalize their unions through marriage, engaging in premarital sex even when they opted for marriage at a later date, and leaving unsuccessful relationships in the face of church and state opposition to the dissolution of matrimony. As Twinam has noted, the relationship between norms and sexual behavior is a complex one and does not always involve a simple correlation between the two.[5]

Both statistical evidence and pervasive popular attitudes recognizing the validity of consensual unions confirm that common-law marriage was widespread and largely socially accepted. Although formal marriage was generally regarded as preferable, consensual unions were widespread enough to constitute a relatively respectable alternative. Couples stayed together for decades, often choosing to formalize their union only on the deathbed of one of the spouses—thus indicating their ultimate preference for ecclesiastical sanction. While bringing somewhat lower social status, consensual unions were, in plebeian eyes, more or less identical to formal marriage. Common-law husbands and wives socialized with and assisted in-laws, formalized their relationships with brothers- and sisters-in-law through *compadrazgo*, and took on orphans from their spouses' families. If formal marriage was ultimately preferred, litigants failed to comment negatively on consensual unions during trials.

Another challenge to official sensibilities was the space for premarital sex in both peasant and urban plebeian lives. While such activities were rarely sanctioned openly by parents, plebeian society was fairly tolerant of them. In certain social environments, and providing that a permanent union ensued, premarital sex was widespread enough to secure the acquiescence and facilitation of friends and sometimes parents. Clemencia Ruiz' mother allowed her daughter's suitor free access to her home in the hope that this might entice him into marriage. Couples used the privacy offered by their tasks, especially pastoral duties, to indulge in romance, which many times led to permanent unions. Although Asencia León lied to her mother in order to hide her liaison with Gerónimo Miranda, she had in fact been seeing her lover regularly for months while pasturing the family's stock and freely visiting friends to purchase *huarapo*.

Even when marriage did not result, plebeian women claimed honor, as in the case of Manuela Villanueva, who established both her and her daughter's claim to honor in court, despite her daughter's illegitimacy and both women's employment as market women. These women's behavior, although far from undisputed, illustrates how far the term "honor" could be stretched.

Such departures from official norms notwithstanding, families at all social levels cared deeply about honor. In some cases, a lover's failure to make good his promise of marriage led to accusations of rape or seduction. Usually, the girl's father or, if he was not around, her mother accused the unsteady wooer of having taken advantage of the girl. In most cases, such suits were less about punishing the offender than about reestablishing the victim's reputation by, ideally, forcing the reluctant fiancé to marry her. A conviction, even if the trial did not result in marriage, demonstrated to the public that the girl had been a victim rather than a willing party to her loss of honor. By documenting her family's claim to respectability and accusing the defendant of using force, drugs, or deceit to "corrupt" her (thus proving her innocent of complicity), the plaintiff sought to salvage the remnants of her family's honor. Even when she failed to obtain a conviction, the complainant hoped that her willingness to defend her family's honor would regain some reputation—if not that of the abandoned bride, at least that of her family.

The actual events underlying the proceedings often remain hidden; as stories were retold, many details were omitted and others embellished. Plaintiffs were rarely entirely honest about events, instead seeking to parrot elite sensibilities in order to obtain the judge's sympathy. Women at the center of events were seldom given the opportunity to speak freely. While their actions reveal some volition—after all, most of them had entered these relationships willingly—their legal representatives spoke for them throughout the proceedings, portraying them as passive and gullible. Despite older relatives' attempts to disguise any hint of female initiative, the transcripts do reveal something of women's sexuality. As Lavrin has noted for the colonial period, if women regarded sexual intercourse as pleasurable, no records attested to such feelings;[6] whatever women's subjective experience was, it remained strictly off the record. However, most of the female protagonists in seduction trials engaged in these affairs of their own volition, usually over a protracted period of time. Some acted in concert with acquiescing parents; others openly defied parental control. Several consciously used their relationship in order to escape unhappy domestic situations and patriarchal control. Their guardians' preoccupation with honor need not blind us to these women's determination and ability to act independently.

With the exception of child rape, genuine incidents of rape mostly went unrecorded. The legal system's preoccupation with honor, combined with the many constraints that prevented peasants and other plebeians from seeking legal recourse, made prosecution of such incidents extremely unlikely. Even when reported, rape led to legal consequences only if the victim met the minimum requirements of social respectability. Instead, the courts documented the outcome of unhappy affairs, as girls' families sought to reconcile loss of virginity with contemporary understandings of honor. The main protagonists of these trials were residents of the small towns and villages of Cajamarca, mostly moderately prosperous, or, if poor, connected to wealthier patrons who could support their suit.

In justifying their claim to honor in the face of forfeited virginity, plaintiffs explicated their own understanding of the concept and attempted to reconcile lower-class sexual practice with official gender norms. By shifting blame and responsibility for the act onto the seducer, they hoped to obtain the court's understanding that the loss of honor had been undeserved. Failing the judge's recognition of this alternative interpretation of honor, complainants hoped that the very act of going to court, as well as the opportunity to broadcast their own version of events, might sway public opinion in their family's favor.

These trials reveal how lower-class and modestly well-to-do citizens of Cajamarca entered negotiations concerning their and their dependents' social standing within the legal system and occasionally succeeded in meeting their needs by subverting the premises on which the system was constructed, as in the case of market woman Manuela Villanueva. Despite the bias against lower-class women, Villanueva succeeded in operating within the elite definition of honor and using it for her own ends. However discriminatory these definitions of respectability were against both women and the poor, both groups succeeded in appropriating and, to some degree, transforming and modifying them in order to suit their own cases.

A measure of honor might yet be salvaged, even when the principal part had to be forfeited. If we view honor as a continuum rather than as the elusive either-or quality it was described as by contemporaries, plaintiffs' wish to obtain a slightly higher honor rating is more easily understood. While plaintiffs did not always sway the judge, we can assume that their arguments had some impact on the public. This is evident from the cases dealing with slander. Slander corrupted marriages, as husbands began to doubt their wives' fidelity and sometimes left wives and children and ruined their businesses. One woman was even jailed by her husband after he heard rumors of her alleged adultery. In response, wives—assisted by male relatives, occasionally their husbands—went to court to accuse slanderers of spreading gossip and ruining their good name. Unlike what happened with victims of rape and seduction, plaintiffs in slander trials hoped to regain their reputation in its entirety by proving the slander untrue.

Abandoned wives, most of them suspected of adultery, did not recriminate their husbands for leaving them in a quandary. Contemporary codes of honor linked a husband's honor to his wife's sexual fidelity, and wives recognized (or claimed to recognize) their husband's need to assert his personal honor in the face of suspicions of female adultery. By separating—albeit briefly—from his wife, a husband maintained the legal option of formally accusing her of adultery and subsequently filing for divorce; even if he had no plans to carry out this threat in practice, distancing himself from the source of dishonor (even if temporarily) helped him protect his honor.

Wives played along by publicly displaying wifely deference. Some spoke of their husband's generosity; all expressed understanding of his choice to turn them out of their home; all blamed the slanderer, who had publicized groundless rumors. Whatever these women felt in private, they had little to gain by making public whatever misgivings they might have had concerning their husbands' behavior. Removing the shadow of scandal and suspicion which rested on them was of paramount importance, and public deference toward their husbands and intransigent pursuit of the offenders who had—they claimed, groundlessly—placed them in this predicament were imperative if they were to regain the public's respect. These women were fighting to vindicate and reestablish themselves as respectable members of the community; challenging established norms of behavior which stipulated wifely submission to patriarchal authority was unlikely to further their cause. Wives' tactics, combining acceptance of the dominant code of honor and their husbands' behavior with legal action against the slanderers, therefore paid dividends. Even if trials were not concluded, husbands returned, presumably because the tarnish of dishonor had been removed by legal action.

Despite its many shortcomings, the legal system therefore seems to have served a purpose. Although it rarely meted out justice and few defendants were sentenced and jailed, the legal arena became a site for the publication of disputes over honor, and of negotiation over honor for those whose claim to reputation was in some way threatened.

The legal debates described in the previous chapters detail the stories of contests on many levels: between spouses (both formal and common-law), parents and children, neighbors, lovers, and—ultimately, leading to the recording of these underlying debates—subalterns and the state. Nineteenth-century citizens of Cajamarca lived with multiple, and often overlapping, layers of gender codes. While their behavior might be questioned and judged dishonorable by many, their actions were typical for their social group, and lower-class women and men claimed honor even when it was not freely offered by their superiors.

By retelling their version of events they emphasized their claim to honorable behavior. Infractions of dominant behavioral codes were placed in a context of extenuating circumstances, as in the case of Rosaura Carbajal, who was allegedly drugged with alcohol by her seducer before he deflowered her. Suspicious circumstances were explained, as in the case of Marcelina Paz, who was accused of being a *rabonera*, but who, according to her father, had assisted her mother in seeking to reclaim beasts of burden appropriated by the army. Misapprehensions of social status were rectified, as in the case of Catalina Pájares, whose rapist described her as a mere servant who had the run of the entire village in order to carry out her employer's errands. Her uncle and guardian assured the court that Pájares was being reared as his ward in his home under the care of (he claimed) a highly reputable woman, and not as a servant.

Most stories contained several of these elements. When Francisco del

Campo recounted his wife's entire life history in order to erase the slur of adulteress, he stressed her youth and innocence at the time of her first seduction, implied a certain social status when he explained that she was removed from the care of an aunt residing in a *beaterio* in Lima, justified her abandonment of her first, common-law, husband on the grounds of his "poor behavior" and made the most of her subsequent respectable life at his side. Although del Campo appears to have succeeded in defending his wife's name, the incident also illustrates how a crack in reputation could resurface years after the initial dishonor. Although Francisca Ramírez "passed" (in Twinam's words) for decades, she and her family were exposed to reminders of a less-respectable past decades later, reminding her that her reputation was more vulnerable than most.

If subaltern gender practice demonstrates the multiplicity of gender norms among the population at large, litigants' attempts to justify their own and their relatives' behavior in terms acceptable to a judge demonstrate the pervasiveness of the elite definition of honor. Klubock notes that "even those practices and identities that appear to subvert or oppose normative gender conventions" are shaped by dominant gender ideologies.[7] The ideal code of honor as preached (if not, as other authors have shown, always followed in practice) by the elites and encoded in legislation became a standard against which deviators measured their own behavior.

Although lower-class gender practice departed from official gender norms, plebeians sought to defend their behavior in elite terms — certainly in court, and also, one suspects, outside it. In doing so, and producing eloquent arguments justifying their claim to honor, plebeians demonstrated a sophisticated knowledge of elite understandings of honor even as they exploited the fissures in these.

Elite perceptions of honor included the favorable treatment accorded women of quality and, where behavior did not too seriously contravene elite norms, married women. Women's sexuality was judged differently and depended on their ethnicity, social class, marital status, and age. While greater decorum was expected from wealthier women in Cajamarca, they were also, if suspected of any misconduct, credited with greater moral sensibility and were exempt from suspicion by reason of their social class. Thus Rosaura Carbajal's seducer was sentenced by the court, whereas Rosario Sichas obtained no satisfaction when her mother accused Lisandro Altamirano of corrupting her daughter. Whereas Marcelina Paz was lambasted as a camp follower by her former suitor after she bore him a child out of wedlock, causing her father to give up proceedings against her former fiancé in order to minimize further damage to the family's name, Francisca Ramírez' husband held his head high in court and defended his wife, three decades after she had borne several illegitimate children fathered by another man. Her subsequent conduct and marriage as well as the status of being married to a scribe had repaired her reputation, indicating just how situationally determined honor could be.

Jacoba Bermúdez was only one of many married women who insisted that her matrimonial status entitled her to the defense of her name, thereby implying that single women were less needy or worthy of such considerations. Bermúdez can fairly be said to be one of the women who stretched contemporary definitions of respectability to their very limits: because she repeatedly engaged in street brawls with her husband's former common-law wife, the judge found it difficult to totally exonerate her from her sworn enemy's countercharges. Both were sentenced to jail for slander, albeit with a slighter sentence for Bermúdez, as she had merely insulted a never-married woman, whereas her enemy had offended a married woman and thus earned herself a heftier punishment. As I have shown, it was women who lived on the edge of codes of honor, who negotiated between different social groups' sensibilities of honor, who were most vulnerable.

Honor thus depended on a large number of variables, and individuals claimed it on different grounds. Living in sin, or earning a living in the market might deny one the right to reclaim honor while other grounds might be deemed worthy. Living among multiple understandings of honor, Cajamarca's citizens negotiated complicated terrain, using the opportunities permitted by this complexity to open new avenues for individual interpretation of established norms.

Plebeians were driven, and aided, in their pursuit of honor by contemporary shifts in its definition. As the nineteenth century progressed, honor was defined increasingly in relation to personal virtue (delimited inevitably, for women, as premarital virginity and conjugal fidelity), and less bound to social preeminence and wealth. Although the sample used here is too small to produce any conclusions about change over time, litigants displayed an awareness of the more "modern" understanding of honor in their arguments in court, particularly in alleging personal concern for public morality in cases of rape and slander.

TOEING THE LINE (OR NOT): MARITAL RELATIONS

Gender behavior was subject to negotiation in other spheres, too. Spouses daily battled violently or—less noticeably—silently over their roles. Both other research and my own sources confirm that husbands and wives interpreted their rights and duties very differently. Lavrin speaks of "sexual relationships fraught by opposite interpretations of domination and submissiveness";[8] Stern has explained the logic of matrimonial arguments with the existence of a "patriarchal pact" according to which sexual and economic rights were intimately bound up with one another. While husbands viewed their rights as absolute, wives considered them contingent on male fulfillment of certain duties, including economic obligations toward their family (but not necessarily absolute sexual fidelity).[9] Tinsman notes that husbands and wives disagreed sharply over what constituted good behavior. Confronted with the Chilean Agrarian Reform's advocacy of gender mutualism, spouses interpreted this ethos differently: while wives expected greater respect and autonomy from their husbands, husbands perceived gender mutualism to mean that women owed their husbands support and obedience.[10] Spouses were similarly eager to interpret state policy to support their personal viewpoint in Cajamarca: when Melchor Figueroa was ordered to return to Raymunda Goicochea's side, he took the judge's injunction not to quarrel anymore to mean that his wife owed him complete obedience—including sex on demand. She did not share this view (and clearly made her point, as he eventually resigned himself to sleeping on his poncho rather than sharing her bed) and took cohabitation to mean no more than sharing the same roof, as well as fulfilling certain domestic duties.[11] If we can take Goicochea's behavior as an indication of the order of importance in which wives ranked their duties toward their husbands, wives accepted domestic chores more readily than a husband's access to their body.

The details of conjugal differences are documented in only a few cases for Cajamarca. Only the most extreme manifestations of marital conflict made their way into the courts, sometimes only following the violent death of one of the spouses, usually the wife. For most victims of battery in marriage there was little to be gained by legal action. Husbands were rarely jailed, and, if they were, seldom for long. Divorce was not an option, and even annulment or separation of board and bed, which could be obtained in Lima, appear to have been rare options in Cajamarca. I could not access the ecclesiastical archive for this study, and there is only one, uncompleted, suit for alimony among the civil suit records, indicating that even if the church's blessing for an annulment was obtained, this had no impact on property arrangements. Even in those cases in which conjugal conflict was recorded, judges were often unsympathetic, giving victims scant hearing, and defendants offered rote explanations of violence.

The preeminence of alcohol and suspicions of infidelity emerge as important factors in those trials dealing directly with domestic abuse as well as those where references to such instances are featured. Female infidelity was often given as an explanation of and justification for battery; how common wives' adultery was is uncertain, as husbands had much to gain from blaming their misconduct on their wives' adultery. As important, if not more important, male infidelity was a cause of conjugal disharmony, as husbands' extramarital affairs appear to have been a bone of contention in many unions. Any threat to the husband's economic contributions to the home touched on a wife's concerns for simple existence. As Boyer has noted for colonial Mexico, many women defined *mala vida* as their husbands' failure to support them, tracing that dereliction to the presence of another woman in his life.[12]

More often than taking on their husbands directly, wives attacked rivals. Although the sample of trials available is too small to draw any conclusions about changes over time, it seems likely that wives' sense of insecurity augmented toward the end of the century, as more men migrated periodically to the coast to work on sugar plantations. Such seasonal absences, many of which became permanent, weakened bonds between spouses, heightening the risk of alternative emotional involvement, especially for men. By the last decades of the nineteenth century, men were becoming a scarce commodity, and women competed acrimoniously for those who remained.

As has been documented for other regions and periods, not all conflicts grew out of such clear-cut causes. Several incidents resulted from conflicts over authority and perceived lack of female deference. Men objected when their wife challenged their authority, all the more so if she did so in public. Men struck out in order publicly to reassert patriarchal authority.

More than the causes of marital conflict, the sources allow us to study husbands' rationale for blows, official responses, and the strategies victims used. Even if the background for conflict might be more complex than detailed above, men commonly justified their behavior on the grounds of female infidelity, or excused their violence as being due to the influence of alcohol. Women rarely resorted to legal action; they knew only too well that the courts were reluctant to interfere in domestic affairs. Even when battering spouses were jailed, sentences tended to be short, when they were carried out all.

Alternative strategies included escaping a marriage, albeit often at a considerable price. Although couples did occasionally dissolve the union even if they were formally married, the church and state opposed this solution, and the spouse who wished to leave usually had to leave the province in order to evade legal orders to resume conjugal life. The difficulty of leaving a formal marriage may have made common-law unions more popular, especially for women, who were at greater risk of maltreatment.

Conclusion

While most women stoically accepted a degree of violence, they did not tolerate extreme abuse silently. As noted by other authors, husbands who went beyond acceptable norms of disciplinary punishment upset the equilibrium of gender reciprocity and were likely to be challenged by their wife, in-laws, and society at large.[13] Although a wife's right to resist was recognized by the community in which she lived, this understanding was not shared by the state, which backed patriarchal power absolutely. There was thus a disjuncture between official and popular understanding of gender rights and marriage. Women fought back, and sometimes succeeded in turning the tables on their husbands if the latter were debilitated by illness, disability, or the element of surprise.

In order to combat male infidelity, the lack of material support, and violence, women resorted to "everyday weapons of resistance," a term I have borrowed from James Scott.[14] These could range from coolness, the symbolic insults conveyed through the serving of food to denial of sex to attacks on mistresses to physical violence (or even, in one case, unprovoked assault). Those women who had family living in the vicinity were in the strongest position, as parents and siblings interfered if their daughter or sister was at risk. While this did not necessarily stop abuse, it could prevent extremes. Antonio Minchán was fearful of his common-law wife's brothers' response after he stabbed her; Asunción Ramírez explained that her husband's beatings had been made more intolerable by her isolation.

The intervention of in-laws was especially contentious; husbands objected, often in the form of further violence, and were backed by the courts. Judges condemned the interference of outsiders in matrimonial affairs and, implicitly, the challenge to patriarchal authority, by warning off meddling mothers-in-law with threats of fines and imprisonment and ordering wives to return to their husbands' sides. Those women who filed charges against their husbands were officially "reconciled" with them and instructed to obey them. Despite official injunctions against such interference, familial intervention was crucial to battered women, and several of the charges against husbands were pressed not by the wife, but by her parents and siblings.

The fact that both relatives and, occasionally, outsiders assisted abused women indicates that there was a widespread climate of disapproval of extreme marital violence. The role played by outsiders also underlines the public nature of such intimate events as conjugal arguments.[15] Although this did not prevent abuse, it stood in marked contrast to the official policy of non-interference in marital conflict, regardless of how serious its consequences. This is one area where common-law unions had the advantage over formal marriage; on no occasion did either church or state insist on the resumption of conjugal relations where couples were not formally married. The trials dealing with marital conflict therefore reveal a discourse of conflicting attitudes toward marital battery: whereas the state sought to uphold the maxim of patriarchal authority within the marriage at all costs, lower-class practice was more pragmatic. While a measure of spousal violence was considered unavoidable, most women had access to a range of informal mechanisms that could help them fight off the worst excesses. Location, translating into proximity or distance from family and other networks, was crucial in determining battered women's position in relation to abusive husbands.

Among the questions which remain to be explored in greater detail is how plebeian men defined *mala vida* and viewed violence. Although battered wives received support, it would be interesting to know more about how batterers discussed their behavior outside of court, beyond justifying their right to chastise their wives. How did men reconcile their perceived right to beat their wives with their defense of their sisters?

The near lacuna in the records on the beating of children is also interesting. Police records allow a mere glimpse of acquiescent plebeian silence concerning such abuse. Clearly, children were beaten, at times with lethal results, but such matters received official attention only in rare cases, such as in the murder of María Jesús Condor.[16]

STRUCTURING SOLIDARITY:
RELATIONSHIPS AMONG WOMEN

The role of networks and other examples of solidarity and cooperation among women (and men) is an area in need of further study. Behind the trials' main story lines lurk many examples of reciprocal assistance, mostly —but not exclusively—from other women. Women assisted each other with loans of tools, food, and money; they helped out with domestic and agricultural tasks; they looked after each other during illness and childbirth; and they fought mutual enemies side by side. Family bonds were also important among women, and sisters, mothers, and daughters figure strongly in these examples; however, other friends and neighbors were important, too.

By collating these many examples, I found certain recurrent meeting places and activities, which shows how women scheduled their social activities to correspond with their many duties. It seems as if the development and expression of female friendship were closely linked to women's daily chores, such as fetching water, washing clothes, cooking, and tending to domestic animals. Typical sites for female socialization were therefore the *pileta* and the marketplace, as well as—especially for servants—the domestic arena, with domestic servants socializing with each other and with their mistresses.

Relationships among women were important in determining their relationships with men, and women's relationships with men influenced relationships among women. Support networks helped battered women cope and, sometimes, resist; cooperation enabled single mothers to survive; assistance during illness and childbirth was essential, and usually provided by other women.

Similarly, the limits of female solidarity added conflict and danger to women's lives, as they used slander, witchcraft, and physical violence as weapons. Interest in this topic has been on the rise, as scholars have come to recognize that gender relations were not universally governed by either conflict or a male-female dichotomy.[17] Tensions among women were prevalent, often resulting in years of mutual hatred, and were often extreme enough to provoke physical—occasionally lethal—fights.

While some conflicts erupted into brutal fights, others were restricted to oral offenses, which—as we saw in the discussion of slander trials—could be a powerful weapon in their own right. Poor and subaltern women in particular were likely to use insults and slander in altercations with wealthier and more powerful women, hitting with uncanny precision where they might cause the greatest pain. Although they were less likely to engage in direct confrontation, their female betters did not shy away from retaliation, dealing both blows and oral offenses, as was evident from the encounter between Manuela Villanueva, Manuela Abanto, and their respective daughters and the treatment experienced by servant women at the hands of their mistresses. As the trials dealing with alleged incidents of poisoning indicate, witchcraft and poisoning were also perceived as a potential threat.

Women also provided mutual support and solidarity in moments of strife. By entering the fray on a friend's or relative's side, intervening in ongoing brawls, or concealing an infant threatened by violence to its mother, women manifested their support of one other in moments of crisis. Friends and relatives shared each other's concerns to the extent of plotting revenge, slandering, or, more rarely, poisoning enemies. Calling the wrath of employers and authorities down on themselves, older servant women helped younger dependents escape positions of near slavery, thereby revealing powerful bonds of empathy and identification across generations. Older women were also known to halt the escalation of conflict between younger women by using their authority over younger relatives and leading them away from scenes of rising tension. The manifestation of friendship and solidarity was thus intimately bound up with conflict among women.

The causes of such tensions are obscure: scribes and judges had little interest in noting the particulars of plebeian women's struggles, and the causes are usually only hinted at. The authorities had less interest in ascertaining the origins of contention than in determining the reasons for marital conflict; female victims of violence met with understanding authorities only if they met elite standards of respectability. Women who committed crimes—including assault—were clearly disqualified.[18]

Perceptive to such views, protagonists were unwilling to reveal their private life to the unsympathetic ears of a judge. However, rivalry over men, competition over property, and the defense of children seem to have been common causes of conflict, probably in that order of frequency (as women did not usually go out of their way to harm each other's children). Women clashed over real or imagined causes for jealousy, choosing to attack a rival rather than the subject of their affections; they were fierce in asserting their and their family's claims to land and money, ready to attack debtors, trespassers (particularly if these staked claim to land they perceived to be theirs), and women whose domestic animals damaged their fields. In addition, *patronas* felt within their rights to punish servants and other dependents for perceived misbehavior; such discipline could vary from a slap to grotesque forms of punishment for misdemeanors.

The intense nature of women's rivalry over men can be partly explained by the latter's migration to the coast and their subsequent relative scarcity; men's material contribution made a significant difference to women's quality of life. However, anthropological and historical evidence from other areas confirms that women's rivalry over men was not exclusive to Cajamarca, and the ways in which women competed for men is a field in need of further exploration.[19]

The more extreme manifestations of conflict among women transgressed the boundaries of accepted behavior, and women who brawled implicitly disqualified themselves as honorable persons. Nevertheless, they had their own perceptions of self-worth, which they were often fighting to defend in the face of challenge. As Stern has pointed out, in the daily battle for survival, a reputation for being willing to fight might be more valuable to subaltern women than any amount of decorum.[20] Just as plebeian men were able to ward off potential challenges to their honor by displaying a willingness to defend their good name with their bare hands, women might ward off potential rivals for their spouses' attention by establishing a reputation for jealousy.

Conclusion

Despite the limitations of the sources, trial transcripts—complemented by police records, wills, notarial records, and, where available, census information—offer insights into plebeian life and how lower-class women and men related to such state institutions as the courts. While the lives of hacienda residents are difficult to access, the urban and semiurban residents of provincial and departmental capitals provide a rich gallery of personages. These include abandoned mistresses, single mothers, protective fathers, loving husbands, neighbors meeting at the *pileta* to collect water and wash laundry, lovers conspiring to steal cattle or elope, and servants forming bonds with other servants and patching up quarrels with their employers while kneading bread. Courtship between youngsters, the parameters of honor amid which they flirted, conjugal conflict, and women's struggle with long-standing enemies are among the themes which appear in the transcripts.

Although a great breadth of both everyday and less-mundane experiences is touched on in the transcripts, the stories lack many details. However, perhaps most striking is the intimate knowledge of elite codes of behavior displayed by lower-class women and men, and their willingness to engage in legal action. Plebeians did not simply appear in court as defendants following cattle theft or drunken assaults; to the contrary, many entered court willingly and proved adept at manipulating the court's understandings of honor and reputation. Artisans, servants, seamstresses, shop owners, and—more rarely—agricultural laborers made shrewd decisions about whether and how to make use of the legal system. Going to court to defend one's name from slander or to force a reluctant fiancé to the altar made sense; accusing one's husband of violence did not. Even when defendants were hauled into court for assault or theft, they opted for arguments and strategies to justify their actions (witness the lines of argumentation used by violent husbands, unfaithful lovers, and fighting women); failing this, many chose escape and permanent relocation.

Both plaintiffs and defendants therefore displayed a remarkable degree of agency. Trial transcripts not only record the events prior to participants' legal involvement, they also document how plebeians interacted with and made use of the local police force, the clergy, and judges. For trial transcripts to be exploited thoroughly as a historical source, they must be analyzed on several levels, however. Both the conflict leading to criminal prosecution and the legal process itself must be examined. In addition, the everyday events and details recorded by litigants and witnesses may shed light on often-unrelated topics, compensating for the sources' tendency to focus on conflict. Such an approach can uncover information on many hitherto understudied topics, including the many ways in which networks of family and friendship operated and what norms governed women's and men's everyday lives.

Marital and Literacy Data from Criminal Trials, 1862–1900

∞

TABLE A1. *Marital status, from trial sample*

	Men		Women	
Marital Status	N	% of Total	N	% of Total
Married	207	45.2	87	31.8
Single	227	49.6	144	52.7
Widowed	24	5.2	42	15.4
Total	458		273	

SOURCE: Archivo Departamental de Cajamarca.

TABLE A2. *Literacy, from trial sample*

	Men		Women	
Literacy	N	% of Total	N	% of Total
Literate	270	69.2	49	19.0
Illiterate	120	30.8	209	81.0
Total	390		258	

SOURCE: Archivo Departamental de Cajamarca.

Data from the National Census Conducted in 1876

TABLE B1. *Ethnicity of males, Province of Cajamarca, 1876*

District	White		Indian		Mestizo		African		Asian		Total
	N	% of District	N	% of District	N	% of District	N	% of District	N	% of District	
Asunción	392	19.4	727	36.1	894	44.3	0	0.0	3	0.1	2,016
Cajamarca	1,198	17.3	3,869	55.8	1,779	25.6	80	1.2	11	0.2	6,937
Chetilla	20	2.9	668	96.8	2	0.3	0	0.0	0	0.0	690
Cospán	379	23.1	787	48.0	473	28.8	2	0.1	0	0.0	1,641
Encañada	69	5.0	715	51.4	596	42.8	10	0.7	1	0.1	1,391
Ichocán	1,936	86.3	206	9.2	99	4.4	2	0.1	0	0.0	2,243
Jesús	605	24.2	988	39.6	900	36.0	4	0.2	1	0.0	2,498
Llacanora	43	6.9	571	92.2	4	0.6	1	0.2	0	0.0	619
Magdalena	23	5.1	376	83.7	5	1.1	39	8.7	6	1.3	449
Matara	38	5.0	131	17.4	577	76.6	7	0.9	0	0.0	753
San Marcos	823	23.8	453	13.1	2,164	62.7	9	0.3	3	0.1	3,452
San Pablo	1,650	44.0	1,540	41.1	429	11.5	25	0.7	102	2.7	3,746
Province total	7,176	27.1	11,031	41.7	7,922	30.0	179	0.7	127	0.5	26,435

SOURCE: Dirección Nacional de Estadística, *Resumen del censo general.*

TABLE B2. *Ethnicity of females, Province of Cajamarca, 1876*

District	White		Indian		Mestiza		African		Asian		Total
	N	% of District	N	% of District	N	% of District	N	% of District	N	% of District	
Asunción	458	20.6	755	33.9	1,013	45.5	1	0.0	0	0.0	2,227
Cajamarca	1,632	19.9	4,195	51.2	2,275	27.8	92	1.1	3	0.0	8,197
Chetilla	30	3.4	852	96.6	0	0.0	0	0.0	0	0.0	882
Cospán	401	24.3	752	45.5	500	30.2	0	0.0	0	0.0	1,653
Encañada	70	4.5	776	50.2	687	44.4	14	0.9	0	0.0	1,547
Ichocán	2,127	85.8	225	9.1	128	5.2	0	0.0	0	0.0	2,480
Jesús	736	26.5	1,033	37.2	1,006	36.2	0	0.0	1	0.0	2,776
Llacanora	42	7.1	541	91.4	8	1.4	1	0.2	0	0.0	592
Magdalena	20	4.8	348	84.1	46	11.1	0	0.0	0	0.0	414
Matara	53	6.4	139	16.8	630	76.1	6	0.7	0	0.0	828
San Marcos	836	22.7	529	14.3	2,315	62.7	10	0.3	0	0.0	3,690
San Pablo	1,179	35.7	1,637	49.6	447	13.6	35	1.1	0	0.0	3,298
Province total	7,584	26.5	11,782	41.2	9,055	31.7	159	0.6	4	0.0	28,584

SOURCE: Dirección Nacional de Estadística, *Resumen del censo general.*

TABLE B3. *Literacy rate of males, Province of Cajamarca, 1876*

District	Literate		Semiliterate		Illiterate		
	N	% of District	N	% of District	N	% of District	Total
Asunción	421	38.3	88	8.0	590	53.7	1,099
Cajamarca	1,539	37.6	184	4.5	2,369	57.9	4,092
Chetilla	317	80.1	6	1.5	73	18.4	396
Cospán	326	38.9	46	5.5	467	55.7	839
Encañada	190	25.0	8	1.1	563	74.0	761
Ichocán	773	61.1	52	4.1	441	34.8	1,266
Jesús	483	28.4	44	2.6	1,172	69.0	1,699
Llacanora	73	20.5	16	4.5	267	75.0	356
Magdalena	64	23.8	11	4.1	194	72.1	269
Matara	185	34.1	89	16.4	268	49.4	542
San Marcos	1,132	55.4	37	1.8	874	42.8	2,043
San Pablo	555	25.0	90	4.1	1,573	70.9	2,218
Province total	6,058	38.9	671	4.3	8,851	56.8	15,580

NOTE: All columns refer to persons above age fifteen.
SOURCE: Dirección Nacional de Estadística, *Resumen del censo general.*

TABLE B4. *Literacy rate of females, Province of Cajamarca, 1876*

District	Literate		Semiliterate		Illiterate		
	N	% of District	N	% of District	N	% of District	Total
Asunción	113	8.3	59	4.3	1,191	87.4	1,363
Cajamarca	1,186	21.4	270	4.9	4,092	73.8	5,548
Chetilla	536	85.4	5	0.8	87	13.9	628
Cospán	75	7.7	25	2.6	868	89.7	968
Encañada	44	4.7	7	0.7	894	94.6	945
Ichocán	148	9.7	78	5.1	1,304	85.2	1,530
Jesús	101	4.9	26	1.3	1,924	93.8	2,051
Llacanora	8	2.2	7	2.0	342	95.8	357
Magdalena	8	3.0	2	0.8	254	96.2	264
Matara	17	2.9	21	3.6	546	93.5	584
San Marcos	205	8.7	34	1.4	2,116	89.9	2,355
San Pablo	154	6.0	89	3.4	2,341	90.6	2,584
Province total	2,595	13.5	623	3.2	15,959	83.2	19,177

NOTE: All columns refer to persons above age fifteen.
SOURCE: Dirección Nacional de Estadística, *Resumen del censo general.*

TABLE B5. *Marital status of males, Province of Cajamarca, 1876*

District	Single N	% of District	Married N	% of District	Widowed N	% of District	Total
Asunción	426	51.8	336	40.9	60	7.3	822
Cajamarca	1,473	49.4	1,303	43.7	207	6.9	2,983
Chetilla	118	36.2	162	49.7	46	14.1	326
Cospán	212	37.1	320	55.9	40	7.0	572
Encañada	226	41.4	287	52.6	33	6.0	546
Ichocán	117	13.5	674	77.8	75	8.7	866
Jesús	454	34.1	760	57.1	118	8.9	1,332
Llacanora	0	0.0	201	88.5	26	11.5	227
Magdalena	146	70.5	50	24.2	11	5.3	207
Matara	60	18.5	224	68.9	41	12.6	325
San Marcos	274	20.2	955	70.5	126	9.3	1,355
San Pablo	736	50.5	617	42.4	103	7.1	1,456
Province total	4,242	38.5	5,889	53.5	886	8.0	11,017

NOTES: Following Deere (*Household and Class Relations*, p. 97), I set twenty-five as the average age at marriage. Census takers defined persons in common-law marriages as single.
SOURCE: Dirección Nacional de Estadística, *Resumen del censo general*.

TABLE B6. *Marital status of females, Province of Cajamarca, 1876*

District	Single N	% of District	Married N	% of District	Widowed N	% of District	Total
Asunción	658	57.6	338	29.6	146	12.8	1,142
Cajamarca	2,664	58.7	1,327	29.2	551	12.1	4,542
Chetilla	266	47.2	161	28.6	136	24.2	563
Cospán	331	44.4	312	41.8	103	13.8	746
Encañada	350	46.7	294	39.3	105	14.0	749
Ichocán	378	30.6	643	52.1	213	17.3	1,234
Jesús	714	41.8	703	41.1	292	17.1	1,709
Llacanora	59	20.6	190	66.2	38	13.2	287
Magdalena	163	71.5	48	21.1	17	7.5	228
Matara	172	37.8	227	49.9	56	12.3	455
San Marcos	690	36.3	933	49.1	279	14.7	1,902
San Pablo	1,019	51.0	638	31.9	343	17.2	2,000
Province total	7,464	48.0	5,814	37.4	2,279	14.6	15,557

NOTES: Following Deere (*Household and Class Relations*, p. 97), I set twenty-one as the average age at marriage. Census takers defined persons in common-law marriages as single.
SOURCE: Dirección Nacional de Estadística, *Resumen del censo general*.

TABLE B7. *Sex of population, by age, District of Asunción, 1876*

Age	Total Population	Men	% of Total Population	Women	% of Total Population
0–15	1,781	917	51.5	864	48.5
15–20	268	126	47.0	142	53.0
20–25	364	157	43.1	207	56.9
25–30	363	148	40.8	215	59.2
30–35	297	100	33.7	197	66.3
35–40	335	165	49.3	170	50.7
40–45	211	102	48.3	109	51.7
45–50	193	94	48.7	99	51.3
50–55	156	81	51.9	75	48.1
55–60	101	55	54.5	46	45.5
60–	180	71	39.4	109	60.6
Total	4,249	2,016	47.4	2,233	52.6

SOURCE: Dirección Nacional de Estadística, *Resumen del censo general.*

TABLE B8. *Sex of population, by age, District of Cajamarca, 1876*

Age	Total Population	Men	% of Total Population	Women	% of Total Population
0–15	5,494	2,845	51.8	2,649	48.2
15–20	1,123	481	42.8	642	57.2
20–25	1,573	629	40.0	944	60.0
25–30	1,324	555	41.9	769	58.1
30–35	1,106	496	44.8	610	55.2
35–40	961	424	44.1	537	55.9
40–45	934	390	41.8	544	58.2
45–50	703	314	44.7	389	55.3
50–55	522	209	40.0	313	60.0
55–60	521	208	39.9	313	60.1
60–	947	386	40.8	561	59.2
Total	15,208	6,937	45.6	8,271	54.4

SOURCE: Dirección Nacional de Estadística, *Resumen del censo general.*

TABLE B9. *Sex of population, by age, District of Chetilla, 1876*

Age	Total Population	Men	% of Total Population	Women	% of Total Population
0–15	548	294	53.6	254	46.4
15–20	100	34	34.0	66	66.0
20–25	114	36	31.6	78	68.4
25–30	101	37	36.6	64	63.4
30–35	124	38	30.6	86	69.4
35–40	99	36	36.4	63	63.6
40–45	126	47	37.3	79	62.7
45–50	57	18	31.6	39	68.4
50–55	71	31	43.7	40	56.3
55–60	56	29	51.8	27	48.2
60–65	221	90	40.7	131	59.3
Total	1,617	690	42.7	927	57.3

SOURCE: Dirección Nacional de Estadística, *Resumen del censo general.*

TABLE B10. *Sex of population, by age, District of Cospán, 1876*

Age	Total Population	Men	% of Total Population	Women	% of Total Population
0–15	1,487	802	53.9	685	46.1
15–20	255	112	43.9	143	56.1
20–25	335	155	46.3	180	53.7
25–30	256	120	46.9	136	53.1
30–35	211	93	44.1	118	55.9
35–40	158	77	48.7	81	51.3
40–45	176	82	46.6	94	53.4
45–50	95	50	52.6	45	47.4
50–55	95	50	52.6	45	47.4
55–60	63	37	58.7	26	41.3
60–	163	63	38.7	100	61.3
Total	3,294	1,641	49.8	1,653	50.2

SOURCE: Dirección Nacional de Estadística, *Resumen del censo general.*

TABLE B11. *Sex of population, by age, District of Encañada, 1876*

Age	Total Population	Men	% of Total Population	Women	% of Total Population
0–15	1,176	630	53.6	546	46.4
15–20	222	93	41.9	129	58.1
20–25	277	112	40.4	165	59.6
25–30	264	108	40.9	156	59.1
30–35	179	85	47.5	94	52.5
35–40	199	104	52.3	95	47.7
40–45	157	79	50.3	78	49.7
45–50	145	62	42.8	83	57.2
50–55	72	40	55.6	32	44.4
55–60	56	25	44.6	31	55.4
60–	141	53	37.6	88	62.4
Total	2,888	1,391	48.2	1,497	51.8

SOURCE: Dirección Nacional de Estadística, *Resumen del censo general.*

TABLE B12. *Sex of population, by age, District of Ichocán, 1876*

Age	Total Population	Men	% of Total Population	Women	% of Total Population
0–15	1,937	982	50.7	955	49.3
15–20	352	173	49.1	179	50.9
20–25	540	217	40.2	323	59.8
25–30	457	215	47.0	242	53.0
30–35	301	143	47.5	158	52.5
35–40	305	145	47.5	160	52.5
40–45	207	97	46.9	110	53.1
45–50	184	81	44.0	103	56.0
50–55	98	41	41.8	57	58.2
55–60	109	41	37.6	68	62.4
60–	234	103	44.0	131	56.0
Total	4,724	2,238	47.4	2,486	52.6

SOURCE: Dirección Nacional de Estadística, *Resumen del censo general.*

TABLE B13. *Sex of population, by age, District of Jesús, 1876*

Age	Total Population	Men	% of Total Population	Women	% of Total Population
0–15	1,524	799	52.4	725	47.6
15–20	288	129	44.8	159	55.2
20–25	570	238	41.8	332	58.2
25–30	492	201	40.9	291	59.1
30–35	530	232	43.8	298	56.2
35–40	434	194	44.7	240	55.3
40–45	450	228	50.7	222	49.3
45–50	265	124	46.8	141	53.2
50–55	293	152	51.9	141	48.1
55–60	136	68	50.0	68	50.0
60–	304	133	43.8	171	56.3
Total	5,286	2,498	47.3	2,788	52.7

SOURCE: Dirección Nacional de Estadística, *Resumen del censo general.*

TABLE B14. *Sex of population, by age, District of Llacanora, 1876*

Age	Total Population	Men	% of Total Population	Women	% of Total Population
0–15	498	263	52.8	235	47.2
15–20	68	32	47.1	36	52.9
20–25	197	97	49.2	100	50.8
25–30	120	58	48.3	62	51.7
30–35	98	51	52.0	47	48.0
35–40	59	28	47.5	31	52.5
40–45	59	29	49.2	30	50.8
45–50	33	20	60.6	13	39.4
50–55	28	9	32.1	19	67.9
55–60	19	14	73.7	5	26.3
60–	30	18	60.0	12	40.0
Total	1,209	619	51.2	590	48.8

SOURCE: Dirección Nacional de Estadística, *Resumen del censo general.*

TABLE B15. *Sex of population, by age, District of Magdalena, 1876*

Age	Total Population	Men	% of Total Population	Women	% of Total Population
0–15	330	180	54.5	150	45.5
15–20	46	28	60.9	18	39.1
20–25	79	34	43.0	45	57.0
25–30	91	44	48.4	47	51.6
30–35	64	32	50.0	32	50.0
35–40	68	37	54.4	31	45.6
40–45	53	28	52.8	25	47.2
45–50	38	18	47.4	20	52.6
50–55	26	15	57.7	11	42.3
55–60	22	12	54.5	10	45.5
60–	46	21	45.7	25	54.3
Total	863	449	52.0	414	48.0

SOURCE: Dirección Nacional de Estadística, *Resumen del censo general.*

TABLE B16. *Sex of population, by age, District of Matara, 1876*

Age	Total Population	Men	% of Total Population	Women	% of Total Population
0–15	500	256	51.2	244	48.8
15–20	148	82	55.4	66	44.6
20–25	209	85	40.7	124	59.3
25–30	137	55	40.1	82	59.9
30–35	116	42	36.2	74	63.8
35–40	101	35	34.7	66	65.3
40–45	116	66	56.9	50	43.1
45–50	50	20	40.0	30	60.0
50–55	64	37	57.8	27	42.2
55–60	45	24	53.3	21	46.7
60–	90	46	51.1	44	48.9
Total	1,576	748	47.5	828	52.5

SOURCE: Dirección Nacional de Estadística, *Resumen del censo general.*

TABLE B17. *Sex of population, by age, District of San Marcos, 1876*

Age	Total Population	Men	% of Total Population	Women	% of Total Population
0–15	2,744	1,409	51.3	1,335	48.7
15–20	538	272	50.6	266	49.4
20–25	830	416	50.1	414	49.9
25–30	582	260	44.7	322	55.3
30–35	516	245	47.5	271	52.5
35–40	419	187	44.6	232	55.4
40–45	372	186	50.0	186	50.0
45–50	303	149	49.2	154	50.8
50–55	215	93	43.3	122	56.7
55–60	168	75	44.6	93	55.4
60–	360	160	44.4	200	55.6
Total	7,047	3,452	49.0	3,595	51.0

SOURCE: Dirección Nacional de Estadística, *Resumen del censo general.*

TABLE B18. *Sex of population, by age, District of San Pablo, 1876*

Age	Total Population	Men	% of Total Population	Women	% of Total Population
0–15	2,842	1,528	53.8	1,314	46.2
15–20	674	321	47.6	353	52.4
20–25	992	441	44.5	551	55.5
25–30	708	345	48.7	363	51.3
30–35	540	266	49.3	274	50.7
35–40	450	231	51.3	219	48.7
40–45	385	164	42.6	221	57.4
45–50	305	137	44.9	168	55.1
50–55	249	99	39.8	150	60.2
55–60	142	65	45.8	77	54.2
60–	306	128	41.8	178	58.2
Total	7,593	3,725	49.1	3,868	50.9

SOURCE: Dirección Nacional de Estadística, *Resumen del censo general.*

Cited Trials

CAUSAS CRIMINALES

ADC/CSJ/CC, legajo 1, 9-1-1862, Proceso judicial seguido de oficio contra Isabel Basauri y su hija Rosaura Cabanillas por maltratos inferidos a Remigia Bermúdes, natural de Cajamarca.

ADC/CSJ/CC, legajo 1, 14-1-1862, Francisco del Campo y su esposa Doña Francisca Ramírez, litigando con Don Manuel Espantoso por agresiones personales e insultos.

ADC/CSJ/CC, legajo 1, 15-1-1862, Don José Nasario Alegrío, vecino de Cajamarca, litigando con Andrea Soto por el robo de una romana perol y otras especies.

ADC/CSJ/CC, legajo 1, 19-1-1862, Lorenza Cabrera vecina de Cajamarca litigando con el capitán de gendermería Don José María Cortés sobre entrega de la menor Manuela Chávez quien fue regalada al susodicho por Tadea Casas y José Manuel Goycochea.

ADC/CSJ/CC, legajo 1, 2-4-1862, Proceso criminal seguido a los indígenas Asencio y Eugenio Tongo por maltratos a Baltazara Minchán, causándole aborto.

ADC/CSJ/CC, legajo 1, 5-4-1862, Criminal de oficio contra Don Manuel Goycochea por flagelación a un niño.

ADC/CSJ/CC, legajo 2, 9-9-1862, Juicio seguido de oficio contra Asunción Eustacio por maltratos a Fernanda Rodríguez.

ADC/CSJ/CC, legajo 2, 17-12-1862, Estefania Marín vecina de Cajamarca con Don Pedro Torres sobre agresión personal.

ADC/CSJ/CC, legajo 3, 1-11-1862, Proceso seguido por la Real Justicia en nombre de Doña Juana Silva contra Lorenzo Horna, Tomás Silva y otros por el homicidio de Don Juan Silva.

ADC/CSJ/CC, legajo 3, 4-3-1863, Antonio Llave, sindico-procurador de la ciudad de Cajabamba en nombre de Doña Estefania Marín litigando con Don Pedro Torres Calderón sobre agresión personal.

ADC/CSJ/CC, legajo 5, 9-6-1863, Criminal por querella de Doña María Natividad Chavarri contra el capitán de cavallería Don Manuel Ortega por delito de rapto y estupro en la persona de la menor Beatriz Chavarri.

ADC/CSJ/CC, legajo 5, 14-7-1863, Proceso judicial seguido de oficio al asiático Manuel de la Cruz, sobre heridas graves cometidos en agravio de Antonia Lamar, sirvienta de Aurora Centurión.

ADC/CSJ/CC, legajo 6, 13-11-1863, José Quevedo y Don Valerio Chávez vecinos de Celendín, litigando con Doña Clara Pita sobre agresiones personales contra María Chávez, esposa del primero.

ADC/CSJ/CC, legajo 6, 5-12-1863, Criminal contra Baltazar Ramos, por haber forzado i violada a la menor inmatura Melchora Sánchez Silva hija de Catalino Saucedo Silva.

ADC/CSJ/CC, legajo 7, 3-3-1864, Proceso judicial seguido de oficio contra la reo profuga Cayetana Salazar vecina de Jesús, por agresiones a Josefa Vallejo.

ADC/CSJ/CC, legajo 9, 29-2-1864, Criminal seguida de oficio contra Fermín Cerdán por heridas a María Isabel Ordóñez.

ADC/CSJ/CC, legajo 9, 21-6-1864, Criminal contra Leandra Álvarez y Narro por aborto de que la acusa Gertrudis Azañero.

ADC/CSJ/CC, legajo 9, 8-8-1864, Criminal de oficio contra Manuela Agip por heridas a Buenaventura Vargas de San Pablo.

ADC/CSJ/CC, legajo 10, 27-10-1864. Luis Llacsa, residente en el pueblo de Chetilla, con el conductor de la hacienda Cadena, por robo, conato de homicidio en la persona e hijos.

ADC/CSJ/CC, legajo 10, 26-11-1864, Proceso judicial seguido de oficio contra Sebastián Ortega por el homicidio a Lorenza Mendoza en la hacienda de Sunchubamba en la Asunción.

ADC/CSJ/CC, legajo 11, 13-1-1865, Raymunda Goicochea con su consorte Melchor Figueroa por adulterio con Dionicia Figueroa.

ADC/CSJ/CC, legajo 11, 2-2-1865, Proceso judicial seguido a Mariana Montenegro y otras por el brebaje que le ha dado a Francisca Marín, natural de Celendín.

ADC/CSJ/CC, legajo 13, 3-8-1865, Calixto Juárez de Huasmín, denunciando a su suegra Josefa Oyarse por agresiones.

ADC/CSJ/CC, legajo 13, 14-9-1865, Marcela Montoya denunciando a su consorte Don José Chávez Velásquez por maltratos.

ADC/CSJ/CC, legajo 13, 20-10-1865, La real justicia procesando a Tomasa Castillo y María Manuela Rodríguez por complicidad en el intento de fuga de los presos de la cárcel pública de Cajamarca.

ADC/CSJ/CC, legajo 14, 4-7-1866, Proceso judicial seguido de oficio contra Gerónimo Miranda por el conato de homicidio, maltratos y estupro perpetrado en la menor María Asencia León.

ADC/CSJ/CC, legajo 17, 9-7-1867, La real justicia procesando criminalmente a Juana Rodríguez por el homicidio del menor José Florentino Miranda.

ADC/CSJ/CC, legajo 17, 1-8-1867, Proceso judicial seguido de oficio al Presbítero Pedro José Infante por prisión arbitraria de Juana Mercado.

ADC/CSJ/CC, legajo 19, 11-4-1868, Proceso judicial seguido de oficio contra

Antolino Álvarez y Manuel Toledo vecinos del pueblo de Ichocán por el homicidio de Tomasa Vásquez.

ADC/CSJ/CC, legajo 19, 25-9-1868, La real justicia procesando judicialmente a María de los Santos Chávez por maltratos a Felipe Leyva del distrito de Ichocán.

ADC/CSJ/CC, legajo 20, 15-10-1868, Proceso judicial seguido de oficio contra Manuel Torres de Ichocán por la muerte de María Albarrón.

ADC/CSJ/CC, legajo 20, 22-10-1868, Doña Eusebia Olórtegui, de Moyobamba, con Augusto Krol por injurias.

ADC/CSJ/CC, legajo 21, 12-1-1869, Proceso judicial seguido de oficio a Asunción Vásquez, alias Shulilo, por el homicidio de Manuela Alimra Urrelo, de Cajamarca.

ADC/CSJ/CC, legajo 22, 10-5-1869, Francisco de las Llagas Ruiz con Vicente Noriega sobre estupro de la menor Clemencia Ruiz en la ciudad de Moyobamba.

ADC/CSJ/CC, legajo 22, 17-6-1869, Proceso judicial seguido de oficio a Antonio Minchán por el homicidio de Josefa Chingal, natural de la ciudad de Cajamarca.

ADC/CSJ/CC, legajo 22, 6-8-1869, María Rosario Villacorta de Moyobamba con Manuel Estevan Rocha por robo y estupro de la menor María Andrea del Aguilar.

ADC/CSJ/CC, legajo 23, 24-1-1870, Proceso criminal seguido de oficio contra José de la Torre y María Arrauco por maltratos y fractura de una pierna en agravio de José Sánchez.

ADC/CSJ/CC, legajo 23, 3-5-1870, José Asunción Portilla de la Asunción con Natividad y María Mercedes Escalante y otros por injurias verbales.

ADC/CSJ/CC, legajo 23, 15-10-1870, Asencio Guaman de Puilucoma, perteneciente a los alrededores de Cajamarca, con Prudencia Chávez y su hija Jesús del Campo por agresiones y prisión arbitraria a su cuñada Matea Gallardo.

ADC/CSJ/CC, legajo 23, 22-10-1870, María de los Santos Linares de la Asunción con María Pasión Sumarán por injurias.

ADC/CSJ/CC, legajo 24, 1-7-1871, José Silva y Soto, de Cajamarca, con Jacoba Arbayza y Rosario Ravines por injurias.

ADC/CSJ/CC, legajo 24, 1-9-1871, Pedro José Chavarri de Cajamarca con Juan Esteban Cabrera por los delitos de rapto y violación de la menor Rosaura Carbajal.

ADC/CSJ/CC, legajo 25, 30-4-1872, Don Pedro Chavarri, vecino de Cajamarca, litigando con Esteban Cabrera por el rapto, estupro y violación en agravio de su menor hija Rosauro Carbajal.

ADC/CSJ/CC, legajo 26, 14-6-1872, Manuel Luna Leiva, vecino del distrito de la Asunción litigando con María León por injurias a su esposa Melchora Álvarez.

ADC/CSJ/CC, legajo 26, 3-7-1872, Proceso judicial seguido de oficio a Andrea Chávez y Natividad Bardoles por maltratos que le ocacionaron el aborto de María Jesús Salazar.

ADC/CSJ/CC, legajo 26, 19-9-1872, Juan Álvarez, vecino de Cajamarca, denunciando a Doña Narcisa Tejada por maltratos en agravio de su hermana Felipa Álvarez lo que ocacionó aborto.

ADC/CSJ/CC, legajo 26, 29-10-1872, Doña Adelaida Sheen litigando con Don Casimiro Basauri por injurias.

ADC/CSJ/CC, legajo 27, 6-11-1872, Bonifacio Alvarado y Doña Candelaria Alvarado, vecinos de la Encañada litigando con Doña Micaela Bringas por injurias.

ADC/CSJ/CC, legajo 27, 19-11-1872, Proceso judicial seguido de oficio a José Adriano Silva, vecino de Matara, por intento de homicidio en agravio de Petrona Correa.

ADC/CSJ/CC, legajo 27, 19-11-1872, Doña María Antonia Mendis, vecina del distrito de San Jorge, litigando con Doña Lorenza Sánchez y Luciano Alcántara por robo de dinero.

ADC/CSJ/CC, legajo 27, 5-12-1872, Doña María Vallejos, vecino de Matara litigando con el ex-juez de paz de dicho pueblo Don Bartolomé Bueno por despojo de un terreno.

ADC/CSJ/CC, legajo 28, 26-3-1872, Francisco Bringas en nombre de Jacoba Bermúdez litigando con Manuela Chávez sobre injurias.

ADC/CSJ/CC, legajo 28, 9-1-1873, Proceso judicial seguido de oficio a Martín y Juan Burgos por el aborto de María Encarnación Bartra.

ADC/CSJ/CC, legajo 28, 28-1-1873, Proceso judicial seguido de oficio a Andrés Mestanza vecino de Cajamarca por agresión personal en agravio de Simona Toculi.

ADC/CSJ/CC, legajo 30, 20-10-1873, María Antonia Vigo, de San Pablo, litigando con Don Máximo Castañeda, José y Toribio Revilla y Gabriel Pérez por agresiones a su esposo Don Juan Arroyo.

ADC/CSJ/CC, legajo 31, 9-2-1874, Proceso judicial seguido de oficio contra José Encarnación por prisión arbitraria en agravio de María Llacsa de Chetilla.

ADC/CSJ/CC, legajo 32, 13-7-1874, Proceso seguido de oficio a Gabriela Mendo por el delito de infanticidio de Francisca Pájares, de Jesús.

ADC/CSJ/CC, legajo 32, 14-7-1874, Francisca Sifuentes de Cepeda, de Cajamarca, con Jacoba Bermúdez sobre injurias verbales.

ADC/CSJ/CC, legajo 32, 23-7-1874, Jacoba Bermúdez con Francisca Sifuentes por injurias.

ADC/CSJ/CC, legajo 32, 10-10-1874, Juan Manuel Vera, de Cajamarca, con Leopoldo, Francisca, Catalina Mestanza y Benito Briones por injurias.

ADC/CSJ/CC, legajo 32, 12-10-1874, Casimiro Salazar con Felipa Bueno por agresión personal.

ADC/CSJ/CC, legajo 33, 14-7-1875, Doña Santosa Quispe de Cajamarca con Aparicio Gruzo sobre entrega de tres cerdos y siete cabezas de ganado vacuno.

ADC/CSJ/CC, legajo 34, 10-11-1876, Natividad Arana con Isabel Encalada y Tomasa Villanueva sobre calumnia.

ADC/CSJ/CC, legajo 34, 13-11-1876, Doña Isabel Encalada y Doña Tomasa Villanueva con don Natividad Arana de Arze por injurias.

ADC/CSJ/CC, legajo 35, 3-3-1877, Proceso judicial seguido de oficio a Máxima, Matilde, Estefania, Baltazara, Andrés y Cecilio Espinoza, de la Asunción, por el delito de infanticidio a Ricardina Sáenz.

ADC/CSJ/CC, legajo 35, 31-10-1877, Doña Josefa Chávez denunciando al gobernador de la Encañada Justo Carranzo por abuso de autoridad en el reclutamiento.

ADC/CSJ/CC, legajo 35, 11-12-1877, Candelaria Arce con Cayetana Mille de Villanueva por injurias graves.

ADC/CSJ/CC, legajo 36, 9-1-1878, Cayetana Mille de Villanueva con Candelaria Arce por injurias verbales.

ADC/CSJ/CC, legajo 36, 10-1-1878, Proceso judicial seguido de oficio a José María Fernandes de Cajamarca por las agresiones a Andrea Díaz.

ADC/CSJ/CC, legajo 37, 12-1-1879, El teniente gobernador José Damoso Guerra denunciando a Agustina de la Cruz por haber envenado a Melchora Azañero de Cajamarca.

ADC/CSJ/CC, legajo 37, 5-6-1879, El presbítero Don Bartolomé Gálvez, residente en el distrito de Chetilla, litigando con Simón Alegría por violación a su sobrina la menor Catalina Pájares.

ADC/CSJ/CC, legajo 37, 22-5-1880, Manuela Mestanza, de Cajamarca, con María Jesús y Gregoria Astopilco por injurias y heridas personales.

ADC/CSJ/CC, legajo 37, 5-11-1880, Isidora Paico de Magdalena con María del Carmen Ducos por incendio de una casa.

ADC/CSJ/CC, legajo 38, 18-9-1882, Josefa Alcántara, de Cajamarca, con Manuel María Alcántara, sobre estupro realizado en la menor Zoila Alcántara.

ADC/CSJ/CC, legajo 39, 11-9-1882, Vicente Briones, de Cajamarca, con Manuel Inocente Gaona, por agresiones con arma blanca en agravio de su sobrina Adela Alcalde.

ADC/CSJ/CC, legajo 39, 30-11-1883, Viviana Rangel con Pedro Villavicencio, Isidoro Mercado, vecinos de Jesús, por el homicidio de su esposo, Don Cruz Guerra y agresiones a Sacramento García.

ADC/CSJ/CC, legajo 40, 31-7-1885, Doña Petronila Astopilco de Quiroz de Cajamarca con María Peralta por injurias verbales.

ADC/CSJ/CC, legajo 40, 7-11-1885, El juez de paz de Ichocán Eduardo Arroyo iniciando proceso judicial contra José Manuel Carrera por agresiones a Tomasa Mendoza.

ADC/CSJ/CC, legajo 41, 6-2-1886, Luis Gamarra, en nombre de su esposa Doña Manuela Villanueva y su hija Doña Asunción Gamarra, de Cajamarca, en juicio con Doña Manuela Abanto y su hija Doña Carmen Bringas por injurias verbales.

ADC/CSJ/CC, legajo 43, 30-6-1886, Virginia Barba en juicio con José María Quiroz, Manuela Quiroz, José Manuel Arroyo y Isardo Arroyo por violación de domicilio.

ADC/CSJ/CC, legajo 44, 15-10-1886, Proceso judicial seguido de oficio a José Uriarte, de Llama, Chota, por el homicidio de la menor María Jamina Guevara.

ADC/CSJ/CC, legajo 44, 18-10-1886, Pedro Roncal de Cajamarca con Juana María Taboada, su esposo Diego Tisnado, Lipona Tisnado y María Carmen Peres por intento de homicidio, agresiones y robo de un pellón.

ADC/CSJ/CC, legajo 45, 13-11-1886, María Encarnación Tirado, de Cajamarca, en nombre de su menor hija Tomasa, litigando con Ana y Cruz Campos por agresiones.

ADC/CSJ/CC, legajo 45, 27-12-1886, Marcos Paz con Cayetano Sánchez por el rapto y estupro de la menor Marcelina Paz.

ADC/CSJ/CC, legajo 46, 14-4-1887, Proceso seguido de oficio a Angelina Chávez y Luis Cabanillas por el homicidio de Sebastián Azañero.

ADC/CSJ/CC, legajo 50, 9-5-1888, [José] Isabel Espinosa de Lulicaja en San Pablo con Bruno Romero y Luisa Cabanillas por intento de homicidio en agravio de Doña Mercedes Cabanillas.

ADC/CSJ/CC, legajo 51, 3-3-1889, Proceso judicial seguido de oficio a Melchora Chavarri acusada de infanticidio en agravio de Zoila Maita.

ADC/CSJ/CC, legajo 51, 11-3-1889, Proceso judicial seguido de oficio a Andrés Espinoza por agresiones a María Asunción Portal, de la Asunción.

ADC/CSJ/CC, legajo 54, 23-9-1899, Asencia Camacho de Cajamarca con Manuel Fernández alias "El Chango" por amenazas y violación de domicilio.

ADC/CSJ/CC, legajo 54, 3-12-1889, Manuel Goicochea, de Cajamarca, con Domingo Ortiz y Manuela Alcalde por robo de la menor María Goicochea.

ADC/CSJ/CC, legajo 55, 24-1-1890, La real justicia procesando a Andrea Camacho, presa en la cárcel pública, por envenamiento en agravio de Juana Chávez.

ADC/CSJ/CC, legajo 55, 20-5-1890, María Isabel Vásquez de Bambamarca con Lizardo Villanueva por el secuestro de Joaquina Vásquez.

ADC/CSJ/CC, legajo 55, 21-5-1890, Rosario R. Vda de Urteaga litigando con Don Rafael Chavarri y Don Artemio Sheen sobre lesiones e intento de violación.

ADC/CSJ/CC, legajo 56, 14-7-1890, Gabriela Mendo de Jesús, con Mariano Rojas, Juan Borgas y Rosendo Meza por el secuestro de Francisco García.

ADC/CSJ/CC, legajo 56, 17-7-1890, Manuela Abanto de Cajamarca con Elías Arribasplata por el intento de homicidio de su hijo Gregorio Bringas.

ADC/CSJ/CC, legajo 56, 26-7-1890, Proceso judicial seguido de oficio al Teniente Alcalde del distrito de la Trinidad, Don Manuel Silva, por delitos contra la religión.

ADC/CSJ/CC, legajo 57, 10-9-1890, Margarita Hidalgo de Matara con María Vigo y su hija Clorinda Sánchez por calumnias.

ADC/CSJ/CC, legajo 57, 22-10-1890, Proceso judicial seguido de oficio a Melchora Martos sobre envenamiento en Margarito Rubio, de la ciudad de Cajamarca.

ADC/CSJ/CC, legajo 57, 6-11-1890, Dionicio Díaz, con José Sánchez—alias Pichaco—por intento de homicidio en agravio de su hija María de los Santos Díaz.

ADC/CSJ/CC, legajo 58, 15-11-1890, La real justicia procesando a Antonio Vargas por maltratos a María Castañeda, natural de Ichocán.

ADC/CSJ/CC, legajo 59, 2-12-1890. La real justicia procesando a Juan Miguel Saldaña por secuestro a la menor María Ezequila, hija de Marcelina Alaya.

ADC/CSJ/CC, legajo 60, 20-1-1891, La real justicia procesando a Juana Peralta por el homicidio de Magdalena Díaz perpetrado en el distrito de Cochabamba, Chota.

ADC/CSJ/CC, legajo 60, 4-3-1891, Proceso judicial seguido de oficio a los menores Julio Castañeda, Pacífico Gastanaduy y Endoro Cerna por el homicidio de la menor Hortencia Mercado.

ADC/CSJ/CC, legajo 61, 10-4-1891, Juana Goicochea, con Manuel Silva por agresiones a su esposo Gabriel Castañeda.

ADC/CSJ/CC, legajo 62, 19-5-1891, Manuel Saldaña y Aurora Chávez de la Encañada con Juan Salazar Estrada por agresiones.

ADC/CSJ/CC, legajo 62, 11-6-1891, Pedro Dilas, de Cajamarca, con Manuel Chalán por agresiones en la persona de su hija Manuela Dilas Chalán.

ADC/CSJ/CC, legajo 63, 22-6-1891, Martina Marreros con Santos y Natividad Centurión, Úrsula Cabanillas por agresiones personales.

ADC/CSJ/CC, legajo 63, 12-9-1891, Denuncia presentada por el juez de paz Don Manuel María Díaz en contra de María Manuela Casas, Magdalena Jara y José V. Sandoval por desacato a la autoridad y agresiones en agravio de Juana Jara dueña de los terrenos de Huayllapampa en Cajamarca.

ADC/CSJ/CC, legajo 63, 9-12-1891, Querella criminal, Don José Jesús Tello contra su esposa Ester Pinedo por el delito de adulterio.

ADC/CSJ/CC, legajo 64, 10-10-1891, Emilia Verástegui, esposa legítima de Don Eulogio Armas, con María Centurión por injurias.

ADC/CSJ/CC, legajo 64, 12-10-1891, Ninfa Revilla de Mosqueira, de Monte Alegre, en nombre de su esposo José Mosqueira, litigando con Manuel Gil, Hilario Burgos, José Manuel Burgos, Rafael Rombo y otros por el intento de homicidio.

ADC/CSJ/CC, legajo 64, 7-11-1891, María Cornelia Pita de Cajamarca en juicio con María Encarnación Cadenillas sobre los delitos agresiones verbales y robo.

ADC/CSJ/CC, legajo 64, 21-11-1891, Don Sebastián Cabrera, de Cajamarca, con Juana Cabanillas y Jacoba N. por robo y secuestro de la menor Bernabé Cabrera.

ADC/CSJ/CC, legajo 64, 8-12-1891, Proceso judicial seguido de oficio a Martina Terán, de la hacienda de Callancas por el homicidio de José Resurrección Cuevas.

ADC/CSJ/CC, legajo 65, 30-1-1892, Juana Miranda de Cajamarca, con Micaela Galarreta, Agueda y Zoila Sorogéstua por violación de domicilio y amenazas a Juana Miranda.

ADC/CSJ/CC, legajo 65, 11-2-1892, María Gelacia Flores de Cajamarca, con Trinidad Asareto por violación de domicilio.

ADC/CSJ/CC, legajo 65, 15-2-1892, Manuela Correa, viuda de Palomino, de San Pablo, con María Jesús Burgos de Cancino y otros por allanamiento de domicilio y amenazas.

ADC/CSJ/CC, legajo 65, 22-2-1892, Proceso judicial seguido de oficio a Aurelito González, preso en la cárcel por la desaparación de su esposa Asunción Ramírez.

ADC/CSJ/CC, legajo 66, 2-4-1892, Agapito Sánchez, con Cipriano Céspedes y otros vecinos de Ichocán por violación de domicilio, robo e intento de homicidio.

ADC/CSJ/CC, legajo 66, 14-5-1892, Proceso judicial seguido de oficio a Fidela Vargas por la muerte de María Vásquez de San Pablo.

ADC/CSJ/CC, legajo 69, 4-1-1893, Doña Santos Casanova, de Cajamarca, con Luisa Cotrina y Natividad López por lesiones y amenazas.

ADC/CSJ/CC, legajo 69, 10-1-1893, Fermina Ramos de Calispuquio, Cajamarca, denunciando al mayoral de la finca del Cumbe y otros por secuestro de su hermano Remigio López y robo de dos caballos.

ADC/CSJ/CC, legajo 69, 29-1-1893, Doña Manuela Alcántara de oficio vivandera denunciando a Miguel Goicochea y Aurelio Barrena por agresiones.

ADC/CSJ/CC, legajo 70, 5-5-1893, Proceso seguido de oficio a Pedro Novoa Jiménez por violación de domicilio de Doña Laura Escuza y amenazas con arma de fuego.

ADC/CSJ/CC, legajo 70, 5-5-1893, Proceso judicial seguido de oficio a los reos Manuel Asencia, María Rosario, y Narciso Sembrano por el aborto provocado de Paula Saucedo y maltratos a José Dolores Olivares.

ADC/CSJ/CC, legajo 73, 22-2-1894, Simona Malaver, de Matara, con Benedicto Glandos, Juan Pérez y Manuel Ruiz sobre violación de domicilio y robo de dinero.

ADC/CSJ/CC, legajo 74, 2-7-1894, Hermegilda Villavicencio de Noriega, de la villa de Jesús, con Doña Juliana Vargas viuda de Aguirre y sus tres hijas por injurias.

ADC/CSJ/CC, legajo 74, 28-8-1894, María Josefa Calderón de Cajamarca con Jacoba Concepción [Castillo] por injurias.

ADC/CSJ/CC, legajo 75, 18-1-1895, Doña Sánchez contra Manuesto Tirado por violación y estupro en la menor Agueda Segura.

ADC/CSJ/CC, legajo 75, 13-2-1895, Francisca Bustamante, de la estancia de Huambocancha, en juicio con Gregoria Bustamante y Bustamante por defraudación de bienes.

ADC/CSJ/CC, legajo 75, 4-3-1895, Carolina Infante de la Asunción, con Santos Sáenz, Daniel Mendoza, Francisco Ángulo y otros, por violación de domicilio e intento de homicidio.

ADC/CSJ/CC, legajo 75, 5-3-1895, Proceso judicial seguido de oficio a Agustín Gurbillón y María Jesús Valderrama, de Cajamarca, sobre violación de domicilio y amenazas a Cecilia Quispe Quiroz.

ADC/CSJ/CC, legajo 78, 15-5-1896, Proceso judicial seguido de oficio a José Bringas Castillo de la Encañada por lesiones y aborto en agravio de Pascuala Vargas.

ADC/CSJ/CC, legajo 79, 2-6-1896, Elena Cruzado de San Pablo en juicio con Don Tadeo Terán y su hijo Segundo Terán sobre injurias.

ADC/CSJ/CC, legajo 79, 15-9-1896, José Dolores Jara, de Ichocán, con Doña María Rosario Tirado, esposa de Don Pedro Horna, por injurias y de flagelación a su menor hija María Aurora Jara.

ADC/CSJ/CC, legajo 80, 29-10-1896, María Trinidad Sánchez de Cajamarca con Juan Delgado y Andrés Gutiérrez, por amenazas, rapto e intento de violación.

ADC/CSJ/CC, legajo 81, 12-12-1896, Melecio Tirado, de Cajamarca, con Manuel María Tirado por injurias.

ADC/CSJ/CC, legajo 83, 6-4-1897, Proceso judicial seguido de oficio a Vicente Sousa sobre secuestro.

ADC/CSJ/CC, legajo 83, 6-5-1897, Proceso judicial de oficio seguido a Nicolás Malca sobre estupro en la menor Mercedes Velesmoro.

ADC/CSJ/CC, legajo 84, 9-7-1897, Doña Rosenda y Patrocina Mugica, de Cajamarca, con Doña Aurora Sánchez y hermanos por injurias inferidas a sus menores hijas Atenodora Alarcón y María Ángeles Rodríguez.

ADC/CSJ/CC, legajo 84, 3-8-1897, Proceso judicial seguido de oficio a Casimiro Chilcote sobre el delito de uxoricidio de María Huaccha perpetrado en la Paccha, distrito de Cajamarca.

ADC/CSJ/CC, legajo 85, 21-9-1897, Manuel Encarnación Llerena de Cajamarca en juicio con José Eduardo Apolitano, su madre de este María Jesús Cepeda sobre violación de domicilio y agresiones.

ADC/CSJ/CC, legajo 88, 27-9-1898, Miguel Quispe y su esposa Juana Torres con José María, Ramón Mille y otros por violación de domicilio y lesiones.

ADC/CSJ/CC, legajo 89, 5-11-1898, María Resurrección Julcamoro viuda de Sichas, en nombre de su menor hija Rosario Sichas, con Lisandro Altamirano sobre rapto y estupro.

ADC/CSJ/CC, legajo 89, 5-12-1898, Doña Ana Quiroz de Abanto en juicio con Manuel María Cabrera por calumnia.

ADC/CSJ/CC, legajo 90, 16-3-1899, Proceso judicial seguido de oficio a María Calla por el homicidio de Don Remigio Pretel.

ADC/CSJ/CC, legajo 90, 19-4-1899, María Isabel Araujo litigando con Manuela Soto de Rodríguez por agresión y aborto.

ADC/CSJ/CC, legajo 91, 4-7-1899, El indígena Mariano Chilón de Cajamarca con Pablo Malimbo, Justo Malquipoma y otros por el secuestro de sus hijos Pedro, José y Rosario Chilón.

CAUSAS ORDINARIAS

ADC/CSJ/CO, legajo 1, 24-3-1862, Vicente Vigo en nombre de su esposa Nicolasa de los Ríos, su cuñada María Petrocila, vecinos de San Pablo, con Isidoro Ríos sobre divisón y partición de los bienes de Gregorio Ríos y Barnardina Correa.

ADC/CSJ/CO, legajo 130, 2-4-1892, Felipe Hernández y su esposa Doña Juana Horna con Manuela Terán y Guillermo Urbina sobre despojo de un tereno nombrado "El Puquio" ubicado en el distrito de San Pablo.

ADC/CSJ/CO, legajo 130, 23-4-1892, Washington Silva Santisteban de Cajamarca, en nombre de José López Llovera y Manuel Llovera con María Eustaquia Llovera sobre derecho a los bienes del intestado Pío Llovera.

ADC/CSJ/CO, legajo 130, 5-5-1892, Manuela Izquierda, con Don Francisco Gálvez Egusquiza sobre entrega de un menor.

ADC/CSJ/CO, legajo 139, 12-7-1893, Don José Pallango representando a su esposa Doña Asunción Ruiz y otros con Estevan Dario, Manuel Ramos Ruiz sobre nulidad de la división y partición de los terrenos de Shirac, Liglipampa y Conapata.

JUECES DE PAZ

ADC/CSJ/Jueces de Paz, legajo 1, Francisca Cotrina, esposa legítima de Eugenio Chávez de esta vecindad.

Notes

1. INTRODUCTION

1. Nazzari, "An Urgent Need to Conceal," p. 105.

2. Pitt-Rivers, *The People of the Sierra*, p. 113.

3. Chambers, *From Subjects to Citizens*, p. 4.

4. Hünefeldt, *Liberalism in the Bedroom*, 2000.

5. For studies of plebeian notions of honor, consult the volume edited by Johnson and Lipsett-Rivera, *The Faces of Honor*.

6. Johnson and Lipsett-Rivera, *The Faces of Honor*, p. 11.

7. Peristiany, *Honour and Shame*; Pitt-Rivers, *The People of the Sierra*, and idem, *The Fate of Shechem*.

8. Although I studied 234 trials closely, in Appendix C I list only the 154 whose stories I relate in some detail here.

9. Martínez-Alier, *Marriage, Class and Colour in Nineteenth Century Cuba*.

10. For Klubock's discussion of these questions, see "Writing the History of Women and Gender in Twentieth-Century Chile."

11. Seventy-nine criminal trial records from the years 1862–1863 remain; the corresponding number for the years 1872–1873 is sixty-two. Only fifteen trial records from the years 1882–1883 exist in the ADC. The number of trial records preserved from 1879 to 1884 is extremely low, only twenty-seven.

12. According to Florencia Mallon (*The Defense of Community in Peru's Central Highlands*, p. 358), "Related to the word *tinta* (ink), this term [*tinterillo*] refers to someone versed in the legal process, sometimes but not necessarily a lawyer, who profits from—and therefore tends to instigate or encourage—litigation."

13. For a description of Cajamarcan power politics and comment on how these impinged on the legal process, see Taylor, "Los orígenes del bandolerismo en Hualgayoc, 1870–1900," p. 223; idem, "Society and Politics in late Nineteenth Century Peru," p. 17.

14. J. Scott, *Domination and the Arts of Resistance*, p. 4.
15. Martínez-Alier, *Marriage, Class and Colour in Nineteenth Century Cuba*, p. 1.
16. ADC/Corte Superior de Justicia (hereafter CSJ)/Causas Criminales (hereafter CC), legajo 34, 10-11-1876. In order to shorten notes I have cited trials only with their *legajo* (dossier number) and date (in day-month-year order); a full list of all criminal and civil trials cited can be found in Appendix C. Other documents, such as wills, police reports, and notarial records, are cited fully in the notes and are therefore not listed at the end.
17. ADC/CSJ/CC, legajo 84, 9-7-1897.
18. Middendorf, *Peru*, p. 212 (all translations are mine unless otherwise noted).
19. ADC/CSJ/CC, legajo 10, 27-10-1864.

2. CAJAMARCAN SOCIETY UNDER THE MAGNIFYING GLASS

1. Peruvian political representation and administration divided the country into *departamentos, provincias* (provinces), and *distritos* (districts). A district usually encompassed a town and its environs and had as its administrative head a *teniente gobernador*, who might well be a local landowner or merchant. Provinces and departments were headed by subprefects and prefects, respectively.
2. Taylor, "Society and Politics in Late Nineteenth Century Peru."
3. Taylor, "Earning a Living in Hualgayoc, 1870–1900."
4. For representatives of these views, see Burga and Flores Galindo, *Apogeo y crisis de la república aristocrática*.
5. Taylor, "Estates, Freeholders and Peasant Communities in Cajamarca, 1876–1972," p. 6, Table 2.
6. Taylor, "Earning a Living in Hualgayoc, 1870–1900," p. 109.
7. Taylor, "Literature as History"; idem, "Main Trends in Agrarian Capitalist Development," p. 81.
8. Ellefsen, "1780," p. 170. Also see Gootenberg, "Population and Ethnicity in Early Republican Peru."
9. Dirección Nacional de Estadística, *Resumen del censo general*, pp. 448–532.
10. Within the province of Cajamarca, variations among districts were pronounced. Whereas 4,063 white inhabitants were counted in Ichocán (of a total of 4,723), equaling 86.1 percent, Llacanora had only 85 white inhabitants, or 7 percent of its 1,211 total. Indians accounted for 91.8 percent of the district of Llacanora's inhabitants. The town of Cajamarca had 8,064 Indian (53.5 percent), 4,054 mestizo (26.7 percent), and 2,830 (18.8 percent) white inhabitants.
11. Gootenberg, "Population and Ethnicity in Early Republican Peru."
12. Taylor, "Main Trends in Agrarian Capitalist Development," p. 50.
13. Taylor, "Cambios capitalistas en las haciendas cajamarquinas, 1900–35," p. 126.

14. Taylor, "Organización económica y social de la hacienda San Felipe de Combayo, 1918," pp. 143–192.

15. The government issued *boletos de ocupación honrosa* (i.e., certificates confirming that men were gainfully employed) to *enganche* laborers in an attempt to regulate the contracting of labor.

16. *Enganche* was a device used by coastal plantation owners to obtain migrant labor from the highlands. Intermediaries, usually landlords or merchants, extended loans to highland peasants, which were later repaid with labor on the coastal plantations. For a fuller account, see Gonzales, "Capitalist Agriculture and Labour Contracting in Northern Peru, 1880–1905."

17. On the impact of temporary migration on women's workload in twentieth-century Cajamarca, see Deere, "The Differentiation of the Peasantry and Family Structure," p. 433. Anne H. Johnson found that capitalist penetration, rising pressure on land, and male labor migration produced a gender imbalance of 120 women to 100 men in nineteenth-century Chile. She notes the high incidence of female-headed households. See "The Impact of Market Agriculture on Family and Household Structure in Nineteenth Century Chile."

18. In Llacanora, on the other hand, seasonal male migration seems to have produced less of a gender imbalance: in no age group under fifty did the percentage of males drop under 47 percent. As most males were ten to fifteen years old it seems more likely that the smallness of the sample (the entire district of Llacanora boasted only 619 male inhabitants) rather than seasonal migration accounts for this.

19. Dirección Nacional de Estadística, *Resumen del censo general.* Also see Appendix B here.

20. Middendorf, *Peru,* p. 163. Earlier in the century William Bennet Stevenson noted of Cajamarca, "This city carries on a considerable trade with Lambayeque and other places on the coast, furnishing them with the different home manufactured articles; such as baizes, bayetones, panetes, a kind of coarse cloth, flannels, tocuyos, etc., and receiving in return European manufactures, soap, sugar, cocoa, brandy, wine, indigo, *hierba de Paraguay,* salted fish, iron, steel, etc." (*A Historical and Descriptive Narrative,* pp. 137–138).

21. Taylor, "Society and Politics in Late Nineteenth Century Peru," p. 12.

22. Manuel Romero, "Datos tomados para la estadística de la provincia de Hualgayoc," *El Peruano* (19 November 1874), cited in Taylor, "Economía y sociedad en la provincia de Hualgayoc, 1870–1900," p. 42.

23. The combined cost of production and transport of barley, beans, and corn from the hacienda San Felipe de Combayo to Celendín exceeded the fetching prices of these products (see Taylor, "Organización económica y social de la hacienda San Felipe de Combayo, 1918," pp. 176–177). Similarly, the transport of wheat to Lima accounted for 59 percent of its total cost, reducing *hacendado* profits.

24. Taylor, "Earning a Living in Hualgayoc, 1870–1900," p. 111.

25. In Hualgayoc, the population was growing rapidly, notes Taylor: for every person who died, three were born (*Bandits and Politics in Peru,* p. 11).

26. Taylor, "Society and Politics in Late Nineteenth Century Peru," p. 15.

27. Taylor, "Los orígenes del bandolerismo en Hualgayoc, 1870–1900," p. 217.

28. Taylor, "Los orígenes del bandolerismo en Hualgayoc, 1870–1900," p. 217.

29. Taylor, *Bandits and Politics in Peru*.

30. The 1861 introduction of decentralized electoral administration, which, as noted, allowed the mayor, the governor, and the district judge to draw up the electoral rolls, increased rivalry for these positions. As a result, it was not unusual for membership to be decided by armed battle. See Taylor, "Los orígenes del bandolerismo en Hualgayoc, 1870–1900."

31. Taylor, "Society and Politics in Late Nineteenth Century Peru," p. 36.

32. Taylor, "Los orígenes del bandolerismo en Hualgayoc, 1870–1900," p. 221.

33. Taylor, "Society and Politics in Late Nineteenth Century Peru," p 17.

34. Taylor, "Los orígenes del bandolerismo en Hualgayoc, 1870–1900," p. 223.

35. While Francisco Plasencia León's son, Francisco Plasencia Cortés, backed the supporters of the Iglesias family, José Mercedes Alva sided with Puga and joined the Cáceres faction.

36. Dammert Bellido, *Cajamarca durante la guerra del Pacífico*, p. 5.

37. Married men, children, and invalids were supposed to be exempt from military service.

38. See, for instance, ADC/CSJ/CC, legajo 73, 22-2-1894, for an account of an entire neighborhood fleeing the village upon the approach of a recruitment force.

39. Mallon, *Peasant and Nation*, p. 238.

40. ADC/Prefectura/Particulares, legajos 224, 225, 226, 227, 229, 231, contain examples of such petitions.

41. Taylor, "Society and Politics in Late Nineteenth Century Peru," p. 36.

42. A central figure in this process was Eleodoro Benel, one of the dominant local bosses in the province of Hualgayoc. Like many such bosses, Benel was not an *hacendado*, but engaged in a series of capital-accumulation activities. He owned several haciendas as well as shops in a number of small towns (Bambamarca, Chota, Hualgayoc, and Santa Cruz). He acted as a labor contractor for several coastal estates and held the post of tax collector, a position which offered him direct economic benefit and political power. Most important, his political clout ensured virtual legal immunity, allowing him to persecute his enemies without fear of legal repercussions. See Taylor, *Bandits and Politics in Peru*.

43. Taylor, "Estates, Freeholders, and Peasant Communities."

44. Taylor, "Estates, Freeholders, and Peasant Communities."

45. Taylor, "Society and Politics in Late Nineteenth Century Peru," p. 7.

46. Raimondi, "Viajes por el departamento de Cajamarca, 1859," p. 199.

47. Eléspuru Bernizón ("La provincia de Cajamarca," p. 154) noted that "almost all the houses [in the town of Cajamarca] have a farmyard and a garden. In addition they have rooms, a hallway, and a large patio" .

48. ADC/CSJ/CC, legajo 1, 9-1-1862; legajo 34, 10-11-1876.
49. ADC/Notarios/Ríos, 1886, 205, 8-10-1886, Testamento de Manuel Ortiz; ADC/Notarios/Ríos, 1887, 254 vta., 31-7-1888, Testamento de José del Carmen Alcalde.
50. Taylor, "Earning a Living in Hualgayoc, 1870–1900," p. 114.
51. Chambers, *From Subjects to Citizens*, p. 9.
52. Middendorf, *Peru*, p. 182.
53. Some 37 men, or 3.4 percent of the economically active male population, noted in legal records that they worked in the textile trade.
54. For more detail on women's involvement in textile production and sale, see Taylor, "Earning a Living in Hualgayoc, 1870–1900," p. 119.
55. For purposes of comparison, 81.4 percent of the economically active male population said that they worked on the land as agriculturalists (6,798, or 43.4 percent), day laborers (3,855, or 24.6 percent), and *labradores* (workers) (2,103, or 13.4 percent).
56. Altogether, 313 men worked as domestic servants in the province of Cajamarca.
57. See Mallon, "Patriarchy in the Transition to Capitalism," p. 385; Dore, "Public Patriarchy in Rural Nicaragua, 1830–1875."
58. See Appendix B, Tables B3 and B4.
59. Dirección Nacional de Estadística, *Resumen del censo general*. Also see Appendix B here, Tables B3 and B4.
60. For examples, see ADC/CSJ/CC, legajo 10, 27-10-1864; legajo 56, 14-7-1890; legajo 59, 2-12-1890; legajo 83, 6-4-1897.
61. Deere supports these conclusions with data from the rental contracts of the hacienda Santa Ursula in 1918 (*Household and Class Relations*, p. 107).
62. Taylor, "Organización económica y social de la hacienda San Felipe de Combayo, 1918," p. 153.
63. Taylor, "Cambios capitalistas en las haciendas cajamarquinas, 1900–35," p. 132.
64. Eléspuru Bernizón, "La Provincia de Cajamarca," p. 157.
65. Bourque and Warren, "Female Participation, Perception and Power," p. 120.
66. See, for example, Tutino, "Power, Class and Family," p. 377; Tinsman, *Partners in Conflict*, p. 27.
67. Deere, *Household and Class Relations*, pp. 104–110.
68. Deere, "The Division of Labor by Sex in Agriculture."
69. Deere, *Household and Class Relations*.
70. Taylor, "Main Trends in Agrarian Capitalist Development," p. 32.
71. Middendorf, *Peru*, p. 182.

3. LEGISLATING GENDER

1. For a study of legislative evolution in Mexico in the same period, see Arrom, "Changes in Mexican Family Law in the Nineteenth Century"; idem, *The Women of Mexico City, 1790–1857*, Chap. 2.

2. Basadre, *Historia de la República del Perú*, p. 1235.

3. For further details on the relationship between church and state in the colonial period, see Klaiber, *The Catholic Church in Peru, 1821–1985;* idem, *Religion and Revolution in Peru, 1824–1976;* and idem, "La reorganización de la iglesia ante el estado liberal en el Perú (1860–1930)."

4. Mannarelli, *Pecados públicos*, pp. 107, 127.

5. Klaiber, *The Catholic Church in Peru, 1821–1985*, p. 179.

6. Hünefeldt, *Liberalism in the Bedroom*, pp. 86–87.

7. Klaiber, "La reorganización de la iglesia," p. 278.

8. Stranger, "Church and State in Peru," p. 151.

9. Calderón, *Diccionario de la legislación peruana*, p. 780; M. A. Fuentes, *Curso de enciclopedia del derecho*, Vol. I, pp. 121, pp. 380–381.

10. Hünefeldt, *Liberalism in the Bedroom*, pp. 150–176.

11. García Calderón, *Diccionario de la legislación peruana*, p. 7.

12. García Calderón, *Diccionario de la legislación peruana*, p. 667.

13. García Calderón, *Diccionario de la legislación peruana*, pp. 161, 271.

14. García Calderón, *Diccionario de la legislación peruana*, pp. 7, 253.

15. For a study of how marriage and widowhood affected women's lives, see Wilson, "Marriage, Property and the Position of Women," pp. 297–325. Also see Lavrin, *Latin American Women*, pp. 23–59; and Lavrin and Couturier, "Dowries and Wills."

16. García Calderón, *Diccionario de la legislación peruana*, p. 129.

17. Chassen-López, "Cheaper than Modernization," pp. 27–50.

18. García Calderón, *Diccionario de la legislación peruana*, p. 565.

19. García Calderón, *Diccionario de la legislación peruana*, p. 531.

20. Denegri, *El abanico y la cigarrera*, p. 40.

21. González de Fanning, *Educación femenina*.

22. For more detailed analysis of these *mujeres ilustradas* (female literati), see Villavicencio, *Del silencio a la palabra;* Denegri, *El abanico y la cigarrera*.

23. Sarmiento Gutiérrez, *La educación en Cajamarca;* Tauzin-Castellanos, "La educación femenina en el Perú del siglo XIX."

24. Villavicencio, *Del silencio a la palabra*, p. 97.

25. Ruggiero, "Honor, Maternity, and the Disciplining of Women."

26. Denegri notes that although upper-class women ceased to use the *saya y manto*, the lower classes continued to do so (*El abanico y la cigarrera*, pp. 62–63).

27. García Calderón, *Diccionario de la legislación peruana*, p. 544. For an analysis of the tendency to understand women's subordination as natural, see Stolcke, "Women's Labours."

28. Lama, *Código civil*, p. 29.

29. García Calderón, *Diccionario de la legislación peruana*, p. 583.

30. Lavrin, *Sexuality and Marriage*, p. 1.

31. Arrom suggests that the state's preoccupation with spelling out women's subordination to men was linked to the corporate view of society which underlay the late-colonial and nineteenth-century views of politics. She points out that the nuclear family was seen as the foundation of the

social structure, and the male head of family as the state's representative within the family. Hence, relationships within the family had to be regulated closely so as to ensure social order. See *The Women of Mexico City, 1790–1857*, pp. 77–78. Also see idem, "Changes in Mexican Family Law in the Nineteenth Century"; and Guy, *Sex and Danger in Buenos Aires*, p. 2.

32. Dore, "The Holy Family," pp. 106–107. Arrom makes a similar suggestion in *The Women of Mexico City, 1790–1857*, p. 97.

33. Guy, "Women, Peonage and Industrialization in Argentina, 1810–1914," p. 69.

34. McCreery, "*This Life of Misery and Shame.*"

35. Hünefeldt, *Liberalism in the Bedroom*, p. 54.

36. Basadre, *Historia de la República del Perú*, 1291.

37. Chambers, *From Subjects to Citizens*, p.244.

38. M. A. Fuentes, *Curso de enciclopedia del derecho*, Vol. I, p. 645.

39. García Calderón, *Diccionario de la legislación peruana*, p. 568.

40. ADC/Notarios/Ríos, 1878, 1, 1-1-1878, Testamento de Lino Rodríguez.

41. This was providing that their mother had not remained otherwise childless and had specifically named them as her heirs (García Calderón, *Diccionario de la legislación peruana*, pp. 250–254). It was relatively common for parents to include illegitimate children in their household as foster children, claiming that they were orphaned and of unknown parentage. Some of these were left property as foster children; others were formally adopted (providing that their parents had no other children) and named as sole heirs.

42. It would seem as though lived practice differed from legal theory in such cases. While the law stipulated that fathers were to retain custody of children in cases of divorce, I have found several examples of husbands throwing out their wives and children, but none of a husband wishing to separate from his wife and retain the children. Lavrin and Couturier, working on colonial Mexico, also note that a number of women complained of husbands who had deserted them, leaving them with the practical and financial responsibility of bringing up their children; see "Dowries and Wills," p. 299.

43. M. A. Fuentes, *Curso de enciclopedia del derecho*, Vol. I, p. 116.

44. Martínez-Alier, *Marriage, Class and Colour in Nineteenth Century Cuba*, pp. 108–109.

45. For a discussion of the importance of legitimacy in the colonial period, see Twinam, "The Negotiation of Honor"; idem, *Public Lives, Private Secrets*.

46. García Calderón, *Diccionario de la legislación peruana*, p. 1078.

47. García Calderón, *Diccionario de la legislación peruana*, p. 199.

48. García Calderón, *Diccionario de la legislación peruana*, p. 353.

49. See Martínez-Alier, *Marriage, Class and Colour in Nineteenth Century Cuba*; Stern, *The Secret History of Gender*, p. 96; Pitt-Rivers, *The Fate of Shechem*, p. 26; Socolow, "Women and Crime," p. 47; Bolton, "The Qolla Marriage Process." Harvey confirms that the idiom of *rapto* continued in

use in the 1980s in southern Peru; see "Domestic Violence in the Peruvian Andes," p. 72.

50. For parallels from colonial Mexico, see Boyer, "Honor among Plebeians," p. 153.

51. García Calderón, *Diccionario de la legislación peruana*, p. 84.

52. Twinam, *Public Lives, Private Secrets.*

53. García Calderón, *Diccionario de la legislación peruana*, p. 242.

4. SURVIVAL STRATEGIES

1. Bolton and Mayer, *Andean Kinship and Marriage*; Miller, "La mujer obrera en Lima, 1900–30." For a summary of informal unions and concubinage in Paraguay, see Potthast-Jutkeit, "The Ass of a Mare and Other Scandals"; for Brazil, consult Ramos, "Single and Married Women in Vila Rica, Brazil, 1754–1838," and Kuznesof, "Sexual Politics," pp. 240–260; for Mexico, see Stern, *The Secret History of Gender*, p. 273.

2. Mannarelli, *Pecados públicos*, pp. 15, 105–107, 122.

3. Macera, "Sexo y coloniaje."

4. On the basis of the 1908 census, Miller concludes that 50 percent of all births were illegitimate ("La mujer obrera en Lima, 1900–30"). Hünefeldt notes that illegitimacy was on the rise during the nineteenth century (*Liberalism in the Bedroom*, p. 23).

5. Eléspuru Bernizón, "La provincia de Cajamarca," p. 157.

6. Torre, *Los dos lados del mundo y del tiempo*, p. 28.

7. Dirección Nacional de Estadística, *Resumen del censo general.*

8. Basadre, *Introducción a las bases documentales*, p. 15; Taylor, "Estates, Freeholders, and Peasant Communities in Cajamarca, 1876–1972."

9. Lobo, who has conducted a sociological study of squatter settlements in Lima, notes that official figures tend to overreport marriage and underreport free unions; see *A House of My Own*, p. 140.

10. Basing myself on Deere, I have defined twenty-one as the average age at marriage for peasant women and twenty-five for men; see Deere, *Household and Class Relations*, p. 97.

11. Of adult women, 37.4 percent were married; 48 percent were single (Dirección Nacional de Estadística, *Resumen del censo general*, pp. 452, 461, 470, 476, 490, 497, 504, 510, 515–516, 522, 530). Also see Appendix B here, Tables B5 and B6.

12. Dirección Nacional de Estadística, *Resumen del censo general*, p. 504.

13. Dirección Nacional de Estadística, *Resumen del censo general*, p. 452.

14. Dirección Nacional de Estadística, *Resumen del censo general*, p. 461.

15. Lauderdale Graham found that servants frequently formed families based on consensual unions rather than formal marriage in nineteenth-century Rio de Janeiro. She concludes that one-fifth of female domestic servants had children, but were single mothers (*House and Street*, p. 77).

16. See Appendix A.

17. Lavrin, *Sexuality and Marriage*, p. 12.

18. For a reference to the failure of Indians to register their marriages and comments on their own wedding and christening rituals, see ADC/CSJ/ Causas Ordinarias (hereafter CO), legajo 130, 23-4-1892.

19. Legitimation secured children's inheritance, but did little to increase the surviving spouse's economic situation. Inheritance was passed on to children, and such last-minute marriages usually did not last long enough for the couple to accumulate shared assets, half of which were passed on to the widow or widower. It was not uncommon, however, for a spouse to push for the formalization of a union on his or her deathbed, only to recover soon after and enjoy the status associated with formal marriage.

20. ADC/Notarios/Ríos 1897, 630, 17-6-1898, Testamento de Manuela Abanto.

21. ADC/Notarios/Ríos, 1878, 77 vta., Testamento de Juan Tomás Gutiérrez; see also ADC/Notarios/Santistevan, 1863, 290 vta., Testamento de Toribio Silva Soto, 17-7-1864; ADC/Notarios/Santistevan, 1863, 215, 19-3-1864, Testamento de José Manuel Vásquez; ADC/Notarios/Santistevan, 1872, 700, 9-4-1872, Testamento de Manuela Pita Vallejos; ADC/Notarios/ Santistevan, 1872, 268, 14-1-1873, Testamento de Francisco Quiroz.

22. ADC/Notarios/Ríos, 1895, 68 vta., 9-8-1895, Testamento de Nicolás Silva Santisteban.

23. ADC/Notarios/Ríos, 1893, 347 vta., 25-5-1894, Testamento de José Barrena Soto.

24. ADC/CSJ/CC, legajo 70, 5-5-1893, Proceso seguido de oficio a Pedro Novoa Jiménez por violación de domicilio de Doña Laura Escuza y amenazas con arma de fuego.

25. ADC/Notarios/Ríos, 1878, 181, 19-3-1879, Testamento de José Sumarán.

26. ADC/Notarios/Chavarri, 76, 10-8-1864, José Santos Zamora; see also ADC/Notarios/Ríos, 1889, 77 vta., 12-5-1889, Testamento de Manuel Quiroz.

27. ADC/Notarios/Santistevan, 1863, 26 vta., 20-3-1863, Testamento de Isabel Cotrina.

28. ADC/CSJ/CC, legajo 39, 11-9-1882.

29. ADC/CSJ/CC, legajo 58, 15-11-1890.

30. ADC/CSJ/CC, legajo 56, 17-7-1890.

31. ADC/CSJ/CC, legajo 1, 19-1-1862.

32. ADC/CSJ/CC, legajo 58, 15-11-1890.

33. ADC/CSJ/CC, legajo 19, 11-4-1868.

34. Hünefeldt, *Liberalism in the Bedroom*, p. 214.

35. ADC/Notarios/Ríos, 1889, 863, 3-1-1889, Testamento de Manuel Miranda; see also ADC/Notarios/Ríos, 1891, 317 vta., 28-10-1892, Testamento de Villacorta.

36. ADC/Notarios/Federico Ríos, 187, 190, 19-1-1888, Testamento de Julián Rubio.

37. ADC/Notarios/Ríos, 1878, 108, 30-12-1878, Testamento de María Mercedes Apaestegui.

38. See ADC/Notarios/Santistevan, 1864, 338, 26-10-1864, Testamento de Barboza Camilo, for several examples of foster and adopted children.

39. M. A. Fuentes, *Curso de enciclopedia del derecho,* Vol. I, p. 27.

40. ADC/Notarios/Ríos, 1879, 133, 19-1-1879, Testamento de Miguel Sánchez Castillo.

41. ADC/Notarios/Chavarri, 1864, 109 vta., Testamento de José María Galvez Tirado.

42. There were data for the number of children married and widowed male testators had in 113 wills: 600 children, of whom 295—or 49 percent—died, were recorded in these. Eighty-three female testators recorded the number of children they had borne—441—267 of whom, or 60.6 percent, had died.

43. Deere, *Household and Class Relations,* p. 96.

44. ADC/Notarios/Chavarri, 1873, 17 vta., 24-3-1873.

45. ADC/Notarios/Ríos, 1878, 6, 12-1-1878, Testamento de Mariano Basauri. See also ADC/Notarios/Ríos, 1878, 112 vta., 28-11-1878, Testamento de Narciso Correa (who lost ten of fourteen children); ADC/Notarios/Santistevan, 1864, 315 vta., 26-8-1864, Testamento de María del Carmen Cabrera; ADC/Notarios/Santistevan, 1864, 51, 21-4-1863, Testamento de Manuel Antonio Mendoza; ADC/Notarios/Santistevan, 1863, 298, 25-7-1864, Testamento de José María Solano, for further examples.

46. ADC/Notarios/Ríos, 1878, 132, 30-1-1879, Testamento de Manuel Quiroz.

47. ADC/Notarios/Ríos, 1878, 237, 7-8-1878, Testamento de Rangel. See also ADC/Notarios/Ríos, 1879, 133, 19-1-1879.

48. ADC/Notarios/Santistevan, 1891, 101 vta., 19-6-1891, Testamento de Gregorio Cubas y Rubio.

49. ADC/Notarios/Ríos, 1880, 74, 7-7-1880; see also ADC/Notarios/Santistevan, 1863, 1114, 31-5-1864, Testamento de Manuel Saldaña Tello.

50. ADC/Notarios/Ríos, 1878, 25, 12-2-1878, Testamento de Rafael Tejada.

51. ADC/Notarios/Santistevan, 1864, 338, 26-10-1864.

52. After the subtraction of *gananciales,* the property accumulated during the marriage, the rest was to be divided among any surviving children and the offspring of deceased children. Testators were free to dispose of up to one-fifth—*el quinto*—of their property freely in order to leave property to someone outside the immediate family or not a descendant, to leave property to any illegitimate offspring they might have, or to improve the share of one or several of the heirs.

53. ADC/Notarios/Chavarri, 1867, 217, 4-8-1868, Testamento de María Bazán.

54. ADC/Notarios/Ríos, 1878, 181, 19-3-1879, José Sumarán.

55. ADC/Notarios/Santistevan, 1894, 324, 16-7-1894; see also ADC/Notarios/Ríos, 1891, 130 vta., 25-11-1891, Testamento de Faustina Novo.

56. ADC/Notarios/Santistevan, 1866, 158, 10-1-1866, Testamento de Jo-

sefa Horna; see also ADC/Notarios/Ríos, 1895, 543 vta., 24-12-1896, Testamento de Gavino Novoa; ADC/Notarios/Ríos, 1893, 64 vta., 5-4-1895, Testamento de José Manuel Pérez.

57. ADC/Notarios/Ríos, 1895, 18, 24-4-1895, Testamento de Melchora Corpa.

58. Deere, *Household and Class Relations*, p. 98.

59. ADC/Notarios/Ríos, 1878, 168 vta., 21-2-1879, Testamento de Antonio García; see also ADC/Notarios/ Santistevan, 1863, 38 vta., 1-4-1863, Testamento de Nicolasa Esparza (she stipulated that those of her three children who were not of age were to receive an additional share of five hundred pesos); ADC/Notarios/Santistevan, 1872, 717, 8-8-1872, Testamento de José Ravines.

60. ADC/Notarios/Chavarri, 1864, 109 vta., Testamento de José María Gálvez Tirado.

61. ADC/Notarios/Chavarri, 1864, 176, 26-9-1864, Testamento de Mariano Eduardo Vargas.

62. See ADC/Notarios/Ríos, 1877, 44 vta., 17-5-1877, Testamento de María de los Santos Sánchez Colorado.

63. ADC/Notarios/Chavarri, 1864, 134, 22-12-1864, Testamento de Manuela Barrantes y Villanueva. See also ADC/Notarios/Ríos, 1877, 66, 21-7-1877, Testamento de Leandra Zepeda; ADC/Notarios/Ríos, 1878, 178, 14-3-1879, Testamento de María Rabines.

64. García Calderón, *Diccionario de la legislación peruana*, p. 224.

65. ADC/Notarios/Santistevan, 1863, 1067, 21-3-1863, Testamento de José Pantaleón Palacios.

66. ADC/Notarios/Santistevan, 1882, 311, 31-5-1882, Testamento de José Tadeo Pita.

67. ADC/Notarios/Ríos, 1899, 284 vta., 1-11-1899, Testamento de Doroteo Villanueva; ADC/Notarios/Santistevan, 1872, 353 vta., 12-5-1873, Testamento de Fernando Reburedo; ADC/Notarios/Santistevan, 1872, 70 vta., 20-4-1872, Testamento de José Tadeo Pita; ADC/Notarios/Ríos, 157, 9-8-1882, Testamento de Manuel Resurrección Pastor; ADC/Notarios/Ríos, 1890, 181, 4-4-1890, Testamento de Miguel Sánchez. Klaiber says that concubinage among the Peruvian priesthood was widespread, but was not a great source of scandal. Most complaints against the priesthood focused on exorbitant charges for mass and high rent for property (*The Catholic Church in Peru, 1821–1985*, p. 189).

68. In his study of *mala vida* (trouble) in colonial Mexico, Boyer confirms that wives resorted to the courts only in cases of extreme abuse; see *Lives of the Bigamists*.

69. Stern found a broad cross section of the population among those whose marital conflicts were recorded as a result of criminal action, but no instances of upper-class marital conflict were found in the court records; see *The Secret History of Gender*, p. 53.

70. ADC/CSJ/CC, legajo 1, 5-4-1862. The other incident I refer to later, in which Nicolás Malca beat his stepdaughter, was not filed as a result of his violence. The trial began following the girl's accusation of rape and was

discontinued after midwives concluded that the girl's hymen had not been ruptured (ADC/CSJ/CC, legajo 83, 6-5-1897).

71. In the only two cases in which violence against children was revealed in criminal trial records, the events were disclosed during the investigation of other trials. When Mercedes Velesmoro claimed that her stepfather had raped her, the case was investigated with unusual diligence by the court in Cajamarca. When it emerged that he had "merely" slung her across the room while drunk, but not raped her, the charges were dropped; see ADC/CSJ/CC, legajo 83, 6-5-1897. The other incident was brought to court after a merchant took into his home an orphaned boy who feared further violence from his grandmother. The grandmother, who regularly beat both her grandchildren with a heavy stick, sued Francisco Gálvez Egusquiza for return of her grandson. No legal action followed the revelation of the grandmother's excessive use of violence; see ADC/CSJ/CO, 130, 5-5-1892.

72. Some modern studies link rural origins with violence toward children. LaJara shows that whereas 60 percent of mothers from the sierra were likely to use physical punishment with their children, only 47 percent of mothers from the coast and 35 percent of mothers from the urban areas were likely to do so. See LaJara, "Socialización de los hijos," p. 93.

73. ADC/CSJ/CC, legajo 2, 9-9-1862; legajo 5, 14-7-1863; legajo 11, 13-1-1865; legajo 13, 3-8-1865; legajo 13, 14-9-1865; legajo 19, 11-4-1868; legajo 19, 25-9-1868; legajo 9, 8-8-1869; legajo 39, 11-9-1882; legajo 58, 15-11-1890; legajo 84, 3-8-1897.

74. ADC/CSJ/CC, legajo 84, 3-8-1897.

75. ADC/Prefectura/Gobernación, legajo 86, Asunción 1887-1890, Gobernador del distrito de la Asunción, mayo de 1887, Oficio del teniente gobernador de dicho distrito, 9-5-1887.

76. ADC/CSJ/CC, legajo 1, 2-4-1862; legajo 10, 26-11-1864; legajo 22, 17-6-1869; legajo 26, 3-7-1872; legajo 32, 14-7-1874; legajo 32, 23-7-1874; legajo 36, 10-1-1878; legajo 37, 22-5-1880; legajo 37, 5-11-1880; legajo 56, 17-7-1890; legajo 64, 8-12-1891; legajo 65, 22-2-1892.

77. ADC/CSJ/CC, legajo 10, 26-11-1864.

78. ADC/CSJ/CC, legajo 1, 2-4-1862.

79. ADC/CSJ/CC, legajo 26, 3-7-1872.

80. ADC/CSJ/CC, legajo 21, 12-1-1869; legajo 27, 19-11-1872; legajo 27, 19-11-1872; legajo 36, 10-1-1878; legajo 44, 18-10-1886; legajo 70, 5-5-1893.

81. ADC/Prefectura/Particulares, legajo 183, Comandancia de Ronda de la Guardia Civil, Cajamarca, 22-7-1887.

82. ADC/Prefectura/Particulares, legajo 183, Comandancia de Ronda de la Guardia Civil, Cajamarca, 21-1-1878.

83. ADC/Prefectura/Particulares, legajo 182, Comandancia de Ronda de la Guardia Civil, Cajamarca, 19-8-1875.

84. ADC/Prefectura/Particulares, legajo 183, Comandancia de Ronda de la Guardia Civil, Cajamarca, 29-1-1878.

85. ADC/Prefectura/Particulares, legajo 183, Comandancia de Ronda de la Guardia Civil, Cajamarca, 15-6-1878.

86. The records for some years—1862 to 1869 and 1872 and 1873—are

missing entirely; most of the records from other years also seem to have disappeared. While 274 reports remain from 1875, there are only 4 reports preserved from 1870 and 2 from 1871.

87. ADC/CSJ/CC, legajo 22, 17-6-1869.

88. ADC/CSJ/CC, legajo 19, 11-4-1868.

89. ADC/CSJ/CC, legajo 84, 3-8-1897.

90. ADC/CSJ/CC, legajo 39, 11-9-1882.

91. ADC/CSJ/CC, legajo 37, 22-5-1880.

92. Hydén, *Woman Battering*, p. ix.

93. ADC/CSJ/CC, legajo 13, 14-9-1865.

94. ADC/CSJ/CC, legajo 5, 14-7-1863.

95. ADC/CSJ/CC, legajo 27, 19-11-1872.

96. ADC/CSJ/CC, legajo 9, 8-8-1869.

97. See ADC/CSJ/CC, legajo 5, 14-7-1863; legajo 13, 14-9-1865; legajo 9, 8-8-1869; legajo 27, 19-11-1872.

98. ADC/CSJ/CC, legajo 11, 13-1-1865; legajo 19, 11-4-1868; legajo 39, 11-9-1882; legajo 84, 3-8-1897.

99. ADC/CSJ/CC, legajo 19, 25-9-1868; legajo 37, 22-5-1880.

100. Asunción Eustacio, ADC/CSJ/CC, legajo 2, 9-9-1862; Antonio Vargas, ADC/CSJ/CC, legajo 58, 15-11-1890.

101. Gayford, "Battered Wives," p. 126.

102. Torre Araujo, *Estudio de campo*, p. 22. Other authors note the link between infidelity and violence: Mannarelli, *Pecados públicos*, p. 14; Stølen, "Gender, Sexuality and Violence in Ecuador." For further references to the link between accusations of sexual misconduct and marital abuse, see Socolow, "Women and Crime," p. 45; Harvey, "Domestic Violence in the Peruvian Andes," p. 75. Bourque and Warren also note the link between jealousy and violence: "Female Participation, Perception and Power."

103. ADC/CSJ/CC, legajo 2, 9-9-1862. The husband was absolved, although apparently on the grounds that the injuries were "light." In his study of battered women in the United States in the 1980s, Gayford also notes that several women reported that their partners beat them in order to extract confessions of infidelity; see "Battered Wives," p. 126.

104. García Calderón, *Diccionario de la legislación peruana*, p. 593. Peruvian law stated that injuries to a spouse caught in the act of adultery could be punished only if healing exceeded thirty days.

105. ADC/CSJ/CC, legajo 27, 19-11-1872.

106. ADC/CSJ/CC, legajo 13, 14-9-1865; also see the case brought by Raymunda Goicochea against her husband, Melchor Figueroa (ADC/CSJ/CC, legajo 11, 13-1-1865), after several attempts on her life. She was forced to undergo two sessions of *reconciliación*. For another example of a fruitless reconciliation imposed by the court, see ADC/CSJ/Jueces de Paz, legajo 1, Francisca Cotrina, esposa legítima de Eugenio Chávez de esta vecindad.

107. ADC/CSJ/CC, legajo 2, 9-9-1862.

108. Stern also notes that courts tried to persuade women to return to their husbands following incidents in which wife beating was reported; see *The Secret History of Gender*, p. 266. Chambers draws similar conclusions

for Arequipa in southern Peru, with judges admonishing wives to obey their husbands; see *From Subjects to Citizens*, p. 210.

109. ADC/CSJ/CC, legajo 5, 14-7-1863.

110. In her study of the Argentinean state's growing interference in private and family life during the nineteenth century, Guy notes that whereas the state protected the privacy of white, male-headed households, it did not define poor households as families, and therefore did not accord them the same degree of privacy; see "Lower Class Families," pp. 518–519.

111. M. A. Fuentes, *Curso de enciclopedia del derecho*, Vol. I, p. 235.

112. ADC/CSJ/CC, legajo 84, 3-8-1897.

113. ADC/CSJ/CC, legajo 37, 22-5-1880.

114. In 1893 Josefa Cadenillas de Ocuña applied for *alimentos*, a maintenance pension, as her husband had abandoned her. The case was never concluded, and no further proceedings followed; see ADC/ CSJ/CO, legajo 139, 12-7-1893.

115. For a study of the technicalities of divorce proceedings, as well as the changing lines of argumentation employed during the nineteenth century, consult Hünefeldt, *Liberalism in the Bedroom*.

116. García Calderón, *Diccionario de la legislación peruana*, pp. 3, 567.

117. ADC/CSJ/CC, legajo 17, 1-8-1867.

118. For another example of a priest adjudicating in a matter of marital conflict—this time by authorizing a young woman to return to her parents— see ADC/CSJ/CC, legajo 65, 22-2-1892. ADC/CSJ/CC, legajo 3, 1-11-1862 describes how the suspects in a murder trial were kept in the priest's house for lack of a local jail. For another trial dealing with conflict between the secular and the ecclesiastical authorities, see ADC/CSJ/CC, legajo 56, 26-7-1890. Manuel Silva was accused of having forbidden the local schoolteacher to teach religion to the children and of having buried the corpse of a dead child without the appropriate religious rituals and the priest's blessing. He was prosecuted in the criminal court and initially sentenced to jail, but subsequently freed.

119. For references to partners who left their spouses and were never heard of again, see ADC/Notarios/Chavarri, 1874, 537, 17-4-1874, Testamento de José Silva Urteaga; ADC/Notarios/Ríos, 1887, 190 vta., 19-1-1888; ADC/Notarios/Ríos, 1895, 51 vta., 14-7-1895, Testamento de Teresa Medina.

120. ADC/CSJ/CC, legajo 65, 22-2-1892.

121. ADC/CSJ/CC, legajo 20, 15-10-1868.

122. ADC/CSJ/CC, legajo 23, 15-10-1870.

123. ADC/CSJ/CC, legajo 26, 3-7-1872.

124. ADC/CSJ/CC, legajo 27, 19-11-1872.

125. Mannarelli, *Pecados públicos*, p. 123.

126. Stern, *The Secret History of Gender*, pp. 87–88.

127. Stern, *The Secret History of Gender*, p. 89.

128. García Calderón, *Diccionario de la legislación peruana*, p. 253.

129. "Como mujer soltera ella sabrá como ha adquirido esta hija y que su padre no es el mencionado Carlos Alcántara" (ADC/CSJ/CC, legajo 33, 14-7-1875).

130. ADC/CSJ/CC, legajo 1, 2-4-1862.

131. ADC/CSJ/CC, legajo 46, 14-4-1887.

132. "Este cholo se ha fingido loco, péro que no tiene ni ha tenido tal enfermedad, lo que sí tenía hera que cuándo se mareaba, salía de su cabal, y muchas veces ha maltratado a mi referida hermana" (ADC/CSJ/CC, legajo 84, 3-8-1897).

133. ADC/CSJ/CC, legajo 36, 10-1-1878.

134. ADC/CSJ/CC, legajo 83, 6-5-1897.

135. ADC/CSJ/CC, legajo 56, 17-7-1890.

136. See Gayford, "Battered Wives." Harris, "Complementaridad y conflicto," confirms the connection between alcohol and violence in late-twentieth-century Bolivia. Stølen does the same for 1970s highland Ecuador; see "Gender, Sexuality and Violence in Ecuador," p. 56. Romanucci-Ross couples the prevalence of alcohol with male violence—against both spouses and peers; see *Conflict, Violence and Morality in a Mexican Village*, p. 136.

137. Torre Araujo, *Estudio de campo*, p. 23.

138. Torre Araujo, *Estudio de campo*, p. 15.

139. Johnson, "Dangerous Words," p. 145.

140. See Stern, *The Secret History of Gender*, p. 161.

141. Tinsman, *Partners in Conflict*, p. 57; also see Lavrin, *Sexuality and Marriage*, p. 78.

142. ADC/CSJ/CC, legajo 11, 13-1-1865.

143. Stern, *The Secret History of Gender*, p. 85. Women also expressed an awareness of the link between male adultery and failure to provide economically for their spouses in seventeenth-century Lima; see Mannarelli, *Pecados públicos*, p. 150.

144. Boyer, "Women, *la mala vida*," p. 263.

145. ADC/CSJ/CC, legajo 11, 13-1-1865.

146. Tomasa Arce's exact words were, "Quítate de aquí puticima pechugona, que por tu culpa mi marido casi me mata" (Get out of here, you shameless full-breasted whore, it is your fault that my husband nearly killed me) (ADC/CSJ/CC, legajo 10, 26-11-1864).

147. ADC/CSJ/CC, legajo 2, 9-9-1862.

148. ADC/CSJ/CC, legajo 37, 5-11-1880.

149. For further discussion of conflict among women over men, see Chapter 7.

150. "Mi dicha consorte procura fastidiarme y aburrirme diariamente sin motivo alguno."

151. "Yo procuré llevar a mi mujer a nuestra cama recordándole continuamente que la fastidia nos tenía amistados y que no sea mandatos . . . pués era mi mujer y no tenía por que llamarme forzador" (ADC/CSJ/CC, legajo 11, 13-1-1865).

152. Tinsman, "Good Wives and Unfaithful Men," p. 601.

153. "Me arollé con mi ponchito en un rincón" ADC/CSJ/CC, legajo 11, 13-1-1865). The incident also hints at the personal price wives and mothers often had to pay for the economic security offered by in-house husbands.

154. ADC/CSJ/CC, legajo 11, 13-1-1865.

155. "Mala voluntad que me tiene y su repugnancia a vivir con su marido" (ADC/CSJ/CC, legajo 11, 13-1-1865).

156. No insults (apart from accusations of adultery) between husband and wife were recorded in trials dealing with marital conflict in Cajamarca. Hünefeldt (*Liberalism in the Bedroom*, pp. 55–56) notes that racial insults were common among spouses in Lima during the nineteenth century; racial insults were conspicuously absent not only from trials dealing with marital squabbles, but from slander trials in general in Cajamarca. See Chapter 5.

157. Stern, *The Secret History of Gender*, p. 97.

158. "En todo la he sufrido y sobrellevando mi desgraciada suerte, he seguido compliendo mis deberes."

159. Stern, *The Secret History of Gender*, pp. 70–111; also see Chambers, *From Subjects to Citizens*, pp. 101, 245; Arrom, *The Women of Mexico City, 1790–1857*, p. 232.

160. ADC/CSJ/CC, legajo 20, 15-10-1868; legajo 63, 9-12-1891. Another example is Ester Pinedo, whose husband refused to maintain her and who was—according to her and several witnesses—driven to adultery to obtain a living; see ADC/CSJ/CC, legajo 63, 9-12-1891.

161. ADC/CSJ/CC, legajo 37, 22-5-1880.

162. ADC/CSJ/CC, legajo 37, 5-11-1880.

163. Johnson, "Dangerous Words," p. 145.

164. Stern argues that a man's right to "symbolic deference" was conditional, and eroded when men failed to fulfill their part of the patriarchal pact—i.e., when they did not provide for the family or refrain from excessive violence; see *The Secret History of Gender*, pp. 70–75.

165. Chambers, *From Subjects to Citizens*, p. 101; see also Stern's discussion of subaltern male honor in *The Secret History of Gender*, p. 170.

166. See Hünefeldt's study of marital relations in Lima for parallel conclusions: *Liberalism in the Bedroom*, p. 73.

167. J. Scott, *Weapons of the Weak*, p. xv; idem, *Domination and the Arts of Resistance*, pp. 14, 22; idem, *Moral Economy*, p. 32.

168. ADC/CSJ/CC, legajo 9, 8-8-1869.

169. ADC/CSJ/CC, legajo 19, 25-9-1868.

170. Gayford, "Battered Wives," p. 124.

171. ADC/CSJ/CC, legajo 1, 2-4-1862.

172. ADC/CSJ/CC, legajo 58, 15-11-1890.

173. ADC/CSJ/CC, legajo 64, 8-12-1891.

174. Hydén, *Woman Battering*, p. 81.

175. Harvey, "Domestic Violence in the Peruvian Andes," p. 66.

176. Torre Araujo, *Estudio de campo*, p. 25.

177. ADC/CSJ/CC, legajo 11, 13-1-1865; legajo 13, 14-9-1865.

178. ADC/CSJ/CC, legajo 9, 8-8-1869; legajo 19, 25-9-1868.

179. ADC/CSJ/CC, legajo 13, 14-9-1865.

180. ADC/CSJ/CC, legajo 11, 13-1-1865.

181. ADC/CSJ/CC, legajo 2, 9-9-1862; legajo 11, 13-1865; legajo 19, 11-4-1868; legajo 39, 11-9-1882.

182. ADC/CSJ/CC, legajo 5, 14-7-1863; legajo 9, 8-8-1869; legajo 19, 25-9-1868; legajo 58, 15-11-1890; legajo 84, 3-8-1897.

183. See also Boyer, *Lives of the Bigamists*.

184. Boyer, "Women, *la mala vida*," p. 268.

185. Hünefeldt (*Liberalism in the Bedroom*) mentions violence among women's grounds for divorce petitions. See also Arrom, *The Women of Mexico City, 1790–1857*, pp. 206–207. Arrom notes that applications for divorce were primarily a female recourse and were used by women to protect themselves. Martín (*Daughters of the Conquistadores*, p. 146) notes that family violence and domestic abuse were a frequent cause of separation in colonial Peru; see also Mannarelli, *Pecados públicos*, pp. 149–151. Romanucci-Ross (*Conflict, Violence and Morality*, p. 62) observes that maltreatment combined with the lack of maintenance were the most common causes for applications for separation in the village she studied in Morelos in the 1970s.

186. ADC/CSJ/CC, legajo 65, 22-2-1892.

187. ADC/CSJ/CC, legajo 36, 10-1-1878.

188. ADC/CSJ/CC, legajo 21, 12-1-1869.

189. ADC/CSJ/CC, legajo 54, 23-9-1899.

190. ADC/CSJ/CC, legajo 9, 29-2-1864.

191. ADC/CSJ/CC, legajo 37, 22-5-1880.

192. ADC/CSJ/CC, legajo 84, 3-8-1897.

193. ADC/CSJ/CC, legajo 26, 3-7-1872.

194. ADC/CSJ/CC, legajo 28, 26-3-1872.

195. The same was true of Lima: the presence of servants (often in the same bed or room) and the proximity of neighbors meant that there were often witnesses to marital conflict—and that outsiders intervened, albeit only in extreme situations (Mannarelli, *Pecados públicos*, p. 94; Hünefeldt, *Liberalism in the Bedroom*, Chapter 2).

196. Chambers, *From Subjects to Citizens*, p. 101; Stern, *The Secret History of Gender*, p. 15.

197. ADC/CSJ/CC, legajo 58, 15-11-1890.

198. ADC/CSJ/CC, legajo 84, 3-8-1897.

199. ADC/CSJ/CC, legajo 11, 13-1-1865.

200. ADC/CSJ/CC, legajo 13, 3-8-1865.

201. Johnson, "Dangerous Words," p. 145. Also see Hünefeldt, *Liberalism in the Bedroom*, p. 70. It is worth noting that I have found no example of conflict between abusive husbands and fathers-in-law. This may indicate the cultural acceptance of paternal intervention in cases where daughters were beaten.

202. ADC/CSJ/CC, legajo 23, 24-1-1870 (Sánchez); legajo 85, 21-9-1897 (Llerena).

203. For references to the role of brothers, see Stavig, *The World of Tupac Amaru*; Harris, "Complementaridad y conflicto." For comments on the alliance between mothers and children when faced with domestic violence, see Stølen, "Gender, Sexuality and Violence in Ecuador"; Torre Araujo, *Estudio de campo*.

204. ADC/CSJ/CC, legajo 19, 11-4-1868.
205. ADC/CSJ/CC, legajo 56, 17-7-1890.
206. ADC/CSJ/CC, legajo 56, 17-7-1890.
207. ADC/CSJ/CC, legajo 2, 9-9-1862. Stølen, working on a mestizo community in the Ecuadorean highlands in the 1970s, also found that the abusers' mothers intervened in order to protect their daughters-in-law on several occasions ("Gender, Sexuality and Violence in Ecuador").
208. Other authors have noted the importance of neighbors' intervention in extreme cases of marital abuse. See Chambers, *From Subjects to Citizens*, pp. 104–106, on neighbors' reluctance to interfere when husbands "corrected" their wives, and all of Chapter 3 on the importance of neighborhood networks in shielding spouses from the most extreme consequences of violence. Hünefeldt (*Liberalism in the Bedroom*, Chapter 2) notes the importance of barrio expectations in shaping marital behavior, including the likelihood that neighbors would interfere before marital violence became fatal. Also see Stern, *The Secret History of Gender*, pp. 98–107, on female weapons such as the "pluralization of patriarchs" and female-female networks.
209. Deere reports that it was customary for the youngest son to live with or close to his parents with his family in order to lend them assistance in their old age. In recompense, he usually inherited the family home (*Household and Class Relations*, p. 98). Anselma Tarma, for instance, recorded in her will that she had built the house she lived in with her daughter (ADC/Notarios/Ríos, 1884, 69, 21-11-1885, Testamento de Anselma Tarma). Another woman told the notary that she and her two grown daughters occupied one room each in a house they owned together (ADC/Notarios/Ríos, 1895, 104 vta., 2-10-1895, Testamento de Manuela Arana Chávez). Dolores Mille recorded that her niece had built a house on her property (ADC/Notarios/Ríos, 1895, 221 vta., 21-2-1896, Testamento de Dolores Mille). In addition, several wills record that heirs frequently subdivided and shared the houses they inherited from their parents or other relatives. See ADC/Notarios/Chavarri, 1864, 76, 10-8-1864, Testamento de José Santos Zamora; 1864, 134, 22-12-1864, Testamento de Manuela Barrantes y Villanueva.
210. ADC/CSJ/CC, legajo 13, 3-8-1865; for another example of the lack of privacy afforded by contemporary architecture, see ADC/CSJ/CC, legajo 1, 2-4-1862. In this trial local tongues gave the lie to Baltazara Minchán's attempts to blame an Indian peon for her miscarriage; according to a different source it was public knowledge that the blows which caused her to miscarry were inflicted by her common-law husband. In another case, Cecilia Quispe Quiroz was surprised by her former boyfriend, Agustín Gurbillón, who climbed over the wall between their houses in order to avenge himself for having been abandoned when he was in jail (ADC/CSJ/CC, legajo 75, 5-3-1895). Hünefeldt points out the public nature of matrimonial conflict in her finding that living arrangements were such that slaves, skilled workers, and apprentices, as well as neighbors, frequently were witnesses to arguments and instances of abuse (*Liberalism in the Bedroom*, pp. 63–68).
211. ADC/CSJ/CC, legajo 51, 11-3-1889.
212. ADC/CSJ/CC, legajo 56, 17-7-1890. Torre, studying peasants in Caja-

marca in the 1990s, notes that men in the *rondas campesinas* (peasant para-militia), which occasionally adjudicate in matters of domestic violence, call wife beaters "fag" [*maricón*] (Torre Araujo, *Estudio de campo*, p. 27).

213. ADC/CSJ/CC, legajo 37, 5-11-1880.

214. ADC/CSJ/CC, legajo 10, 26-11-1864.

215. ADC/CSJ/CC, legajo 13, 3-8-1865.

216. Harvey, "Domestic Violence in the Peruvian Andes," p. 77.

217. See Stølen, *A media voz*, for similar examples from highland Ecuador.

218. J. Scott, *Weapons of the Weak*, pp. 35, 301.

219. J. Scott, *Weapons of the Weak*, p. 234.

220. Chambers, *From Subjects to Citizens*, p. 101.

221. Hünefeldt, *Liberalism in the Bedroom*, p. 69. Chambers notes neighbors' reluctance to intervene actively on behalf of battered wives in Arequipa, but observes that they willingly offered them refuge (*From Subjects to Citizens*, p. 104).

222. Harvey, "Domestic Violence in the Peruvian Andes," p. 77.

223. Hünefeldt, *Liberalism in the Bedroom*, p. 70.

224. ADC/CSJ/CC, legajo 13, 14-9-1865.

225. ADC/CSJ/Jueces de Paz, legajo 1, Francisca Cotrina, esposa legítima de Eugenio Chávez de esta vecindad.

226. Hünefeldt, *Liberalism in the Bedroom*, p. 325.

227. Chambers, *From Subjects to Citizens*.

5. *INJURIAS VERBALES Y CALUMNIAS*

1. Twinam, *Public Lives, Private Secrets*.

2. Chambers, *From Subjects to Citizens*, p. 192; Hünefeldt, *Liberalism in the Bedroom*, p. 149.

3. "Because reputation and honor are more highly esteemed . . . than wealth, because they win society's respect, it is necessary to punish actions which diminish honor, for the same reason that actions which damage property must be punished. Therefore the penal laws deal with crimes against honor, and count slander and insults among these" (García Calderón, *Diccionario de la legislación peruana*, p. 242).

4. Dore, who has studied the village of Diriomo in nineteenth-century Nicaragua, notes that most of the trials involving women dealt with matters related to honor ("Patriarchy and Private Property in Nicaragua").

5. For the use of *ramera* and *abandonada*, see ADC/CSJ/CC, legajo 26, 14-6-1872.

6. ADC/CSJ/CC, legajo 23, 22-10-1870; legajo 84, 9-7-1897.

7. ADC/CSJ/CC, legajo 41, 6-2-1886.

8. ADC/CSJ/CC, legajo 1, 14-1-1862; legajo 32, 14-7-1874; legajo 74, 2-7-1894.

9. ADC/CSJ/CC, legajo 23, 22-10-1870; legajo 79, 2-6-1896.

10. ADC/CSJ/CC, legajo 34, 13-11-1876.

11. ADC/CSJ/CC, legajo 65, 30-1-1892.

12. ADC/CSJ/CC, legajo 23, 15-10-1870 and legajo 79, 15-9-1896.

13. ADC/CSJ/CC, legajo 1, 14-1-1862; legajo 20, 22-10-1868; legajo 23, 22-10-1870; legajo 27, 6-11-1872; legajo 79, 15-9-1896.

14. Interestingly, there are no cases of racial insults in the sample, contrasting with findings by Chambers for Arequipa (*From Subjects to Citizens*, p. 171) and Hünefeldt for Lima. Hünefeldt notes that most defamation suits were related to racial slurs (*Liberalism in the Bedroom*, p. 55). If most of these dealt with imputations of African blood, the near-absence of African descendants in the highland department of Cajamarca may account for this contrast. See ADC/CSJ/CC, legajo 1, 14-1-1862; legajo 6, 13-11-1863; legajo 20, 22-10-1868; legajo 23, 3-5-1870; legajo 23, 22-10-1870; legajo 24, 1-7-1871; legajo 26, 14-6-1872; legajo 26, 29-10-1872; legajo 27, 6-11-1872; legajo 28, 26-3-1872; legajo 32, 14-7-1874; legajo 32, 23-7-1874; legajo 34, 13-11-1876; legajo 35, 11-12-1877; legajo 40, 31-7-1885; legajo 41, 6-2-1886; legajo 45, 13-11-1886; legajo 57, 10-9-1890; legajo 64, 10-10-1891; legajo 74, 2-7-1894; legajo 79, 2-6-1896; legajo 79, 15-9-1896; legajo 84, 9-7-1897.

15. ADC/CSJ/CC, legajo 28, 26-3-1872; legajo 34, 10-11-1876; legajo 35, 11-12-1877; legajo 57, 10-9-1890; legajo 64, 7-11-1891.

16. ADC/CSJ/CC, legajo 28, 26-3-1872.

17. ADC/CSJ/CC, legajo 34, 10-11-1876.

18. ADC/CSJ/CC, legajo 35, 11-12-1877, Candelaria Arce con Cayetana Mille de Villanueva por injurias graves; ADC/CSJ/CC, legajo 36, 9-1-1878, Cayetana Mille de Villanueva con Candelaria Arce por injurias verbales.

19. ADC/CSJ/CC, legajo 34, 10-11-1876; legajo 64, 7-11-1891.

20. ADC/CSJ/CC, legajo 57, 10-9-1890.

21. ADC/CSJ/CC, legajo 35, 11-12-1877.

22. ADC/CSJ/CC, legajo 6, 13-11-1863.

23. The same applied to the other typically feminine insult, "witch." None of the three women I found who were called "witch" pressed charges merely on the basis of this insult, but because it was uttered in conjunction with the word *whore*, or because it was accompanied by physical assault, as in the case of Elena Cruzado: ADC/CSJ/CC, legajo 79, 2-6-1896. The insult of calling Manuela Chávez a witch was documented only during the trial which her opponent initiated against her (ADC/CSJ/CC, legajo 28, 26-3-1872). For the third example of the use of the word *witch* as an insult, see ADC/CSJ/CC, legajo 32, 14-7-1874.

24. The only reference to the insult "fag" being used was in relation to a man beating his common-law wife; see ADC/CSJ/CC, legajo 56, 17-7-1890.

25. ADC/CSJ/CC, legajo 27, 6-11-1872.

26. ADC/CSJ/CC, legajo 34, 10-11-1876.

27. Pitt-Rivers (*The Fate of Shechem*, p. 18) also notes the tendency to damage reputations with insults unrelated to the argument's subject matter. See also ADC/CSJ/CC, legajo 23, 22-10-1870; legajo 34, 10-11-1876; legajo 79, 15-9-1896.

28. ADC/CSJ/CC, legajo 41, 6-2-1886.

29. ADC/CSJ/CC, legajo 24, 1-7-1871.

30. Demos, *Entertaining Satan*, p. 249.

31. For an analysis of a rape or seduction trial which turned out to the victim's disadvantage, see Boyer, "Honor among Plebeians," p. 175.

32. ADC/CSJ/CC, legajo 79, 15-9-1896.

33. See Stern, *The Secret History of Gender*, pp. 142–147, for an exploration of the politics of gossip and the weapon of scandal.

34. ADC/CSJ/CC, legajo 20, 22-10-1868.

35. ADC/CSJ/CC, legajo 20, 22-10-1868.

36. ADC/CSJ/CC, legajo 6, 13-11-1863.

37. ADC/CSJ/CC, legajo 34, 10-11-1876.

38. ADC/CSJ/CC, legajo 24, 1-7-1871.

39. ADC/CSJ/CC, legajo 27, 6-11-1872.

40. ADC/CSJ/CC, legajo 32, 10-10-1874.

41. ADC/CSJ/CC, legajo 26, 29-10-1872.

42. ADC/CSJ/CC, legajo 74, 2-7-1894.

43. ADC/CSJ/CC, legajo 32, 10-10-1874.

44. ADC/CSJ/CC, legajo 81, 12-12-1896.

45. ADC/CSJ/CC, legajo 64, 10-10-1891.

46. ADC/CSJ/CC, legajo 35, 11-12-1877.

47. "Con semejante difamación se me ha muerto moralmente en la sociedad" (ADC/CSJ/CC, legajo 23, 22-10-1870).

48. Twinam, *Public Lives, Private Secrets*, pp. 32–33.

49. ADC/CSJ/CC, legajo 23, 3-5-1870.

50. ADC/CSJ/CC, legajo 26, 14-6-1872.

51. ADC/CSJ/CC, legajo 34, 10-11-1876.

52. ADC/CSJ/CC, legajo 27, 6-11-1872.

53. Porter, "And That It Is Custom Makes It Law," p. 137.

54. For a review of perceived links between sexual morality and public order in nineteenth-century Latin America, see Chapter 3 here. Concerning the ways in which the public transcript can be used to obscure the hidden transcript, see J. Scott, *Domination and the Arts of Resistance*.

55. These were Candelaria Alvarado (ADC/CSJ/CC, legajo 27, 6-11-1872); Jacoba Bermúdez (legajo 28, 26-3-1872); Francisca Sifuentes (legajo 32, 14-7-1874); and Candelaria Arce (legajo 35, 11-12-1877; legajo 35, 11-12-1877).

56. These were Eusebia Olortegui (ADC/CSJ/CC, legajo 20, 22-10-1868); Jacoba Bermúdez (ADC/CSJ/CC, legajo 32, 23-7-1874); Petronila Astopilco (ADC/CSJ/CC, legajo 40, 31-7-1885); and Emilia Verástegui (ADC/CSJ/CC, legajo 64, 20-10-1891).

57. ADC/CSJ/CC, legajo 32, 14-7-1874.

58. ADC/CSJ/CC, legajo 32, 23-7-1874. The marriage between Jacoba Bermúdez and Manuel Quiroz was also referred to in Quiroz' will, written seven years later, in which he stated that all their nine children had died (ADC/Notarios/Ríos, 1878, 30-1-1879, Testamento de Manuel Quiroz).

59. ADC/CSJ/CC, legajo 64, 10-10-1891. See Chapter 4 here for further examples of the links between suspicions of infidelity and domestic abuse.

60. ADC/CSJ/CC, legajo 40, 31-7-1885. In cases of divorce, women were allowed to retain custody of the children only if they could prove that their conduct was irreproachable. Women convicted (or suspected) of adultery

were thus excluded. As well as facing the possible breakup of her family, María Peralta may have feared losing custody of her children.

61. "Me querello a fin de que la acusada prueve los ladronios y adulterios de mi esposa, poniendola en un depocito mientras sea provada pues de lo contrario desde esta fecha quedo separado de hella."

62. ADC/CSJ/CC, legajo 6, 13-11-1863.

63. ADC/CSJ/CC, legajo 27 6-11-1872.

64. ADC/CSJ/CC, legajo 28, 26-3-1872.

65. See Pitt-Rivers, *The People of the Sierra*, pp. 113–115, for an exploration of this argument concerning Andalusia.

66. ADC/CSJ/CC, legajo 28, 26-3-1872.

67. Pitt-Rivers, referring to Andalusia in the 1950s, found that the wife's "unfaithfulness is proof of . . . her shamelessness, . . . it defiles . . . [the husband's] manliness. In a sense it testifies to his lack of manliness, since had he proved an adequate husband and kept proper authority over her she would not have deceived him" (*The People of the Sierra*, p. 116).

68. Stern, *The Secret History of Gender*, pp. 161–170; also see Chambers, *From Subjects to Citizens*, Chapters 3 and 4.

69. Hünefeldt (*Liberalism in the Bedroom*, p. 72) also notes the ability of gossip to ruin marriages, reporting that husbands left their wife after hearing her branded as an adulteress. Chambers (*From Subjects to Citizens*, p. 103) observes that husbands attempted to assert their control over their wives by restricting their movements to the private arena and forbidding them to gossip.

70. ADC/CSJ/CC, legajo 27, 6-11-1872.

71. ADC/CSJ/CC, legajo 26, 14-6-1872.

72. ADC/CSJ/CC, legajo 28, 26-3-1872.

73. ADC/CSJ/CC, legajo 74, 2-7-1894.

74. ADC/CSJ/CC, legajo 74, 2-7-1894.

75. García Calderón, *Diccionario de la legislación peruana*, p. 63; see Chapter 4 here for a discussion of the limits of wives' endurance with regard to husbands' infidelity.

76. Twinam, "The Negotiation of Honor," p. 79; idem, *Public Lives, Private Secrets*.

77. ADC/CSJ/CC, legajo 6, 13-11-1863.

78. ADC/CSJ/CC, legajo 27, 6-11-1872.

79. ADC/CSJ/CC, legajo 1, 14-1-1862.

80. ADC/CSJ/CC, legajo 23, 3-5-1870.

81. ADC/CSJ/CC, legajo 26, 14-6-1872.

82. Chambers, *From Subjects to Citizens*, pp. 192–198.

83. ADC/CSJ/CC, legajo 35, 11-12-1877.

84. ADC/CSJ/CC, legajo 40, 31-7-1885.

85. ADC/CSJ/CC, legajo 28, 26-3-1872.

86. ADC/CSJ/CC, legajo 27, 6-11-1872.

87. ADC/CSJ/CC, legajo 24, 1-7-1871.

88. Lauderdale Graham, *House and Street*, p. 77.

89. See Socolow, "Women and Crime," for further examples of women

going to court to defend their honor following slander. Also see Boyer, "Honor among Plebeians," p. 161, for an example of a slave woman who claimed honor on the basis of her married status. Ramos, commenting on colonial Brazil, describes marriage as "an affirmation of status" ("Single and Married Women in Vila Rica, Brazil, 1754–1838").

90. ADC/CSJ/CC, legajo 28, 26-3-1872.

91. "En esta virtud las dos son criminalmente responsable con la diferencia de que el amancebamiento imputado a la Bermúdes imparte un delito de adulterio penado por la ley, en tanto que la injuria hecha a la Chávez, que es soltera, no es más que una falta de moralidad" (ADC/CSJ/CC, legajo 28, 26-3-1872).

92. ADC/CSJ/CC, legajo 23, 22-10-1870.

93. ADC/CSJ/CC, legajo 45, 13-11-1886.

94. Porter, "And That It Is Custom Makes It Law," p. 127.

95. Dore, "The Holy Family," p. 109.

96. "Debido a mi honra y a mis buenas costumbres alcancé casarme con Don Manuel Quiroz, persona notoriamente honrada" (ADC/CSJ/CC, legajo 28, 26-3-1872).

97. "Sin atender a nuestro sexo y a los miramientos que se debe a la virtud de que hasta ahora felizmente conserva mi hija Tomasa" (ADC/CSJ/CC, legajo 34, 13-11-1876). For another example of a single mother demonstrating concern over her daughter's rather than her own reputation, see ADC/CSJ/CC, legajo 45, 13-11-1886.

98. ADC/CSJ/CC, legajo 27, 6-11-1872.

99. ADC/CSJ/CC, legajo 20, 22-10-1868.

100. ADC/CSJ/CC, legajo 26, 14-6-1872.

101. As I noted above, Bermúdez was also sentenced, as the insults were mutual. It is unclear whether either woman ever served her sentence (ADC/CSJ/CC, legajo 28, 26-3-1872).

102. ADC/CSJ/CC, legajo 32, 10-10-1874. There is no information as to whether this sentence was actually served.

103. ADC/CSJ/CC, legajo 26, 14-6-1872.

104. ADC/CSJ/CC, legajo 20, 22-10-1868.

105. ADC/CSJ/CC, legajo 27, 6-11-1872.

106. ADC/CSJ/CC, legajo 64, 10-10-1891 (Verástegui); legajo 37, 22-5-1880 (Astopilco).

107. ADC/CSJ/CC, legajo 6, 13-11-1863.

108. Johnson notes that the failure of a man to defend his female relatives' honor was interpreted by his peers as an admission that their honor could not be defended ("Dangerous Words," p. 130). Lipsett-Rivera writes, "Only women who had honor could fight the slights that could stain their reputation" ("A Slap in the Face of Honor," p. 181).

109. ADC/CSJ/CC, legajo 28, 26-3-1872.

110. "De dejar impune un hecho de trascendencia seria para dar lugar a que la sociedad me mire, como a persona indigna de estar entre ella (. . .) me he visto precisada a ocurrir al unico medio legal." ADC/CSJ/CC, legajo 32, 14-7-1874.

111. ADC/CSJ/CC, legajo 64, 10-10-1891.
112. ADC/CSJ/CC, legajo 34, 10-11-1876.
113. Twinam, *Public Lives, Private Secrets*, p. 65.
114. ADC, "Necrología," *El Ferrocarril*, 17-3-1899, no. 132.
115. ADC/CSJ/CC, legajo 1, 14-1-1862.
116. Twinam suggests that individuals who had been stained with dishonor might nevertheless succeed in being accepted as honorable. She labels this "passing." Although they might, to all intents and purposes, be considered respectable, they would always continue to be vulnerable to challenge ("The Negotiation of Honor," pp. 88–91).
117. Pitt-Rivers, *The Fate of Shechem*, p. 27.
118. ADC/CSJ/CC, legajo 26, 29-10-1872.
119. ADC/CSJ/CC, legajo 41, 6-2-1886.
120. For a comment on how plebeian women and men refrained from using the term "honor" in their dealings with the authorities in order to avoid disputing the elite's claim to a monopoly on the commodity in colonial Buenos Aires, see Johnson, "Dangerous Words," pp. 128–129.
121. For an analysis of gossip and scandalmongering in colonial Mexico, see Stern, *The Secret History of Gender*, pp. 107–110, 142. Romanucci-Ross, in an anthropological study of a Morelos, Mexico, village in the 1970s (*Conflict, Violence and Morality*, p. 147) confirms the power of oral insults and notes that the verbal component of the morality contest could frequently be more destructive than physical blows.
122. Stern, *The Secret History of Gender*, p. 15.
123. Johnson, "Dangerous Words," p. 130.

6. *RAPTO, SEDUCCIÓN, VIOLACIÓN,* AND *ESTUPRO*

1. See Chapter 3.
2. ADC/CSJ/CC, legajo 37, 5-6-1879 (Gálvez); legajo 45, 27-12-1886 (Paz); legajo 25, 30-4-1872 (Chavarri).
3. García Calderón, *Diccionario de la legislación peruana*, p. 353.
4. ADC/CSJ/CC, legajo 5, 9-6-1863; legajo 6, 5-12-1863; legajo 14, 4-7-1866; legajo 22, 10-5-1869; legajo 22, 6-8-1869; legajo 24, 1-9-1871 and legajo 25, 30-4-1872 (dealing with the same case of seduction); legajo 37, 5-6-1879; legajo 38, 18-9-1882; legajo 44, 15-10-1886; legajo 45, 27-12-1886; legajo 55, 21-5-1890; legajo 62, 11-6-1891; legajo 75, 18-1-1895; legajo 80, 29-10-1896; legajo 83, 6-5-1897; legajo 83, 6-5-1897.
5. The victims were Catalina Pájares, Zoila Alcántara, Rosario Sichas, Mercedes Velesmoro, and María Jamina Guevara.
6. ADC/CSJ/CC, legajo 55, 21-5-1890; legajo 73, 22-2-1894; legajo 80, 29-10-1896.
7. ADC/CSJ/CC, legajo 14, 4-7-1866; legajo 22, 6-8-1869; legajo 37, 5-6-1879; legajo 38, 18-9-1882; legajo 44, 15-10-1886; legajo 83, 6-5-1897; legajo 83, 6-5-1897. As charges were routinely mislabeled by plaintiffs for dramatic effect, the actual number of rape cases reported was even lower.

8. ADC/CSJ/CC, legajo 55, 21-5-1890; legajo 62, 11-6-1891; legajo 73, 22-2-1894; legajo 80, 29-10-1896.

9. ADC/CSJ/CC, legajo 22, 10-5-1869; legajo 45, 27-12-1886.

10. ADC/CSJ/CC, legajo 5, 9-6-1863; legajo 24, 1-9-1871; legajo 25, 30-4-1872.

11. See ADC, "Clamor a la justicia," *La Opinión: Periódico Popular*, 8-10-1862, no. 50. Of the 15 trials that dealt primarily with sex-related crime, only 4 led to convictions. This neglect of sex-related crime was not unique to Cajamarca; Dore notes that in Diriomo, Nicaragua, 83 of 102 cases of rape, sexual assault, and battery brought before the court were dismissed ("Property, Households and Public Regulation," p. 599).

12. Violent rape by strangers was recorded on a few, anomalous, occasions. See ADC, Prefectura, legajo 176, Gobernación Asunción, 16-12-1901, containing a report about "a young man, Abel Espino, whose conduct is scandalous, as I am continuously informed that he assaults and rapes women both here and in the countryside, by his behavior inciting others to follow his example." The official, Isaac Yepes, added that "a *mujer desgraciada* [unfortunate woman/girl], called Beatriz Narro [was raped last night]. The crime has been reported, but undoubtedly the justice of the peace will claim that the matter is outside of his field of authority." The report thus indicates how difficult it could be to press charges of rape.

13. Pitt-Rivers, *The People of the Sierra*, p. 113.

14. ADC/CSJ/CC, legajo 37, 5-6-1879.

15. ADC/CSJ/CC, legajo 45, 27-12-1886.

16. ADC/CSJ/CC, legajo 22, 6-8-1869.

17. ADC/CSJ/CC, legajo 38, 18-9-1882.

18. ADC/CSJ/CC, legajo 45, 27-12-1886.

19. "El autor de la deshonra de mi hija, de la mía, de mi familia" (ADC/CSJ/CC, legajo 24, 1-9-1871).

20. "La pobre madre de ésta, cuyo corazón laserado con la perdida de la pureza de una hija y de la honra de ésta y de toda su familia lo ha compadecido y compadece todo este vecindario" (ADC/CSJ/CC, legajo 24, 1-9-1871).

21. ADC/CSJ/CC, legajo 22, 10-5-1869.

22. ADC/CSJ/CC, legajo 38, 18-9-1882.

23. J. Scott, *Domination and the Arts of Resistance*, p. 3.

24. ADC/CSJ/CC, legajo 22, 10-5-1869.

25. ADC/CSJ/CC, legajo 75, 18-1-1895.

26. "[Estoy lejos] de creer que Altamirano posea dotes seductivos para captarse afectos en el sexo femenino."

27. ADC/CSJ/CC, legajo 89, 5-11-1898.

28. See Martínez-Alier, *Marriage, Class and Colour in Nineteenth-Century Cuba*, for her pathbreaking study of marriage and class, and the custom of using marriage to repair the damage to honor resulting from cases of seduction and elopement in Cuba.

29. "Este mozo vago [sin] más oficio que palanquanear creyendose un gran personaje."

30. "Una mujer se niegue tenazmente a los actos que la sociedad respeta . . . prefiriendo su prostitución" (ADC/CSJ/CC, legajo 24, 1-9-1871).

31. ADC/CSJ/CC, legajo 22, 6-8-1869.

32. ADC/CSJ/CC, legajo 5, 9-6-1863.

33. ADC/CSJ/CC, legajo 24, 1-9-1871.

34. Sarmiento Gutiérrez, *La educación en Cajamarca.*

35. "La situación dolorosa de mi consorte que handa de casa en casa y de chacra en chacra buscando a su hija."

36. ADC/CSJ/CC, legajo 24, 1-9-1871.

37. ADC/CSJ/CC, legajo 14, 4-7-1866.

38. ADC/CSJ/CC, legajo 38, 18-9-1882. Zoila Alcántara and Manuel María Alcántara were cousins.

39. ADC/CSJ/CC, legajo 37, 5-6-1879.

40. ADC/CSJ/CC, legajo 25, 30-4-1872.

41. ADC/CSJ/CC, legajo 24, 1-9-1871.

42. ADC/CSJ/CC, legajo 38, 18-9-1882. For a further example, see ADC/Prefectura/Particulares, legajo 182, Comandante de la Ronda de la Guardia Civil, Cajamarca, enero 16 de 1877.

43. García Calderón, *Diccionario de la legislación peruana,* p. 199.

44. ADC/CSJ/CC, legajo 89, 5-11-1898 (Sichas); legajo 14, 4-7-1866 (León).

45. Boyer, "Honor among Plebeians," p. 172.

46. ADC/CSJ/CC, legajo 24, 1-9-1871.

47. Twinam, *Public Lives, Private Secrets,* p. 64.

48. ADC/CSJ/CC, legajo 24, 1-9-1871.

49. ADC/CSJ/CC, legajo 22, 6-8-1869.

50. ADC/CSJ/CC, legajo 22, 10-5-1869.

51. ADC/CSJ/CC, legajo 22, 10-5-1869.

52. Boyer, "Honor among Plebeians," p. 152. Socolow also notes the danger of increased dishonor by publicizing rape through legal action ("Women and Crime," p. 46).

53. Johnson, "Dangerous Words," p. 146.

54. Seed, "Marriage Promises," p. 265. Seed's article is of particular interest as she notes a change in the attitude toward male and female honor. She argues that women's claims that they had been given oral promises of marriage were usually accepted as valid during the seventeenth century, but were questioned increasingly throughout the eighteenth century. The value of women's testimony, in other words, declined, as did men's concern with behaving honorably and fulfilling their part of the bargain. Instead, men more and more often refused to marry their fiancées, accusing them of not having been virgins prior to their seduction. Martínez-Alier notes that men used similar tactics in trying to evade marriage after deflowering young women (*Marriage, Class and Colour in Nineteenth Century Cuba,* p. 111).

55. ADC/CSJ/CC, legajo 5, 9-6-1863.

56. ADC/CSJ/CC, legajo 37, 5-6-1879.

57. ADC/CSJ/CC, legajo 89, 5-11-1898.

58. ADC/CSJ/CC, legajo 6, 5-12-1863.

59. ADC/CSJ/CC, legajo 45, 27-12-1886.

60. See Seed, "Marriage Promises," pp. 258, 263, for references to gift giving as part of the engagement process in colonial Mexico.

61. "Que virginidad puede haber en una mujer corrida, que se ha encontrado con montoneras? La que se dice virgen y menor de edad, es pues . . . una muger de mundo, y mayor de veinte años."

62. ADC/CSJ/CC, legajo 38, 18-9-1882.

63. ADC/CSJ/CC, legajo 24, 1-9-1871.

64. ADC/CSJ/CC, legajo 22, 10-5-1869 (Noriega) and legajo 5, 9-6-1863 (Ortega).

65. ADC/CSJ/CC, legajo 14, 4-7-1866. She recanted on her deathbed.

66. ADC/CSJ/CC, legajo 45, 27-12-1886.

67. ADC/CSJ/CC, legajo 37, 5-6-1879.

68. ADC/CSJ/CC, legajo 24, 1-9-1871.

69. ADC/CSJ/CC, legajo 22, 6-8-1869.

70. ADC/CSJ/CC, legajo 45, 27-12-1886.

71. ADC/CSJ/CC, legajo 89, 5-11-1898. For further analysis of how exposure in the public sphere threatened women's reputations, see Porter, "And That It Is Custom Makes It Law," p. 134.

72. ADC/CSJ/CC, legajo 45, 27-12-1886.

73. ADC/CSJ/CC, legajo 83, 6-5-1897.

74. ADC/CSJ/CC, legajo 6, 5-12-1863.

75. ADC/CSJ/CC, legajo 5, 9-6-1863.

76. ADC/CSJ/CC, legajo 75, 18-1-1895.

77. ADC/CSJ/CC, legajo 38, 18-9-1882.

78. Among these was Manuel María Alcántara, who told friends that he had raped his cousin and fathered a child, but was not sentenced for either rape or seduction.

79. ADC/CSJ/CC, legajo 24, 1-9-1871.

80. ADC/CSJ/CC, legajo 44, 15-10-1886.

81. "Violar" seems to have been used to describe the rape of a nonvirgin —in this case a married woman—while "estuprar" here implies the rape and deflowering of a virgin (ADC/CSJ/CC, legajo 73, 22-2-1894).

82. ADC/CSJ/CC, legajo 89, 5-11-1898.

83. ADC/CSJ/CC, legajo 37, 5-6-1879.

84. Kuznesof, "Sexual Politics," p. 242.

85. Lauderdale Graham, *House and Street*, p. 46.

86. ADC/CSJ/CC, legajo 24, 1-9-1871. Hünefeldt also notes that victims of rape and seduction received legal support only if they were of the same social class as their rapist or seducer. Lower-class women received little sympathy (*Liberalism in the Bedroom*, p. 185).

87. ADC/CSJ/CC, legajo 38, 18-9-1882.

88. Twinam, "The Negotiation of Honor," p. 83.

89. ADC/CSJ/CC, legajo 55, 21-5-1890. Whereas this is the only reference to the rape—attempted or completed—of a married woman I have found, Socolow has found several such cases in her sample of approximately seventy criminal trials in colonial Buenos Aires. Moreover, she notes that it was only the rape of married women which was treated seriously by judges, as such

crimes affected the husband's honor. Rape of unmarried women, particularly if they lacked a male protector or guardian, rarely resulted in sentences, or, if it did, only light sentences. It would seem that legal practice in nineteenth-century Peru and in colonial Buenos Aires differed with regard to how the finer details of the code of honor were worked out. See Socolow, "Women and Crime," p. 48.

90. See Lipsett-Rivera, "A Slap in the Face of Honor," p. 195.

91. Socolow, "Women and Crime," also notes the authorities' distress when faced with incidents of child rape. While she notes that the burden of proof rested on the girl in question in eighteenth-century Buenos Aires, and that complete physical penetration had to have taken place for a sentence to be levied, legal practice in Cajamarca differed from case to case. Although the man Mercedes Velesmoro, age eight, accused of raping her was absolved as the midwives could find no sign of penetration, the man who failed to complete the rape of fourteen-year-old Melchora Sánchez Silva was sentenced to jail for four years. See ADC/CSJ/CC, legajo 83, 6-5-1897 (Velesmoro) and legajo 6, 5-12-1863 (Sánchez Silva).

92. ADC/CSJ/CC, legajo 44, 15-10-1886.

93. ADC/CSJ/CC, legajo 83, 6-5-1897 (Velesmoro). For another example of the rape of a minor, see ADC/Prefectura/Particulares, legajo 182, Comandante de Ronda de la Guardia Civil, Cajamarca, 12-3-1877: "Sr. Teniente Coronel Mayor de Guardias. Parte. Tengo el honor de poner en el conocimiento de U. que en la noche de ayer ha sido tenido preso a ese cuartel, José Alcántara, acusado de haber querido estrupar una chica de ciete años de edad, llamadase Josefa Solano, hija de Don Pedro Solano, siendo el padre el que acusa de este delito al espresado Alcántara. Diós Guarde a U. Belisario Pájares" [Colonel, Major of the Guards. I have the honor to inform you that José Alcántara was imprisoned in these barracks, having wanted to rape a girl aged seven years, named Josefa Solano, daughter of Don Pedro Solano, who is the one indicting the said Alcántara. God save you. Belisario Pájares]

94. ADC/CSJ/CC, legajo 38, 18-9-1882.

95. ADC/CSJ/CC, legajo 14, 4-7-1866.

96. For example, ADC/CSJ/CC, legajo 22, 10-5-1869.

97. ADC/CSJ/CC, legajo 24, 1-9-1871; legajo 25, 30-4-1872.

98. ADC/CSJ/CC, legajo 24, 1-9-1871.

99. It certainly seems that this applied to plebeian men. Twinam observes that this was not the case for colonial elite men who entered relationships with their peers. Many safeguarded their mistress' honor, arranging for private pregnancies and assuming full responsibility for the upbringing of their children (*Public Lives, Private Secrets*, p. 94).

100. ADC/CSJ/CC, legajo 74, 22-2-1894.

101. ADC/CSJ/CC, legajo 38, 18-9-1882.

102. ADC/CSJ/CC, legajo 62, 11-6-1891.

103. ADC/CSJ/CC, legajo 1, 14-1-1862.

104. Chambers notes that plebeian single women could lay claim to honor, providing they lived in a stable, long-term union, ideally with an expectation of marriage (*From Subjects to Citizens*, p. 177).

105. ADC/CSJ/CC, legajo 22, 10-5-1869.

106. For similar conclusions about the colonial period, see Twinam, *Public Lives, Private Secrets*, p. 39; Lipsett-Rivera, "A Slap in the Face of Honor," p. 83.

107. Harvey, "Domestic Violence in the Peruvian Andes."

108. Hünefeldt, *Liberalism in the Bedroom*, pp. 181–184. Martínez-Alier (*Marriage, Class and Colour in Nineteenth Century Cuba*, p. 113) argues the reverse, namely, that the taint of racial inferiority was considered more serious than that of lost virginity, showing that parents in Cuba preferred a daughter's dishonor to bringing colored blood into the family.

109. ADC/CSJ/CC, legajo 5, 9-6-1863.

110. ADC/CSJ/CC, legajo 14, 4-7-1866.

111. ADC/CSJ/CC, legajo 5, 9-6-1863.

112. Stern and Johnson and Lipsett-Rivera argue that the notion of a single honor/shame code as a guide to gender values and social relations must be discarded. See Stern, *The Secret History of Gender*, p. 110; Johnson and Lipsett-Rivera, *The Faces of Honor*, p. 15.

7. CONFLICT AND COOPERATION AMONG WOMEN

1. ADC/CSJ/CC, legajo 1, 9-1-1862.

2. The only two cases in which the abuse of servant girls by their mistresses resulted in criminal proceedings were cases in which the girls died following their maltreatment. See ADC/CSJ/CC, legajo 14, 22-6-1866 and legajo 51, 3-3-1889. The other four references to tension between mistresses and female servants were recorded after an employer complained of a servant's abduction or escape. See the trials dealing with Manuela Chávez (ADC/CSJ/CC, legajo 1, 19-1-1862), Beatriz Chavarri (ADC/CSJ/CC, legajo 5, 9-6-1863), Bernabé Cabrera (ADC/CSJ/CC, legajo 64, 21-11-1891), and Manuela Goicochea (ADC/CSJ/CC, legajo 54, 3-12-1889).

3. See the section on poisoning and witchcraft, below.

4. See the case dealing with the dispute between Isidora Paico and Carmen Ducos, below. Paico started an argument with Ducos during a village fiesta and was later suspected of having set fire to Ducos' barn, which burned down the same evening (ADC/CSJ/CC, legajo 37, 5-11-1880).

5. For examples of women killed in fights with other women, see ADC/CSJ/CC, legajo 60, 20-1-1891 and legajo 66, 14-5-1892. See the following trials for examples of miscarriages: ADC/CSJ/CC, legajo 26, 3-7-1872; legajo 26, 19-9-1872; legajo 32, 13-7-1874; legajo 90, 19-4-1899. For the death of infants as a result of assaults on their mothers, see ADC/CSJ/CC, legajo 17, 9-7-1867 and legajo 35, 3-3-1877. As the example of Fermín Cerdán's attack on his pregnant common-law wife, Manuela Urrelo (which I describe in Chapter 4), shows, pregnant women were at risk from men as well as women.

6. "Creyendo que allí hubiera pelea, me acerqué, y como había vastante luna vi a Manuela Mestanza y sobre ella a Gregoria Astopilco, recíprocamente agarrada de los pelos y la Jesús Astopilco . . . le daba tambien de patadas a la tal Mestanza . . . apenas se levantó la Mestanza le vi toda la cara

bañada en sangre, y una herida en la frente que parecía se habian sacado un pedazo de carne" (ADC/CSJ/CC, legajo 37, 22-5-1880).

7. Several cases of assault were reported only following near-lethal attacks. See, for instance, the case of Dionicio Díaz, who pressed charges against his daughter's former lover and the latter's new wife only after they started trying to shoot his daughter (ADC/CSJ/CC, legajo 57, 6-11-1890).

8. See, for instance, descriptions of fights in the following trials: ADC/CSJ/CC, legajo 17, 9-7-1867; legajo 32, 13-7-1874; legajo 37, 22-5-1880; legajo 63, 22-6-1891; legajo 69, 4-1-1893. Pulling hair was not an exclusively female practice. Pascuala Vargas said that José Bringas Castilla initiated his assault on her by pulling her hair: ADC/CSJ/CC, legajo 78, 15-5-1896.

9. For a description of peasant women's appearance, see Eléspuru Bernizón, "La provincia de Cajamarca," p. 154.

10. ADC/CSJ/CC, legajo 1, 9-1-1862 and legajo 17, 9-7-1867.

11. For examples of stone throwing as an effective attack and defense, see ADC/CSJ/CC, legajo 10, 26-11-1864; legajo 32, 13-7-1874; legajo 39, 11-9-1882; legajo 65, 11-2-1892. For examples of men using stones, see ADC/CSJ/CC, legajo 28, 9-1-1873 and legajo 28, 28-1-1873.

12. ADC/Prefectura/Comandancia General, legajo 195, Capitanía de la 2a compañía de la columna de voluntarios [sic] de Bambamarca, 1-5-1865.

13. ADC/CSJ/CC, legajo 17, 9-7-1867 and legajo 63, 22-6-1891.

14. Torre Araujo, *Estudio de campo*, p. 23.

15. ADC/CSJ/CC, legajo 35, 3-3-1877.

16. ADC/CSJ/CC, legajo 37, 22-5-1880.

17. ADC/CSJ/CC, legajo 63, 22-6-1891.

18. ADC/CSJ/CC, legajo 32, 23-7-1874.

19. ADC/CSJ/CC, legajo 65, 30-1-1892.

20. ADC/CSJ/CC, legajo 37, 22-5-1880. For more examples of oral insults preceding physical attacks, see ADC/CSJ/CC, legajo 23, 3-5-1870; legajo 23, 22-10-1870; legajo 90, 19-4-1899.

21. ADC/CSJ/CC, legajo 79, 2-6-1896.

22. ADC/CSJ/CC, legajo 23, 31-5-1870.

23. ADC/CSJ/CC, legajo 74, 2-7-1894.

24. Romanucci-Ross, *Conflict, Violence and Morality*, p. 147.

25. Stern, *The Secret History of Gender*, pp. 108–109, 142.

26. For a similar example, see ADC/CSJ/CC, legajo 23, 15-10-1870; legajo 55, 20-5-1890.

27. Lipsett-Rivera, "A Slap in the Face of Honor," p. 197.

28. ADC/CSJ/CC, legajo 41, 6-2-1886.

29. ADC/CSJ/CC, legajo 90, 19-4-1899.

30. ADC/CSJ/CC, legajo 23, 15-10-1870.

31. ADC/CSJ/CC, legajo 64, 21-11-1891.

32. ADC/CSJ/CC, legajo 51, 3-3-1889; also see the case of Remigia Bermúdes, mentioned earlier (ADC/CSJ/CC, legajo 1, 9-1-1862).

33. ADC/CSJ/CC, legajo 1, 19-1-1862.

34. ADC/CSJ/CC, legajo 11, 2-2-1865.

35. Fairchilds, *Domestic Enemies*, p. 131. Also see Demos, *Entertaining*

Satan, p. 54, who points out that blaming supposed witches for incomprehensible disasters served a social function. Also, blaming such individuals could be more convenient than facing up to personal incompetence.

36. Demos (*Entertaining Satan*, p. 80) also notes the connection between midwifery and witchcraft.

37. ADC/CSJ/CC, legajo 55, 24-1-1890.

38. Marín was subsequently diagnosed as suffering from epilepsy. Her seizures subsided when she returned to her home province of Celendín (ADC/CSJ/CC, legajo 11, 2-2-1865).

39. ADC/CSJ/CC, legajo 37, 12-1-1879.

40. Stern, *The Secret History of Gender*, p. 107.

41. ADC/CSJ/CC, legajo 23, 3-5-1870.

42. ADC/CSJ/CC, legajo 57, 6-11-1890.

43. See, for instance, ADC/CSJ/CC, legajo 32, 14-7-1874; legajo 32, 23-7-1874; legajo 35, 11-12-1877; legajo 36, 9-1-1878; legajo 65, 11-2-1892.

44. ADC/CSJ/CC, legajo 65, 30-1-1892 (second trial).

45. See, for instance, the trial concerning the fight between Bernardina Sáenz and Máxima, Matilde, Estefania, and Baltazara Espinoza—ADC/CSJ/CC, legajo 35, 3-3-1877—and the comments of Micaela Galarretea and Agueda and Zoila Sorogéstua in ADC/CSJ/CC, legajo 65, 30-1-1892.

46. ADC/CSJ/CC, legajo 64, 10-10-1891.

47. ADC/CSJ/CC, legajo 28, 28-1-1873.

48. ADC/CSJ/CC, legajo 75, 4-3-1895.

49. ADC/CSJ/CC, legajo 3, 1-11-1862.

50. Torre Araujo, *Estudio de campo*, p. 23.

51. ADC/CSJ/CC, legajo 26, 3-7-1872.

52. ADC/CSJ/CC, legajo 32, 14-7-1874; legajo 35, 3-3-1877; legajo 65, 30-1-1892.

53. ADC/CSJ/CC, legajo 79, 15-9-1896.

54. ADC/CSJ/CC, legajo 66, 14-5-1892.

55. ADC/CSJ/CC, legajo 26, 3-7-1872.

56. ADC/CSJ/CC, legajo 26, 19-9-1872. For another example of conflict between close relatives, see ADC/CSJ/CC, legajo 9, 21-6-1864.

57. ADC/CSJ/CC, legajo 75, 13-2-1895.

58. ADC/CSJ/CC, legajo 45, 13-11-1886.

59. ADC/CSJ/CC, legajo 74, 28-8-1894.

60. ADC/CSJ/CC, legajo 57, 22-10-1890.

61. Johnson, "Dangerous Words," p. 135.

62. ADC/CSJ/CC, legajo 35, 3-3-1877.

63. In a male parallel, Juan Salazar Estrada refused to join in a drinking party which took place in the house in which he lived, because two of the party's members had "been enemies of mine for some time." Although he left the room where the group settled, a mêlée ensued. Isidoro Fernández broke a bottle over Manuel Saldaña's head, and Saldaña accidentally shot his own brother-in-law, Estrada, in the chest (ADC/CSJ/CC, legajo 62, 19-5-1891). Family obligations and the small social milieux of the villages and towns were likely to produce continual encounters and hence confrontations with

opponents, with the result that antagonistic relationships regularly boiled over into violence.

64. ADC/CSJ/CC, legajo 79, 15-9-1896.

65. ADC/CSJ/CC, legajo 7, 3-3-1864. Also see ADC/CSJ/CC, legajo 37, 22-5-1880; legajo 57, 6-11-1890.

66. ADC/CSJ/CC, legajo 37, 5-11-1880.

67. ADC/CSJ/CC, legajo 26, 3-7-1872.

68. ADC/CSJ/CC, legajo 65, 15-2-1892.

69. ADC/Prefectura/Particulares, legajo 230, 16-4-1891, Nota de Asunción Medina.

70. ADC/CSJ/CC, legajo 37, 12-1-1879; also see ADC/CSJ/CC, legajo 11, 2-2-1865.

71. ADC/CSJ/CC, legajo 37, 5-11-1880.

72. Millones and Pratt, *Amor brujo*, p. 46.

73. Torre Araujo, *Estudio de campo*, p. 23.

74. Romanucci-Ross, *Conflict, Violence and Morality*, p. 148; Chambers, *From Subjects to Citizens*, p. 92.

75. Deere, *Household and Class Relations*, pp. 95, 286–287.

76. ADC/CSJ/CC, legajo 1, 15-1-1862.

77. ADC/CSJ/CC, legajo 23, 15-10-1870.

78. Stern, *The Secret History of Gender*, p. 134.

79. Taylor, "Earning a Living in Hualgayoc, 1870–1900," p. 116; also see idem, "Society and Politics in Late Nineteenth Century Peru," p. 15; Deere, *Household and Class Relations*, p. 45.

80. See, for instance, Gerónimo Miranda's flight to the coast to escape a charge of rape (ADC/CSJ/CC, legajo 14, 4-7-1866).

81. See Tables B7–B18, Appendix B.

82. Romanucci-Ross, *Conflict, Violence and Morality*, p. 64.

83. Stern, *The Secret History of Gender*, pp. 79–80, 85.

84. ADC/CSJ/CC, legajo 6, 13-11-1863; legajo 9, 21-6-1864.

85. ADC/CSJ/CC, legajo 34, 10-11-1876.

86. ADC/CSJ/CC, legajo 90, 19-4-1899.

87. ADC/CSJ/CC, legajo 75, 13-2-1895.

88. ADC/CSJ/CC, legajo 63, 12-9-1891.

89. ADC/CSJ/CC, legajo 43, 30-6-1886.

90. ADC/CSJ/CC, legajo 9, 21-6-1864.

91. ADC/CSJ/CC, legajo 60, 20-1-1891; for other examples of rows over pigs, see ADC/CSJ/CC, legajo 64, 7-11-1891; legajo 32, 13-7-1874; legajo 23, 31-5-1870.

92. ADC/CSJ/CC, legajo 6, 13-11-1863.

93. Torre Araujo, *Estudio de campo*, p. 24.

94. Lapiedra, "Roles y valores de la mujer andina," pp. 47–48.

95. ADC/CSJ/CC, legajo 17, 9-7-1867 and legajo 23, 15-10-1870.

96. Bermúdes appeared in the Basauri household in order to prevent her son José Trinidad from being punished for the loss of two eggs (ADC/CSJ/CC, legajo 1, 9-1-1862).

97. ADC/CSJ/CC, legajo 23, 15-10-1870.

98. See ADC/CSJ/CC, legajo 65, 11-2-1892.

99. ADC/CSJ/CC, legajo 32, 14-7-1874 (Sifuentes); legajo 32, 23-7-1874 (Bermúdez).

100. Romanucci-Ross, *Conflict, Violence and Morality*, p. 148.

101. Remigia Bermúdes claimed that none of the judges in the town of Cajamarca were willing to act on her complaint (ADC/CSJ/CC, legajo 1, 9-1-1862). The charges against Isabel Basauri were dealt with only after she sent a letter to the prefect (ADC/CSJ/CC, legajo 1, 9-1-1862).

102. See ADC/CSJ/CC, legajo 28, 26-3-1872 and legajo 24, 1-7-1871.

103. ADC/CSJ/CC, legajo 65, 30-1-1892.

104. ADC/CSJ/CC, legajo 37, 22-5-1880.

105. ADC/CSJ/CC, legajo 35, 3-3-1877.

106. ADC/CSJ/CC, legajo 65, 15-2-1892. For other allegations of corruption impeding justice, see ADC/CSJ/CC, legajo 7, 3-3-1864.

107. See, for instance, ADC/CSJ/CC, legajo 45, 13-11-1886 and legajo 69, 4-1-1893.

108. ADC/CSJ/CC, legajo 1, 9-1-1862.

109. ADC/CSJ/CC, legajo 26, 3-7-1872.

110. ADC/CSJ/CC, legajo 70, 5-5-1893, Proceso judicial seguido de oficio a los reos Manuel Asencio, María Rosario, y Narciso Sembrano por el aborto provocado de Paula Saucedo y maltratos a José Dolores Olivares. For another example of delayed and unreliable medical conclusions, see ADC/CSJ/CC, legajo 32, 13-7-1874. Although the first medical examination concluded that Francisca Pájares' miscarriage was the result of a stone thrown by the accused, a second opinion, formed six months after the event, blamed illness for the termination.

111. ADC/CSJ/CC, legajo 41, 6-2-1886.

112. ADC/CSJ/CC, legajo 34, 13-11-1876.

113. See ADC/CSJ/CC, legajo 35, 3-3-1877 (Sáenz); legajo 37, 22-5-1880 (Mestanza).

114. ADC/CSJ/CC, legajo 10, 26-11-1864.

115. ADC/CSJ/CC, legajo 65, 15-2-1892. For another example of a woman being threatened by two sisters, see ADC/Prefectura/Particulares, legajo 230, 16-4-1891, Nota de Asunción Medina.

116. ADC/CSJ/CC, legajo 35, 3-3-1877.

117. ADC/CSJ/CC, legajo 63, 22-6-1891 and legajo 74, 28-8-1894.

118. Stern draws similar conclusions in *The Secret History of Gender*, p. 125. Torre Araujo also notes that female relatives usually assist each other when they become embroiled in violent conflict; see *Estudio de campo*, p. 23.

119. ADC/CSJ/CC, legajo 26, 19-9-1872.

120. ADC/CSJ/CC, legajo 26, 19-9-1872. For another example of a mother intervening to lead her daughter away from conflict, see ADC/CSJ/CC, legajo 28, 26-3-1872.

121. ADC/CSJ/CC, legajo 26, 3-7-1872.

122. ADC/CSJ/CC, legajo 35, 3-3-1877.

123. ADC/CSJ/CC, legajo 37, 5-11-1880.

124. ADC/CSJ/CC, legajo 51, 11-3-1889.

125. Stern, *The Secret History of Gender*, p. 185.

126. ADC/CSJ/CC, legajo 17, 9-7-1867. For another example of such assistance, read Baltazara Espinoza's statement in ADC/CSJ/CC, legajo 35, 3-3-1877.

127. ADC/CSJ/CC, legajo 75, 5-3-1895.

128. ADC/CSJ/CC, legajo 34, 10-11-1876.

129. ADC/CSJ/CC, legajo 57, 22-10-1890.

130. ADC/CSJ/CC, legajo 14, 22-6-1866.

131. Miller, "La mujer obrera en Lima, 1900–30," p. 67.

132. Streicker, "Sexuality, Power and Social Order in Cartagena, Colombia," p. 361.

133. ADC/CSJ/CC, legajo 26, 3-7-1872.

134. ADC/CSJ/CC, legajo 9, 21-6-1864.

135. Mannarelli, *Pecados públicos*, p. 295.

136. Barrantes and Urteaga note how the "dramatic situation in which a number of abandoned girls found themselves, because of their parents' irresponsible behavior or their death, [led to the establishment of] the Asilo de Huérfanas orphanage" in 1890 (*Mirando más de un siglo*, p. 125).

137. ADC/CSJ/CC, legajo 1, 19-1-1862.

138. Tadea Casas stated that she had expressed her desire to nurse Chávez of her own accord and approached the girl's uncle herself. Mannarelli observes that women of all social classes began to breast-feed abandoned, frequently illegitimate, children following the death of their own infants (*Pecados públicos*, p. 295).

139. ADC/CSJ/CC, legajo 64, 21-11-1891. For another example of a trial dealing with a similar subject, see ADC/CSJ/CC, legajo 54, 3-12-1889.

140. See ADC/CSJ/CC, legajo 54, 23-9-1899. The rape of Simona Malaver's daughters was averted only through the intervention of neighbors; see ADC/CSJ/CC, legajo 73, 22-2-1894.

141. ADC/CSJ/CC, legajo 74, 2-7-1894. For another example of passersby fearing to intervene, see ADC/CSJ/CC, legajo 40, 7-11-1885. Although José Manuel Carrera attacked Tomasa Mendoza with a machete, a witness stated that he decided to walk on, past the injured woman, out of fear of being attacked.

142. ADC/CSJ/CC, legajo 9, 29-2-1864. For another example of outsiders intervening in order to defuse an escalating situation, see ADC/CSJ/CC, legajo 51, 11-3-1889.

143. ADC/CSJ/CC, legajo 26, 19-9-1872.

144. ADC/CSJ/CC, legajo 9, 21-6-1864.

145. Romanucci-Ross found that the washing fountain played much the same role in the Mexican village she studied: "The washing fountain provides one of the main centers for female contact, gossip, and a kind of brawling that sober men avoid" (*Conflict, Violence and Morality*, p. 79). See Pitt-Rivers (*The People of the Sierra*, p. 88) for a note on women's encounters at water fountains.

146. ADC/CSJ/CC, legajo 26, 19-9-1872.

147. ADC/CSJ/CC, legajo 89, 5-12-1898.

148. Mallon, *Peasant and Nation*, p. 69. Mallon also includes the tasks of gathering food, fetching water, and washing clothes among those that provided an opportunity for women to break out of the seclusion of the household.

149. Lauderdale Graham, *House and Street*, p. 52.

150. ADC/CSJ/CC, legajo 74, 2-7-1894.

151. ADC/CSJ/CC, legajo 41, 6-2-1886.

152. ADC/CSJ/CC, legajo 69, 29-1-1893.

153. For an analysis of contrasting definitions of market women by the women themselves and the local intelligentsia, see Cadena, "The Political Tensions of Representations and Misrepresentations" (p. 114): "Whereas the local elite call the market women *cholas*, and define them as poor, immoral, and culturally inferior, the women themselves describe themselves as *mestizas*, implying that they consider themselves successful urbanites." Cadena also notes that in Cuzco market women's definition of personal worth is built on honorable work and boldness, which conflicts sharply with elite definitions of female respectability, which do not consider boldness a decent female attribute.

154. For an account of another incident in which market women clashed with municipal officials, see Lipsett-Rivera, "A Slap in the Face of Honor," p. 188.

155. J. Scott, *Domination and the Arts of Resistance*, p. 119.

156. Stern, *The Secret History of Gender*, p. 15.

157. Stern, *The Secret History of Gender*, p. 79.

8. CONCLUSION

1. Tinsman notes that campesino men lived under the pressure of conflicting ideals, namely, those of responsible husband and worker; militancy, male assertiveness, and combativeness; loyalty to other men; and sexual prowess ("Good Wives and Unfaithful Men," p. 619). Exploring the pressures exerted by conflicting gender ideals under which both men and women labored—including the question of how men's and women's social ideals differed, with men's socializing very likely earning greater acceptance in society at large than women's—would be extremely interesting.

2. Klubock, "Writing the History of Women and Gender in Twentieth-century Chile," p. 503.

3. Trazegnies Granda, *Ciriaco de Urtecho*, p. 81.

4. Klubock, "Writing the History of Women and Gender in Twentieth-century Chile," p. 514.

5. Twinam, *Public Lives, Private Secrets*.

6. Lavrin, *Sexuality and Marriage*, p. 12.

7. Klubock, "Writing the History of Women and Gender in Twentieth-century Chile," p. 517.

8. Lavrin, *Sexuality and Marriage*, p. 76; also see Boyer, "Women, *la mala vida*," p. 264.

9. Stern, *The Secret History of Gender*, p. 82.

10. Tinsman, "Good Wives and Unfaithful Men," p. 602.

11. See Chapter 4.

12. Boyer, "Women, *la mala vida*," p. 263.

13. Lavrin, *Sexuality and Marriage*, p. 20.

14. J. Scott, *Weapons of the Weak*, p. xv.

15. Also see Lavrin, *Sexuality and Marriage*, p. 64.

16. ADC/CSJ/CC, legajo 14, 22-6-1866.

17. Klubock, "Writing the History of Women and Gender in Twentieth-century Chile," p. 516.

18. Chambers, *From Subjects to Citizens*, pp. 207–209.

19. Romanucci-Ross, *Conflict, Violence and Morality*, p. 148; Stern, *The Secret History of Gender*, p. 134; Torre Araujo, *Estudio de campo*, p. 24.

20. Stern, *The Secret History of Gender*, p. 15.

Bibliography

Alegría, Ciro. *El mundo es ancho y ajeno*. Madrid: Espasa-Calpe, 1982.

Arrom, Silvia Marina. "Changes in Mexican Family Law in the Nineteenth Century: The Civil Codes of 1870 and 1884." *Journal of Family History* 10 (1985): 305–317.

———. *The Women of Mexico City, 1790–1857*. Stanford: Stanford University Press, 1985.

Barrantes Zurita, Cecilia, and Rossina Urteaga Guerrero. *Mirando más de un siglo: Organizaciones femeninas en Cajamarca*. Cajamarca: Asociación Mujer Familia, 1994.

Basadre, Jorge. *Historia de la República del Perú*, Vol. 3. 5th ed. Lima: Editorial Peruamérica, 1964.

———. *Introducción a las bases documentales para la historia de la República del Perú*, Vol. 1. Lima, 1971.

Behar, Ruth. "Sexual Witchcraft, Colonialism, and Women's Powers: Views from the Mexican Inquisition." In *Sexuality and Marriage in Colonial Latin America*, ed. Asunción Lavrin, pp. 178–206. Lincoln: University of Nebraska Press, 1989.

Bolton, Ralph. "The Qolla Marriage Process." In *Andean Kinship and Marriage*, ed. Ralph Bolton and Enrique Mayer, pp. 217–238. Washington, DC: American Anthropological Association, 1977.

———, and Charlene Bolton. *Conflictos en la familia andina (un estudio antropológico entre los campesinos Quollo)*. Cuzco: Centro de Estudios Andinos, 1975.

Bolton, Ralph, and Enrique Mayer, eds. *Andean Kinship and Marriage*. Washington, DC: American Anthropological Association, 1977.

Bourque, Susan C., and Kay B. Warren. "Female Participation, Perception and Power: An Examination of Two Andean Communities." In *Political Participation in Latin America*, Vol. 2, *Politics and the Poor*, ed. John A. Booth and Mitchell A. Seligson, pp. 116–133. New York: Holmes and Meier, 1978.

Boyer, Richard. "Honor among Plebeians: *Mala Sangre* and Social Reputation." In *The Faces of Honor: Sex, Shame and Violence in Colonial Latin America*, ed. Lyman L. Johnson and Sonya Lipsett-Rivera, pp. 152–178. Albuquerque: University of New Mexico Press, 1998.

———. *Lives of the Bigamists: Marriage, Family and Community in Colonial Mexico*. Albuquerque: University of New Mexico Press, 1995.

———. "Women, *la Mala Vida* and the Politics of Marriage." In *Sexuality and Marriage in Colonial Latin America*, ed. Asunción Lavrin, pp. 252–286. Lincoln: University of Nebraska Press, 1989.

Burga, Manuel, and Alberto Flores Galindo. *Apogeo y crisis de la república aristocrática: Oligarquía, aprismo y comunismo en el Perú, 1895-1932*. Lima: Ediciones Rickhay Perú, 1979.

Burkett, Elinor. "Indian Women and White Society: The Case of Sixteenth Century Peru." In *Latin American Women: Historical Perspectives*, ed. Asunción Lavrin, pp. 101–128. Westport, CT: Greenwood Press, 1978.

———. "In Dubious Sisterhood: Class and Sex in Spanish Colonial South America." *Latin American Perspectives* 4, nos. 12–13 (Winter/Spring 1977): 18–26.

Cadena, Marisol de la. "The Political Tensions of Representations and Misrepresentations: Intellectuals and *Mestizas* in Cuzco, 1919-1990." *Journal of Latin American Anthropology* 2, no. 1 (1996): 112–147.

Caulfield, Sueann. "The History of Gender in the Historiography of Latin America." *Hispanic American Historical Review* 81, nos. 3–4 (August–November 2000): 449–490.

Celani, David. *The Illusion of Love: Why the Battered Woman Returns to the Abuser*. New York: Columbia University Press, 1994.

Chambers, Sarah C. *From Subjects to Citizens: Honor, Gender, and Politics in Arequipa, Peru, 1780-1854*. University Park: Pennsylvania State University Press, 1999.

Chassen-López, Francie R. "Cheaper than Modernization: Women and Agriculture in Porfirian Oaxaca, 1880-1911." In *Women of the Mexican Countryside, 1850-1990*, ed. Heather Fowler-Salamini and Mary Kay Vaughan, pp. 27–50. Tucson: University of Arizona Press, 1994.

Couturier, Edith. "Women and the Family in Eighteenth Century Mexico: Law and Practice." *Journal of Family History* 10, no. 3 (Fall 1985): 294–304.

Dammert Bellido, José. *Cajamarca durante la guerra del Pacífico*. Cajamarca: Imp. MACS, 1983.

Deere, Carmen Diana. "Changing Social Relations of Production and Peruvian Peasant Women's Work." *Latin American Perspectives* 4, nos. 12–13 (1977): 48–69.

———. "The Differentiation of the Peasantry and Family Structure: A Peruvian Case Study." *Journal of Family History* 3 (1978): 422–438.

———. "The Division of Labor by Sex in Agriculture: A Peruvian Case Study." *Economic Development and Cultural Change* 30 (1981-1982): 795–811.

———. *Household and Class Relations: Peasants and Landlords in Northern Peru*. Berkeley & Los Angeles: University of California Press, 1990.

Deere, Carmen Diana, and A. de Janvry. "Demographic and Social Differentiation among Northern Peruvian Peasants." *Journal of Peasant Studies* 8, no. 3 (1981): 335–366.

De la Cadena, Marisol. *See* Cadena, Marisol de la.

De la Lama, Miguel Antonio. *See* Lama, Miguel Antonio de la.

De la Torre, Ana. *See* Torre, Ana de la.

Demos, John Putnam. *Entertaining Satan: Witchcraft and the Culture of Early New England.* New York: Oxford University Press, 1982.

Denegri, Francesca. *El abanico y la cigarrera: La primera generación de mujeres ilustradas en el Perú.* Lima: IEP Ediciones, 1996.

Dirección Nacional de Estadística. *Resumen del censo general de habitantes del Perú hecho en 1876,* Vol. 3. Lima, 1878.

Dore, Elizabeth. "The Holy Family: Imagined Households in Latin American History." In *Gender Politics in Latin America: Debates in Theory and Practice,* ed. Elizabeth Dore. New York: Monthly Review Press, 1997.

———. "Patriarchy and Private Property in Nicaragua." In *Patriarchy and Development,* ed. Valentine M. Moghadam, pp. 56–79. Oxford: Clarendon Press, 1996.

———. "Property, Households and Public Regulation of Domestic Life: Diriomo, Nicaragua, 1840–1900." *Journal of Latin American Studies* 29, no. 3 (1997): 591–611.

———. "Public Patriarchy in Rural Nicaragua, 1830–1875." Paper presented at the Latin American Centre, St. Antony's College, Oxford, February 1995.

Ellefsen, Bernardo. "1780: Movimientos antifiscales en la sierra norte de la audiencia de Lima y repercusiones tupamaristas en la misma zona: Nuevas perspectivas." *Allpanchis* (Instituto de Pastoral Andina, Cuzco) 17–18 (1981): 169–201.

Eléspuru Bernizón, Eulogio. "La provincia de Cajamarca." In *Ensayos geográficos,* Vol. 2, ed. Javier Pulgar Vidal, pp. 146–310. Lima: Pontificia Universidad Católica del Perú, 1939.

Fairchilds, Cissie. *Domestic Enemies: Servants and Their Masters in Old Regime France.* Baltimore: Johns Hopkins University Press, 1984.

Fuentes, M. A. *Curso de enciclopedia del derecho.* 3 vols. Lima: Imprenta del Estado, 1876.

———. *Manual práctico de medicina legal.* Lima: Imprenta del Estado, 1869.

García Calderón, Francisco. *Diccionario de la legislación peruana, 2da edición, corregida y aumentada con las leyes y decretos dictados hasta 1877.* Lima: Librería Laroque, 1879.

Gayford, J. J. "Battered Wives." In *International Perspectives on Family Violence,* ed. Richard J. Gelles and Flaire Pedrick Cornell. Lexington, MA: Lexington Books, 1983.

Gilmore, David D. *Aggression and Community: Paradoxes of Andalusian Culture.* New Haven: Yale University Press, 1987.

———. "Honor, Honesty and Shame: Male Status in Contemporary Andalusia." In *Honor and Shame and the Unity of the Mediterranean,* ed.

David G. Gilmore, pp. 90–103. Washington, DC: American Anthropological Association, 1987.

Gonzales, Michael. "Capitalist Agriculture and Labour Contracting in Northern Peru, 1880–1905." *Journal of Latin American Studies* 12, no. 2 (1980).

González de Fanning, Teresa. *Educación femenina: Colección de artículos pedagógicos, morales y sociológicos.* Lima: Tipografía El Lucero, 1905.

González del Riego Espinoza, Delfina. "Divorcio y violencia doméstica: Lima en los siglos XVI y XVII." Paper presented at the IV Coloquio Internacional de Estudiantes de Historia, Pontificia Universidad Católica, Lima, 1993.

Gootenberg, Paul. "Population and Ethnicity in Early Republican Peru: Some Revisions." *Latin American Research Review* 26, no. 3 (1991): 109–157.

Guy, Donna J. "Lower Class Families, Women and the Law in Nineteenth Century Argentina." *Journal of Family History* 10 (1985): 318–331.

———. *Sex and Danger in Buenos Aires: Prostitution, Family and Nation in Argentina.* Lincoln: University of Nebraska Press, 1991.

———. "Women, Peonage and Industrialization in Argentina, 1810–1914." *Latin American Research Review* 16, no. 3 (1981): 65–90.

Harris, Olivia. "Complementaridad y conflicto: Una visión andina del hombre y la mujer." *Allpanchis* 25, no. 21 (1985).

Harvey, Penelope. "Domestic Violence in the Peruvian Andes." In *Sex and Violence: Issues in Representation and Experience,* ed. Penelope Harvey and Peter Gow, pp. 66–89. London: Routledge, 1994.

Herzfeld, Michael. "As in Your Own House: Hospitality, Ethnography, and the Stereotype of Mediterranean Society." In *Honor and Shame and the Unity of the Mediterranean,* ed. David G. Gilmore, pp. 75–89. Washington, DC: American Anthropological Association, 1987.

Hünefeldt, Christine. *Liberalism in the Bedroom: Quarrelling Spouses in Nineteenth-Century Lima.* University Park: Pennsylvania State University Press, 2000.

Hydén, Margareta. *Woman Battering as a Marital Act: The Construction of a Violent Marriage.* Oslo: Scandinavian University Press, 1994.

Jacobsen, Nils. *Mirages of Transition: The Peruvian Altiplano, 1780–1930.* Berkeley & Los Angeles: University of California Press, 1993.

Johnson, Ann Hagerman. "The Impact of Market Agriculture on Family and Household Structure in Nineteenth Century Chile." *Hispanic American Historical Review* 58, no. 4 (1978): 625–648.

Johnson, Lyman L. "Dangerous Words, Provocative Gestures, and Violent Acts: The Disputed Hierarchies of Plebeian Life in Colonial Buenos Aires." In *The Faces of Honor: Sex, Shame and Violence in Colonial Latin America,* ed. Lyman L. Johnson and Sonya Lipsett-Rivera, pp. 127–151. Albuquerque: University of New Mexico Press, 1998.

Johnson, Lyman L., and Sonya Lipsett-Rivera, eds. *The Faces of Honor: Sex, Shame and Violence in Colonial Latin America,* Albuquerque: University of New Mexico Press, 1998.

Klaiber, Jeffrey. *The Catholic Church in Peru, 1821–1985: A Social History.* Washington, DC: Catholic University of America Press, 1992.

———. *Religion and Revolution in Peru, 1824–1976.* Notre Dame, IN: University of Notre Dame Press, 1977.

———. "La reorganización de la iglesia ante el estado liberal en el Perú (1860–1930)." In *Historia general de la iglesia en América Latina,* ed. E. Dussel, Vol. 8, *Perú, Bolivia y Ecuador.* Spain: CEHLA; Salamanca: Ediciones Sígueme, 1987.

Klubock, Thomas Miller. "Writing the History of Women and Gender in Twentieth-century Chile." *Hispanic American Historical Review* 81, nos. 3–4 (August–November 2000): 493–517.

Kuznesof, Elizabeth. "Sexual Politics, Race and Bastard Bearing in Nineteenth Century Brazil: A Question of Culture or Power?" *Journal of Family History* 16, no. 3 (1991): 241–260.

LaJara, E. "Socialización de los hijos del migrante de la sierra." In *Divisions and Solidarities: Gender, Class and Employment in Latin America,* ed. Alison MacEwen Scott, p. 250. London: Routledge, 1994.

Lama, Miguel Antonio de la. *Código civil: Anotado y concordado e índice alfabético de sus artículos.* 3rd ed. Lima: Librería e Imprenta Gil, 1905.

Lapiedra, Aurora. "Roles y valores de la mujer andina." *Allpanchis* 21, no. 25 (1985).

Lauderdale Graham, Sandra. "Honor among Slaves." In *The Faces of Honor: Sex, Shame and Violence in Colonial Latin America,* ed. Lyman L. Johnson and Sonya Lipsett-Rivera, pp. 201–228. Albuquerque: University of New Mexico Press. 1998.

———. *House and Street: The Domestic World of Servants and Masters in Nineteenth-century Rio de Janeiro.* Cambridge: Cambridge University Press, 1988.

Lavrin, Asunción. "In Search of the Colonial Women in Mexico: The Seventeenth and Eighteenth Centuries." In *Latin American Women: Historical Perspectives,* ed. Asunción Lavrin, pp. 23–59. Westport, CT: Greenwood Press, 1978.

———. *Sexuality and Marriage in Colonial Latin America.* Lincoln: University of Nebraska Press, 1989.

———, and Edith Couturier. "Dowries and Wills: A View of Women's Socio-Economic Role in Colonial Guadalajara and Puebla, 1640–1790." *Hispanic American Historical Review* 59, no. 2 (1979): 280–304.

Lavrin, Asunción, ed. *Latin American Women: Historical Perspectives.* Westport, CT: Greenwood Press, 1978.

Lipsett-Rivera, Sonya. "A Slap in the Face of Honor: Social Transgression and Women in Late-Colonial Mexico." In *The Faces of Honor: Sex, Shame and Violence in Colonial Latin America,* ed. Lyman L. Johnson and Sonya Lipsett-Rivera, pp. 179–200. Albuquerque: University of New Mexico Press, 1998.

Lobo, Susan. *A House of My Own: Social Organization in the Squatter Settlements of Lima, Peru.* Tucson: University of Arizona Press, 1986.

Lynch, John. "The Catholic Church in Latin America, 1830–1930." In *Cambridge History of Latin America*, Vol. 4, ed. Leslie Bethell, pp. 525–595. Cambridge: Cambridge University Press, 1986.

Macera, Pablo. "Sexo y coloniaje." In *Trabajos de historia*, Vol. 3, pp. 297–352. Lima: Instituto Nacional de Cultura, 1977.

Málaga Santolalla, Fermín. *Departamento de Cajamarca: Monografía geográfica-estadística.* Lima, 1906.

Mallon, Florencia. *The Defense of Community in Peru's Central Highlands: Peasant Struggle and Capitalist Transition, 1860–1940.* Princeton, NJ: Princeton University Press, 1983.

———. "Patriarchy in the Transition to Capitalism: Central Peru, 1830–1950." *Feminist Studies* 13, no. 2 (1987): 379–408.

———. *Peasant and Nation: The Making of Postcolonial Mexico.* Berkeley & Los Angeles: University of California Press, 1995.

Mannarelli, María Emma. *Pecados públicos: La ilegitimidad en Lima, siglo XVII.* Lima: Ediciones Flora Tristán, 1994.

Margadant, Guillermo. "La familia en el derecho novohispano." In *Familias novohispanas: Siglos XVI al XIX*, ed. Pilar Gonzalbo Aizpuru, pp. 27–58. Mexico City: Seminario de Historia de la Familia, Centro de Estudios Históricos, El Colegio de México, 1991.

Martín, Luis. *Daughters of the Conquistadores: Women and the Viceroyalty of Peru.* Albuquerque: University of New Mexico Press, 1983.

Martínez-Alier, Verena. *Marriage, Class and Colour in Nineteenth Century Cuba: A Study of Racial Attitudes and Sexual Values in a Slave Society.* Cambridge: Cambridge University Press, 1974.

McCreery, David. "*This Life of Misery and Shame:* Female Prostitution in Guatemala City, 1880–1920." *Journal of Latin American Studies* 18, no. 2 (November 1986): 333–353.

Middendorf, E. W. *Peru: Beobachtungen und Studien über das Land und seine Bewohner während eines fünfundzwanzigjährigen Aufenthalts.* Berlin: Robert Oppenheim (Gustav Schmidt), 1895.

Miller, Laura. "La mujer obrera en Lima, 1900–30." In *Lima obrera, 1900–1930*, Vol. 2, ed. Steve Stein. Lima: Ediciones el Virrey, 1987.

Millones, Luis, and Mary Pratt. *Amor brujo: Imagen y cultura del amor en los Andes.* Lima: Instituto de Estudios Peruanos, 1989.

Nazzari, Muriel. "An Urgent Need to Conceal: The System of Honor and Shame in Colonial Brazil." In *The Faces of Honor: Sex, Shame and Violence in Colonial Latin America*, ed. Lyman L. Johnson and Sonya Lipsett-Rivera, pp. 103–126. Albuquerque: University of New Mexico Press, 1998.

Parker, D. S. *The Idea of the Middle Class: White-collar Workers and Peruvian Society, 1900–1950.* University Park: Pennsylvania State University Press, 1998.

Peristiany, J. G. *Honour and Shame: The Values of Mediterranean Society.* Chicago: University of Chicago Press, 1966.

Phillips, Lynne. "Rural Women in Latin America: Directions for Future Research." *Latin American Research Review* 25, no. 3 (1990): 89–108.

Pike, Fredrick B. "Church and State in Peru and Chile since 1840: A Study in Contrasts." *American Historical Review* 73, no. 1 (1967): 30–51.

———. "Heresy, Real and Alleged, in Peru: An Aspect of the Conservative-Liberal Struggle, 1830–75." *Hispanic American Historical Review* 47 (1967): 50–74.

Pitt-Rivers, Julian. *The Fate of Shechem or the Politics of Sex: Essays in the Anthropology of the Mediterranean.* Cambridge: Cambridge University Press, 1977.

———. *The People of the Sierra.* 2nd ed. Chicago: University of Chicago Press, 1971.

Porter, Susie S. "And That It Is Custom Makes It Law": Class Conflict and Gender Ideology in the Public Sphere, Mexico City, 1880–1910." *Social Science History* 24, no. 1 (Spring 2000): 111–140.

Potthast-Jutkeit, Barbara. "The Ass of a Mare and Other Scandals: Marriage and Extra-marital Relations in Nineteenth Century Paraguay." *Journal of Family History* 16, no. 3 (1991): 216–232.

Raimondi, Antonio. "Viajes por el departamento de Cajamarca, 1859." In *Historia de Cajamarca,* Vol. 4, comp. Fernando Silva Santisteban, Waldemar Espinoza Soriano, and Rogger Ravines. N.p.: Consejo Nacional de Ciencia y Tecnología, n.d.

Ramos, Donald. "Single and Married Women in Vila Rica, Brazil, 1754–1838." *Journal of Family History* 16, no. 3 (1991): 261–282.

Romanucci-Ross, Lola. *Conflict, Violence and Morality in a Mexican Village.* Palo Alto, CA: National Press Books, 1973.

Ruggiero, Kristin. "Honor, Maternity, and the Disciplining of Women: Infanticide in Late Nineteenth-Century Buenos Aires." *Hispanic American Historical Review* 72, no. 3 (Aug. 1992): 353–373.

Sarmiento Gutiérrez, Julio. *La educación en Cajamarca, Colonia–Siglo XIX.* Cajamarca: Edición EDAC-CIED, 1992.

Scott, Alison MacEwen. *Divisions and Solidarities: Gender, Class and Employment in Latin America.* New York: Routledge, 1994.

Scott, James C. *Domination and the Arts of Resistance: Hidden Transcripts.* New Haven: Yale University Press, 1990.

———. *Moral Economy: Rebellion and Subsistence in Southeast Asia.* New Haven: Yale University Press, 1976.

———. *Weapons of the Weak: Everyday Forms of Peasant Resistance.* New Haven: Yale University Press, 1985.

Seed, Patricia. "Marriage Promises and the Value of a Woman's Testimony in Colonial Mexico." *Signs: Journal of Women in Culture and Society* 13, no. 2 (1988): 253–276.

Silva Santisteban, Fernando. *Los obrajes en el virreinato del Perú.* Lima: Publicaciones del Museo Nacional de Historia, 1964.

Snell, J. R.; R. Rosenwald; and A. Robey. "The Wifebeater's Wife: A Study of Family Interaction." *Archives of General Psychiatry* 11 (1964): 107–113.

Socolow, Susan. "Women and Crime: Buenos Aires, 1757–97." *Journal of Latin American Studies* 12 (1980): 39–54.

Stavig, Ward. *The World of Tupac Amaru: Conflict, Community and Identity in Colonial Peru*. Lincoln: University of Nebraska Press, 1999.

Stern, Steve J. *The Secret History of Gender: Women, Men, and Power in Late Colonial Mexico:* Chapel Hill: University of North Carolina Press, 1995.

Stevenson, William Bennet. *A Historical and Descriptive Narrative of Twenty Years' Residence in South America, Containing the Travels in Arauco, Chile, Peru, and Colombia; with an Account of the Revolution, Its Rise, Progress, and Results*. London: Hurst, Robinson & Co., 1825.

Stolcke, Verena. "Women's Labours: The Naturalisation of Social Inequality and Women's Subordination." In *Of Marriage and the Market: Women's Subordination Internationally and Its Lessons*, ed. Kate Young, Carol Wolkowitz, and Roslyn McCullagh, pp. 159–177. London: Routledge, 1991.

Stølen, Kristi Anne. *A media voz: Relaciones de género en la sierra ecuatoriana*. Quito: CEPLAES, 1987.

———. "Gender, Sexuality and Violence in Ecuador." *Ethnos* 56, nos. 1–2 (1991): 82–100.

Stranger, Francis Merriman. "Church and State in Peru during the First Century of Independence." In *The Conflict between Church and State in Latin America*, ed. Fredrick B. Pike. New York: Alfred E. Knopf, 1964.

Streicker, Joel. "Sexuality, Power and Social Order in Cartagena, Colombia." *Ethnology* 32, no. 4 (Fall 1993): 359–374.

Tauzin-Castellanos, Isabelle. "La educación femenina en el Perú del siglo XIX." In *Peruanistas contemporáneos I*, ed. Wilfredo Kapsoli, pp. 97–109. Lima: Concytec, 1988.

Taylor, Lewis. *Bandits and Politics in Peru: Landlord and Peasant Violence in Hualgayoc, 1900-30*. Cambridge: Centre of Latin American Studies, 1986.

———. "Cambios capitalistas en las haciendas cajamarquinas, 1900–35." In *Estructuras agrarias y cambios sociales en Cajamarca, siglos XIX-XX*, pp. 105–142. Cajamarca: EDAC, 1994.

———. "Earning a Living in Hualgayoc, 1870–1900." In *Region and Class in Modern Peruvian History*, ed. Rory Miller. Institute of Latin American Studies, Monograph Series no. 14. Liverpool: University of Liverpool, 1987.

———. "Economía y sociedad en la provincia de Hualgayoc, 1870–1900." In *Estructuras agrarias y cambios sociales en Cajamarca, siglos XIX-XX*, ed. Lewis Taylor. Cajamarca: EDAC, 1994.

———. "Estates, Freeholders, and Peasant Communities in Cajamarca, 1876–1972." Working Paper, Centre of Latin American Studies, Cambridge University, 1986.

———. "Literature as History: Ciro Alegría's View of Rural Society in the Northern Peruvian Andes." *Ibero-American Archives* 10, no. 3 (1984): 349–378.

———. "Main Trends in Agrarian Capitalist Development, Cajamarca, Peru, 1880–1976." PhD diss., University of Liverpool, 1979.

———. "Organización económica y social de la hacienda San Felipe de Combayo, 1918." In *Estructuras agrarias y cambios sociales en Cajamarca, siglos XIX-XX*, ed. Lewis Taylor, pp. 143-192. Cajamarca: EDAC, 1994.

———. "Los orígenes del bandolerismo en Hualgayoc, 1870-1900." In *Bandolerismo, abigeos y montoneros: Criminalidad y violencia en el Perú, siglos XVIII-XX*, ed. Carlos Aguirre and Charles Walker, pp. 213-248. Lima: Instituto de Apoyo Agrario, 1990.

———. "Society and Politics in Late Nineteenth Century Peru: Contumazá, 1876-1900." University of Liverpool Institute of Latin American Studies, Working Paper no. 11, 1990.

Tinsman, Heidi. "Good Wives and Unfaithful Men: Gender Negotiations and Sexual Conflicts in the Chilean Agrarian Reform, 1964-1973." *Hispanic American Historical Review* 81, nos. 3-4 (2001): 587-619.

———. *Partners in Conflict: The Politics of Gender, Sexuality and Labor in the Chilean Agrarian Reform, 1950-1973*. Durham: Duke University Press, 2002.

Torre, Ana de la. *Los dos lados del mundo y del tiempo: Representaciones de la naturaleza en Cajamarca indigena*. Lima: Centro de Investigación, Educación y Desarrollo, 1986.

Torre Araujo, Ana de la. *Estudio de campo: Violencia contra la mujer rural en Cajamarca*. Cajamarca: APRISABAC, 1995.

Trazegnies Granda, Fernando de. *Ciriaco de Urtecho, litigante por amor: Reflexiones sobre la polivalencia táctica del razonamiento judicial*. Lima: Pontificia Universidad Católica del Perú, Fondo Editorial, 1981.

Tutino, John. "Power, Class and Family: Men and Women in the Mexican Elite, 1750-1810." *The Americas* 39, no. 3 (1983): 359-382.

Twinam, Ann. "The Negotiation of Honor: Elites, Sexuality, and Illegitimacy in Eighteenth-Century Spanish America." In *The Faces of Honor: Sex, Shame and Violence in Colonial Latin America*, ed. Lyman L. Johnson and Sonya Lipsett-Rivera, pp. 68-102. Albuquerque: University of New Mexico Press, 1998.

———. *Public Lives, Private Secrets: Gender, Honor, Sexuality, and Illegitimacy in Colonial Spanish America*. Stanford: Stanford University Press, 1999.

Villavicencio, Maritza. *Del silencio a la palabra: Mujeres peruanas en los siglos XIX-XX*. Lima: Ediciones Flora Tristán, 1992.

Walker, Leonore. *The Battered Woman*. New York: Harper & Row, 1979.

———. "Battered Women and Learned Helplessness." *Victimology* (1978).

Wilson, Fiona. "Marriage, Property and the Position of Women in the Central Peruvian Andes." In *Kinship Ideology and Practice in Latin America*, ed. R. T. Smith, pp. 297-325. Chapel Hill: University of North Carolina Press, 1984.

Witt, Heinrich. *Diario y observaciones sobre el Perú, 1824-1890*. Lima: Oficina de Asuntos Culturales, COFIDE, 1987.

NEWSPAPERS

ADC: *La Opinión: Periódico Popular*, no. 50 (8-10-1862).

ADC: *El Ferrocarril*, no. 120 (17-12-1898); no. 123 (7-1-1899); no. 132 (17-3-1899).

BN: Mariano Amezaga, "Instrucción de la mujer." *El Nacional* (13-7-1869).

BN: R. B., "Escuelas normales para las mujeres." *El Correo del Perú* (1873), número extraordinario.

Index

LaVergne, TN USA
11 January 2011
212090LV00002B/156/P